Writing Spe

APPROACHES TO WRITING
Series Editor: Graeme Harper

PUBLISHED

Eugen Bacon

Writing Speculative Fiction

Creative and Critical Approaches

First published 2019 by
RED GLOBE PRESS

Red Globe Press in the UK is an imprint of Springer Nature Limited,
registered in England, company number 785998, of 4 Crinan Street,
London, N1 9XW.

Red Globe Press® is a registered trademark in the United States,
the United Kingdom, Europe and other countries.

ISBN 978–1–352–00616–2 hardback
ISBN 978–1–352–00605–6 paperback

This book is printed on paper suitable for recycling and made from fully
managed and sustained forest sources. Logging, pulping and manufacturing
processes are expected to conform to the environmental regulations of the
country of origin.

A catalogue record for this book is available from the British Library.

A catalog record for this book is available from the Library of Congress.

To Da for sowing in me a thirst for knowledge, and dear Ma ...
Both of you forever on my mind ...
To the sum of who I am.

Contents

List of Figures

Acknowledgements

I would like to thank the following mentors who were crucial to locating the best form of this work and guiding me to an articulate product: Associate Professor Dominique Hecq, who once told me: 'Writing is your life line. But never think it is your life.' Hecq came along with knowledge of discipline and worked closely with me to build on my strengths in a safe and harmonious environment, a warm and professional one that helped funnel my desire for mastery. Dr Lucy Nicholas came with critical interrogations and a background in social sciences and theory to channel the experimental creative writer in me to the right language for scholarly dissertation.

A huge thank you to the students I taught at Swinburne University of Technology, Australia. To Mikaela Brown, Jessica Cunha, Sam Everaardt, Jakeb Fair, Alexandra Fraser, Sandra Azkari and Tristan Singh—thank you for allowing me to showcase your stimulating pieces in my book. To Matthew Hargreaves—thank you for your witty essay on postmodern attitudes versus originality that alas! ran out of room for this book. To all, you are gems in practice—keep writing, and may harsh critics fuel rather than quell your spirits. I am privileged to have crossed your paths.

Thank you to Roland Barthes, Ursula Le Guin, Ray Bradbury, Octavia Butler, Mary Shelley, Margaret Atwood, Anthony Doerr, George R. R. Martin and all you influential writers—who offer me models to benchmark against.

Thank you Dr Margaret Johnson, my critical friend and editor as mentor. You challenge my ideas, make me think deeper, help me render my vision and pat my back when I startle you with good writing.

Thank you to series editor Professor Graeme Harper, commissioning editor Rachel Bridgewater, editorial assistant Emily Lovelock for such patience and brilliant service, all the diligent people involved in the production process and my blind referees for your enthusiasm about my project and your guidance that came from a good place and helped shape this book. To National Galleries Scotland for allowing the reproduction in this book of *A Girl* by Australian hyperrealist sculptor Ron Mueck, whose sculpting allowed reflective enquiry drawn from fascination in ekphrasis—the perception of an image, visualizing it and conveying it to others;[1] the sculpting became a poem, a flash fiction, an essay ... a transfer of the image's 'evocative emotional presence'[2] from form to mind in speculative fiction. To publishers and authors whose works appear in fair use as examples or exercises in this publication.

Throughout the writing of this book, I have been overwhelmed by the love, sacrifice and support of my son Nicki, who noticed I went 'absent' in writerly immersion as I juggled parenthood and creative practice and nearly missed the cusp as he broke through childhood to young adulthood.

Preface

It is my deep pleasure to write the foreword to Eugen Bacon's book, *Writing Speculative Fiction: Creative and Critical Approaches*. Speculative fiction is not my area of expertise; I am first and foremost a poet and short-fiction writer with a novel and two plays to my name. My scholarly books and papers explore creative writing and poetics as avenues for investigating creativity while examining the relevance of psychoanalysis for the arts. The nature of our partnership, Bacon's and mine, was at first pedagogical: I supervised her doctoral thesis. We have come full-circle. Bacon is now the fervent expert on speculative fiction, and I, the eager apprentice. On Bacon's authoritative request, this foreword will be a fiction. But first, a few words about the book: its contribution to knowledge and singular vision—these words are non-fiction!

Writing Speculative Fiction helps to erode further the already crumbling boundaries between genres, and more specifically between mimesis and fantasy. In an influential monograph titled *Fantasy and Mimesis: Responses to Reality in Western Literature* (2014[1984]), Kathryn Hume writes:

> Literature is the product of two impulses. They are mimesis, felt as the desire to imitate, to describe events, people, situations and objects with such verisimilitude that others can share your experience; and fantasy, the desire to change givens and alter reality—out of boredom, play, vision, longing … or need for metaphoric images that will bypass the audience's verbal defences. We need not try to claim a book as a fantasy any more than identify a work as a mimesis. Rather we have many genres and forms—each with a characteristic blend or range of blends of the two impulses.[3]

Hume's work exposes the cultural bias inherent in long-lasting critical approaches to Western literature that led to the polarization of realism and fantasy, and in turn, to the privileging of mimesis over fantasy. Hume proposes an alternative approach: rather than isolating fantasy as a distinct literary form, she argues for a dual vision, one that would confer equal status to mimesis and fantasy as different, but equally legitimate. This rethinking of 'traditional' boundaries is at the heart of *Writing Speculative Fiction*. In theory and in practice, it promotes and performs a 'departure from consensus reality'.[4] Notions of genre, gender, selfhood, agency are here imbued by difference.

Let us now humbly try our hand at what this might look like.

*

There is a mountain beside Mount Olympus. We call it Parnassus, the space where earth and sky meet; where the sublime and the grotesque coalesce; where gods and humans converse. It is where we encounter the Muse. Here, the daughters of Mnemosyne turn in two opposite directions to delight the hearts of both men and gods. It is beside Olympus that the Muses replicate the authority of Zeus, their father through the *différance*[5] implicit in their act of memory, turning, as they do, duplicity into enjoyment. It is here that the poet receives her gift, and turns back towards her peers, to amuse and delight them. There, too, is where the solidity of truth is challenged by new forms; their differences generic, though these might not be called genres as such yet—or have ceased to be.

The mythical theory of genres would lead us to believe that the Muses are immobile, each located at a given point in time and space, obeying arbitrary rules of oppositions of high forms to low forms, anticipating Plato's extrapolations and, among others, Hélène Cixous' critique of both. Yet even in mythic times the names of the Nine do not conform to this principle of homogeneity, and their dance denies it absolutely.

The task of the Muse is to mediate between the divine and the human worlds, between essential truth and the appearances of reality, between flesh and spirit—matter and form. The narrative of inspiration is always the story of the Muse's visit, and the Poet's call, at a place where they might coincide both to mark and to suspend the operation of the radical otherness of each other's spaces. It is the story of a magic, dimensionless space: dreams, visions, mirrors and the theatre are the metaphors of Parnassus, itself metaphor of the real. It is not the narrative of the Muse that is mimicked by the theory of genres, but the tableau of a universe structured by opposition: of gods and men, of its moral correlate, the noble and the ignoble, and of the social stratification.

The myth of the Muse is a myth of transgression, and the relation of this myth to the theory of genres is the story of a parody and its denial. Like all stories, it requires relating, for in it emerge the genres, and by necessity they are mixed and sexed.

There is another mountain beside Olympus, and the principle of heterogeneity is already inscribed in its geography, geology, geophysics. Set over against that space whose function is to exclude the middle, Parnassus is the space of layering fictions and genre bending.

This is where you dwell.

You stand on top of the hill looking out over the paddocks. It feels like a holiday. You've seen the sun rise across the valley a thousand times, but from the other side. You notice how the shadows move across the road below and how the road stretches long and narrow in the distance. The smell of gum trees sharp in the air.

There is a white speck visible on either side of the road, the painted wooded handrails of the bridge. A meagre stream meanders across the open paddocks, through a tunnel below the road and off again in the distance. You used to stroll barefoot through the sun-bleached grass and watch the water. You'd dip your feet, and its coolness would take you far away. You might do that on the way back.

From high up here, the road seems smaller and larger at once. You cup your hands. Call out *Cooo-eee*, and your voice echoes across the emptiness. Heading home, you stroll down the winding gravel track. A koala sleeps in the top branches of a blue gum.

You stop before you step onto the road. A wild bird calls from high up in the sky, its long neck and wings extended in flight. You squint. From here you can just see where your driveway ends because of the lambs darting around in the fields on each side of the driveway. In springtime they frolic with youthful energy, bleating *beeh beeh beeh*. A crow flies over a river gum lost on the side of the road. It has survived bushfires, heatwaves and freakish winter storms for over a hundred years. Families of magpies live in its branches, warbling to one another in melodious song. Adults. They teach their young how to fly and extract worms from the ground. They squabble and play like children.

The bitumen road stretches its length, straight and long out to the hills. There are mirages of water on its surface. The stream beckons you to stay a while and listen to the water. You lie in the grass and enjoy the warmness of the late morning sun on your face. A northerly blows in from the desert. For a split second, you remember *pepo la moto*, the wind of fire. You remember a much larger river winding through the alluvial plain of Africa, real or imagined, where seeds of stories were sown.

From the house it is a long walk to the end of the road and back. You listen to the crunch of your steps. Take in the wild flowers hidden in clusters behind red, volcanic rock: golden belly buttons, creamy stackhousia, tufted bluebells—how you love the names. Ruins from a bluestone house among she-oaks and stringy barks. A dog barks in the distance. The wind blows curling smoke from someone's chimney. You smell it. Soon, it will sting your eyes.

And then, you realise your hair is on fire …

The above homage does not do justice to the ardent doctoral student become passionate author. It does not capture Eugen Bacon's candid reassessment of otherness with regard to gender and race. It does not capture the scholarly author's fierce engagement with, and critique of, postmodern discourses.

Writing Speculative Fiction is an invaluable guide in the realms of theory and practice. First, it provides a map for reassessing the respective components of the fantastic and mimetic elements of a text—and indeed of its 'literariness'. The projection of this map offers a framework on which the main components of speculative fiction rest, including the conventions of storytelling. This projection also highlights relief shadings and angles of flight from fantasy to science fiction, horror to the paranormal and suggests the linework of what a cross generic approach to speculative fiction might entail. Second, drawing on works by both established and emerging writers, including students, it offers signposts for recognizing and implementing the 'speculative' in fiction. Third, it broadens the horizon by dissolving artificially constructed distinctions such as those between young adult and adult fiction. Here, speaking from her own experience, Eugen Bacon provides practical advice on how to write for different markets. At every step, through expositions, examples and guided exercises, student, teachers and lovers of speculative fiction will delight in works that point to new writing trajectories.

Associate Professor Dominique Hecq

*

Dominique Hecq worked as Research Leader in her capacity as Associate Professor in Writing at Swinburne University of Technology. She has a PhD in literature and a background in French and Germanic languages, with qualifications in translating. Hecq has published in the areas of literary studies, translation, creative writing, psychoanalysis and pedagogy. She is the author of one novel, three collections of short stories, eight books of poetry and two one-act plays. She co-edited *Female Sexuality: The Early Psychoanalytic Controversies* (1998, 2015) and *Creative Writing with Critical Theory: Inhabitation* (2018), edited *The Creativity Market: Creative Writing in the 21st Century* (2013) and wrote *Towards a Poetics of Creative Writing* (2016). *Hors limites, Crypto* and *After Cage* are her most recent publications. *Air: Dreamwork of a Novel* is forthcoming.

1

The non-introduction

In a humpbacked island of three suns and a split moon, in a place locked away from the rest of the world, lived a widower named Tusk.

He had a daughter named Lunar. She was a velvet-eyed bear hug who approached and put her arms around you for three heartbeats, and your ribs burned a boatload of heartbeats later. The bear entered those arms the very moment the girl's mother died from wasp bite as the tot on her breast suckled. Tusk pulled the bub from his wife's cold body and it clutched him until he passed out. The poison in the milk did nothing to harm the child and, story had it, it became a charm that protected Lunar from whichever harm.

But in this world there wasn't much to bring harm, so the potion was of little use to the girl and no one questioned anything. They did not wonder about much, really, like perhaps ask why the moon was shaped like half the shell of a cracked egg; they had seen nothing different. Its glow put shimmers in their eyes and overwhelmed the shooting stars that whooshed past on their way to nowhere. At day islanders stretched out like lizards on the sand under the blonde beams of triplet suns that smiled, merry sunflowers in an emerald sky.

The young women especially looked luscious sprawled like that on the gentle land, but Tusk firmly decided never to wed again. It was not often that fate came about, and a long-lashed pretty turned out to be a fairy godmother who made chariots out of pumpkins. The stepmother thing was the most risky affair, he resolved, and his Lunar might wind up unclogging toilets and cleaning cinders from a chimney. Figuratively speaking. His mud and straw hut held no chimney.

Housed within the same unsophisticated hut was his Lunar who, five moons ago, became a woman. Tusk was sure of this, no? That's the truth. He watched as Lunar's hips swelled, as her chest softened and her moods swung in tune to the dazzle of the north east star. Now heat in the velvet of her eyes told Tusk that his daughter was in love. He hoped she was about to kiss a frog that would turn into a rich and handsome prince shipwrecked to the island from a faraway land. So he was on standby for her proclamation when it came.

'Baba. I have found my rib,' she said.

'Your rib?'

'Yes. Baba.'

He went silent as a shadow. And then he said: 'Who?'

'Clouds.'

'Clouds?'

'Yes Baba.'

'The one who is a fisherman?'

'Yes Baba.'

'The one who was raised by a hag named Miriam, she found him in a basket by some tall grass in the lip of the ocean, and she left him nothing but farts and the debt of three black roosters for her funeral when she died?'

'That one.'

Clouds was no frog. But he was no big bad wolf either. He was a bald head with a single tuft of ginger on his crown. He owned a hut beside the chameleon green ocean that turned to cinder at dusk and spread licks of ash along the forlorn coastline where the lovers had met. And he was penniless, not a rusted penny to his belt.

Tusk, who had singly cared for his girl since fate in the fangs of a wasp snatched his wife, desired the best, only the best for Lunar, and understood she would live hand to mouth with the fisherlad. He considered Clouds. He was a decent lad, no? That's the truth. An honest face, that mattered.

So Tusk did something random: He said 'yes' to the marriage.

Perhaps, he later thought, Clouds might bring the luck of a lad who put a bean in the ground and it grew into a stalk that twined into the sky where a giant abode with a goose that laid golden eggs.

As the wedding loomed, Tusk scratched palmfuls of receding hair, in edginess about the wedding feast. He did not have three little pigs to spare. Not by any power of the chinny chin chin. And it was not like he had a magic lamp to rub and produce a genie that granted wishes.

He cast his eyes outside the hut and settled his gaze on a goat named Spirit.

Spirit was Tusk's only goat, a prized possession. It was birthed from a lineage of goats handed down for generations. Spirit was the last of its kind. In three moons, Tusk was proposing to coax the island chief's doe for a kid. And there was more to his attachment to Spirit. Lunar, from the moment she could crawl, had developed such a bond with the goat, it was like a mother. When the toddler vanished, all one had to do was find the goat and there was Lunar, sucking her thumb and fast asleep, tucked between its hooves.

Tusk pondered for a moment, thought no. But his daughter's future unfrocked his misgiving. A fine celebration brought with it good fortune. You could not invite people to a wedding and keep them famished. Well, invitations were not necessary—invited or not, everybody would attend. And that was exactly the point. Tusk could not do a miracle of five loaves and two fishes and hope to feed a whole island.

He took to the kitchen, seized a huge paring knife. Hands behind his back, he approached the goat. As if intuiting its fate, the usually amenable goat dodged his reach and trotted away with a heart-wringing bleat. Frankly, it galloped really fast and the sound was more like a bray.

A short burst of speed and a leap: Tusk delivered his blow. The goat's final cry shook the skies and pulled out a roar of thunder. As the animal slumped to the ground, a spray of crimson stained the rustic earth.

*

Straight from rendezvous with the pauper prince to whom she was betrothed, Lunar found Tusk bent over red clay and skinning a corpse. She cast herself at the slain goat, hair floating in a sheet around her face. She fastened the bear around the corpse's belly. 'Why. Baba. No.'

Tusk looked at his daughter toppled over the goat. Her hair soaked up blood like a towel until the crimson crystallized into a crown of rubies. Her injured eyes, her wet voice, her words a whip: 'That's savage.'

'Someone had to do it, no? That's the truth.'

'Baba. He was family.'

He closed his eyes. Spirit was a necessary sacrifice. Still Tusk felt a little angry. No hand of the gods had appeared to spare the goat, swap it from the altar with the right sacrificial lamb. When he looked, Lunar's face was laid against the goat. She put a finger to the animal and tried, with no success, to close those unblinking white-as-white eyes that had glassed.

'It is what it is,' he said.

'He was your favourite!'

'I never have favourites. I always ask questions.'

Gently, but firmly, he pried her off the carcass, and even the bear in her arms was too distraught to resist.

Liquid velvet shimmered in Lunar's eyes. Her cry was tortured as she ran.

Tusk picked his knife. But he could not bring himself to dismember the animal. Instead he skinned it, dressed it with herbs and quinoa, placed its head back so the animal looked whole. He set it overnight by the hearth to marinate.

It was the eve of the wedding.

*

Tusk's sleep was a dance of shadows. Silhouettes swept towards him from the shores.

He awoke dazed, roaring flames all around. His panic turned to horror as people leapt from the flames and exploded one after another, airborne. Just then a raven hopped out of the orange tongues. It morphed and turned into a shark that lunged at Tusk's galloping heart. He shrank, raised his hands, but before the creature snapped him in a gobble, a sound rushed at Tusk like hungry waves: *Baaa!*

He blinked.

His relief was so pure, it brought a tear to his eye. The flames, the people, the raven, the shark … It was all a dream.

Baaa! The bleat was real.

Baaa! It came from the hearth.

A moonlit window cast a filter of light upon the beast.

Lunar arrived quietly behind Tusk. Together they considered the goat, its jaw stretched into a death smile. Its ribs heaved. Was that a wink?

The surreal moment unlocked something, and Lunar touched his hand.

But white-as-white eyes, glassed, melted his doubt. Or was it hope?

He waited for a blast of flame to shoot from its mouth, a volcano that rumbled and lit the room violet, pyres of flame from which Spirit would leap out like a phoenix, reborn.

Nothing happened.

'I could have sworn it was alive, no? That's the truth.'

'I'm tired.' Lunar put her arms around him in an enfold that suffocated.

As he neared passing out, his gaze went out the window. He saw to his astonishment that the generally halved moon had grown whole. Not whole as in a mango-flesh coloured bracelet with a pith in the middle, but a fleshy, hearty egg yolk ensconced in the sky. This was the first of several anomalies he was to observe.

He went to bed but sat up for hours. Rather than collapse into sleep like his daughter, Tusk examined dawn as it arrived. One sun unsheathed from the tomb of a faraway galaxy and climbed to the surface. Slowly its light stretched across the jewel-hued horizon. Tusk's brow furrowed. A single sun; the other two were gone. This was the second anomaly.

*

Guests arrived in throngs. Fishermen and their wives, fisherlads, girls and tots. The old chief came wrapped in feathers. Bracelets and anklets tinkled. He walked skewy, a little tipsy from banana brew. He was the celebrant. Eager footfalls from the islanders soared up billows of dust. Outside Tusk's hut, naked waists stood taut with impatience for the gamey taste of a home-grown wild goat descended from generations. Second best to manna from the heavens.

The chief began his rumblings but folk dived into the spit roast way before he announced it was time for an exchange of vows. People marvelled at how the meat melted in the mouth, how the mushrooms and flowers tendered in the goat's breast and belly.

Tusk scratched his head; he'd left the innards intact, no? That's the truth. He never swapped the goat's kidneys, heart or liver for floral tasters, never set out for the balance of fragrance and bitter now rife in the meat he had tasted in courtesy as a host. Those mushrooms and flowers were the third anomaly, and three was unlucky. No? That's the truth.

It was unthinkable to expect that Lunar might touch the feast. And neither did Clouds, whose ginger crown, on this day, blinked like a shooting star.

The next day, still single-sunned, was moody. Alone, in his hut, Tusk lit a fire but was so overwhelmed with weariness he collapsed in sleep.

Later islanders would tell stories, varied, of how the hut caught fire and orange flames licked the man alive. There was nothing left of Tusk for a princess to kiss and wake up.

That same day a toothy shark leapt from the calm water and ate up a boat, Lunar and Clouds in it. Miraculously they survived. Remember the wasp? Somehow its sorcery was potent enough to also save Clouds.

Clouds sourced a fisherlad to help dig a three-foot-wide, eight-foot-long hole to bury his father-in-law. Together they ploughed and loosened soil at the back of the hut. Then Lunar summoned the islanders.

The old chief began the last rites. Just then, a northern raven crashed from the sky and all eyes turned to the big sooty bird beating its wings as it hopped about the grave. Every now and then it gave an echoing croak. People were still speechless at the bird when it croaked at the ancient chief and he staggered back and tripped on an anklet. He fell *thud!* into the dug hole and bashed his head on a rock. Death was instant.

Before anyone could accommodate this new grieving, news arrived of a family that was sprouting. *Sprouting?* someone said. *Whoever heard of such a thing. Sprouting.*

But all forsook the funeral and dashed to the lip of the island. There, indeed, they witnessed mushrooms and flowers growing out of the eyes, nose and ears of a family of four. Horrified, helpless, islanders watched the father, mother, a fisherlad and his sister writhe and gasp as their bodies bloated with innards turned to vegetables, until the bodies exploded.

And so it was. One by one, all who feasted on the roast spit goat, basically the whole village, succumbed to unusual deaths. All, but Lunar and Clouds.

She sometimes wraps her arms around him so tight he faints. You might catch a glimpse of them, she with her velvet eyes and curtain hair, he with his devotion and a ginger crown, as they tread along an ash-licked shore.

To this day Spirit floats in quiet vigil over the heartbroken but lovestruck couple, hands entangled, and a hunchback island forever lost to history.

*

Perhaps this story of Tusk, Lunar, Clouds and Spirit does not work for you—close this book and give it to someone else; it's not for you. Or you can be curious. There is playfulness in this text, and much imagination that borrows from myth, fable and the Bible. Adopting the narrative device of 'show, don't tell' that allows the reader to experience the story, this fictional piece is not self-indulgent but is rather an active illustration of where you can go with a dollop of whimsical thinking. It is a 2,200-word story that captures the essence of this book: vibrant storytelling of speculative fiction that is fun to write, and potentially to read, and it crosses genre. It is a story about imagining and examining possibilities of bending from traditional paradigms of genre fiction that comes along with 'rules' and convictions of how it should be written. It crosses genre with its fantasy (a child protected by a dead mother's charm) and science fiction (an alien land of three suns and a split moon, whose physical transformations foretell fate) and horror (the horrific death of Tusk burnt alive, and people 'sprouting', their bodies bloating with innards turned to vegetables until they explode). At the same time it borrows from postmodernism with its metafiction—the self-conscious narrative that interacts directly with the reader's consciousness through the author's thought (Remember the wasp?)—and the addition of new wine into old skins: there is a recasting of stories from the Bible (baby Moses in a reed basket retrieved by the Pharaoh's daughter); from English fairy tales (the concept of the three little pigs: 'not by the hair on my chinny chin chin'; and a big bad wolf); and from African or other culture (a chief and his trinkets and the ceremonial burial, and superstition objectified in the black bird at the gravesite). In its cross genre form it also offers the 'literary'—a term later contextualized in this book—enlivened with imagery (sleep as a dance of shadows) and personification (the hug as a bear).

It offers up a world where myth and fairy tale are twisted and recontextual-ized, are rendered postmodern to give the text some feminist or postcolonial or subversive political edge... Or perhaps it is just 'extraordinary' storytelling in the literal sense of the word: odd, unexpected?

Speculative fiction allows this type of question and encourages a response in fiction that is an immeasurable frontier where nothing is a limit. Speculative fiction has over decades equipped authors like Octavia Butler with the foundations to cultivate inclusive worlds and characters. In speculative fiction Butler discovered a place and a voice to write 'herself in' because novels and short stories of her time in a male-dominated world of genre fiction did not feature an 'other' like her.[1] Through a different kind of writing, in speculative fiction, Butler was able to write about change, about sexism, power and politics, and find—in the figments of her imagination—settings and charac-ters she could identify with.

Speculative fiction allows the invention of immersive worlds that may be strange yet believable, like J. R. R. Tolkien's fictional world in the Elven town of Rivendell located in Middle Earth that hosted remarkable characters like the hobbit Bilbo Baggins and the wizard Gandalf the Grey ... Like Mount Doom in the Black Land of Mordor and its Sauron and his army of dark creatures, including trolls, goblins and Orcs—potentially made of stone and slime through sorcery. In his epic imagination and fondness for storytelling, Tolkien still today in his long-lived writing hurls the reader into an 'other' world of light and darkness, a world that is absorptive, and in its depths and complexities engulfs the reader who is so submerged in it, there is no moment to question: What is real? The unreal?

Fiction is a figment of our imagination, or as French literary theorist, critic and philosopher Roland Barthes would have it, text is a tissue of quotations, arising from thousands of sources of culture, and both the writer and the reader extrapolate meaning from it.[2] Enter mimesis—that imitative representation of the real world in art and literature that renders it incon-clusive for someone to say, 'The story I am telling you is fiction,' and true to Hume's words in the preface of this book, the desire to imitate reality thins the boundary between real and the hyperreal. Later, in autobiographical theory, you'll see that fiction can be a creative response to the world around you. As writer and academic Amanda Boulter suggested in her book *Writing Fiction* (2007), authors are consciously or subconsciously building upon fragments of the real, using the world as a way of discovery, as a bridge to imaginary worlds, imaginary characters.[3] As authors we steal from the world—our characters, dialogue, events ... We steal from ourselves—our fears and our dreams. And then we speculate. Speculative fiction is growing in recognition. My work with students invigorated me to appreciate the captivation this area of writing generates in new and established writers.

Speculative fiction writer Michael Pryor in an introduction to *Aurealis*, a magazine of fantasy and science fiction, described fantasy and science fiction as 'the most challenging forms of writing to undertake', types of writing whose authoring involves integrating tremendously imaginative elements atop 'everything that other writers do, like have convincing, multi-dimensional characters and engaging, lucid prose'.[4] As the speculative imagination runs riot, the brain's mental workspace becomes a playground of impulses on triple time, neurons and their billions of connections choreographing images, ideas and theories that shape these type of stories. The quality of 'limitless' that Pryor attributed to the genres of fantasy and science fiction equally applies to speculative fiction, where nothing is out of bounds.

In this book that explores fundamentals of writing speculative fiction and discusses deviants, speculative fiction is broken into four 'genres':

- Fantasy
- Science fiction
- Horror and the paranormal
- Cross genre.

There are those who may argue that speculative fiction is not a genre: By whose standards? Who determines the rules of where an author's work fits? Publishers? Agents? Librarians? Book store owners? Fans? Genre-based organizations such as the Association of Science Fiction and Fantasy Artists?[5], The World Science Fiction Society?[6] The editors of a magazine? Take the submission guidelines of *Aurealis*:

> Aurealis is looking for science fiction, fantasy or horror short stories between 2000 and 8000 words. All types of science fiction, fantasy and horror that are of a 'speculative' nature will be considered, but we do not want stories that are derivative in nature, particularly those based on TV series. We do not publish horror without a supernatural element.[7]

The latter condition for horror is one with which Stephen King, whose horror books like *Carrie* (1974), *The Running Man* (1982), *Under the Dome* (2009) and *11/22/63* (2011) contain 'unrealistic' elements but are not paranormal, might disagree. But in regarding horror and the supernatural as complementary to each other, the magazine is, in effect, illustrating that cross genre works in the speculative do exist. *Aurealis* does not go to lengths to prescribe what is text of a 'speculative' nature.

This book includes a balance of the creative and the critical and is suited to creative writing and literature programmes that teach genre fiction, including speculative fiction. It is a versatile book for aspiring writers to hone their craft, for established writers to explore crossing genre, for teachers to use in an educational setting, for general readers rapt with genre fiction to gain insight to its writing.

What is special about this book? It is an entertaining yet intellectual product by a scholar and an artist who writes across genres and is captivated by R&B: critical thinker Roland Barthes and revolutionary author Ray Bradbury. It is a new kind of book on speculative fiction that is both practical and critical in its evaluative gaze at other practitioners' views on their methods of working, their whys of writing and their artistic approaches to storytelling. It connects theory with how it applies to elements of speculative fiction and, at the end of each chapter, includes exercises for students. The core of this book is heart and passion, an insistence on writing as liberation from the pedantic approach and on reading as fluidity, a flowing with the text and a discovery of the enchantment and wonderment that speculative fiction offers in its 'illogic'.

This is a book about storytelling, and it assumes a sturdy focus on examples not simply because a good writer shows rather than tells, but because there is no accord or judgement on how speculative fiction 'works'; a reasonable approach to reveal its machinations is through anecdotes and excerpts and stories relating to speculative fiction and its writing. The book includes genre examples in print, television and film, and captures mesmeric stories from a diversity of practitioners: pundits, award winners and novices. And showcased in this book are insights and excerpts of stories by students who adore reading fiction. Some at the time of this writing were unpublished writers plugging out text as an interlude, private jottings divulged to trusted family and friends. Some at the end of this writing had placed their texts and become published writers. Draft forms of their explorations found room in reading, writing and criticism workshops. Sharing the student work is valuable because, as stated, this book is for teachers and students of writing courses, it is for potential and established writers of any form and genre, it is for the general readership, and it is about enchantment and curiosity. As Sue Norton discovered, and recounted in her article 'Betwixt and Between: Creative Writing and Scholarly Expectations' (2012),[8] students—young and mature—revel in the creative expression that writing affords them. They are eager to tell their stories, to immerse themselves in the composition space from which they resurface invigorated, dumbfounded by their prose. Master storyteller Le Guin in her essays on fantasy and science fiction defined maturity as a growing up, not an outgrowing; the adult as a child who has survived, not a dead child; the best faculties of a mature human being exist in the child.[9] Study children and they will cast you back to enchantment and curiosity in the everyday. Notice the sparkle in their eyes at the flutter of a butterfly's wings. Heed the tinkle in their mirth at the pop of a bubble. Trace the 'o' of their lips at the 'kroo' of a hen or the wetness of first rain.

To you, dear tutor, invite this sense of marvel in your writing workshop. To you, dear novice, connect and reconnect with language, play and vision, and find stimulation in speculation. To you, dear publisher (or agent), make a case against logic, hesitancy or fear, and find stories that stir and electrify, writing imbued with the kind of illogic that queers the straight thinker. To you, dear reader, discover perspective: perspective and insight to literary expression. Allow a space of imaginings in which to trace your longings or questions. This is a book for lovers of stories. You don't have to be Ray Bradbury or Patricia McKillip to cartwheel in the glory of speculative fiction.

This book is for you.

There's something about speculative fiction …

Nigel Krauth in *Creative Writing and the Radical: Teaching and Learning the Fiction of the Future* (2016)[10] paid attention to radical writing, experimentation in creative writing, the shift of fiction from its traditional forms on paper to the visual, audio and sensory forms of a digital age. Krauth's book is not just about survival, writing in a world of composite media. It is about new approaches to writing as part of postmodernist thought because it is about remodelling: finding a keener sense of awareness, deeper meaning behind art. It is also about play.

The conjecturing in speculative fiction, in whichever genre, however sombre its theme, makes this kind of fiction a work of art that is playful to the writer, to the reader. This book invites you to play, to bend forms of writing or reading to which you may be accustomed and find affection in deviants. Loosen up, frolic in the sand of an upside-down world where the tide washes out and fishermen in hovercrafts cast nets to the sea, and the silhouette of a tall palm tree, its mop of leaves facing down against a melon sky, reaches you so high in your dreams.

This book toys with definitions and considers the recognition or mis-recognition of speculative fiction, where the term 'speculative' here does not denote the flexible and loose definition of what publishers and marketers in the publishing industry may refer to as a 'speculative genre', arguably no more than a commercial tool, a convenient lumping of books on the shelf so that readers may readily find their preferred type of reading.

Orson Scott Card in his book *How to Write Science Fiction and Fantasy* (1990) said:

> unless you are already established as a science fiction or fantasy writer, you do not have the power to decide unilaterally that your work belongs in the category. You must persuade at least one editor that your novel or story is science fiction or fantasy—and with rare exceptions, editors have a finely discriminating eye.[11]

What Card was saying is that subjectivity prevails: there is no hard and fast rule. Unlike a typical genre studies work, this is a cross-disciplinary book whose larger ambition is to encourage a fuller appreciation of crossing genre.

Learn through the influences of others with their blueprints of the experimental and the adventurous from which your reading or writing may borrow. Find a safe place to interrogate complex and unsettling themes, and learn from theorists and philosophers like Roland Barthes, who, in *The Grain of the Voice* (1985), found pleasure in text; for whom text is a multidimensional space where 'things are made and unmade', where 'language is infinite' and literature is a 'deepening and extension of language'; and from existentialists like Simone de Beauvoir, who understood the power of literature, where a novel, its characters and how they interact with each other, is a bridge to inside out: an author or reader's self-understanding and world experience.

Most of all have fun. Approach your reading and writing as you would a dazzling adventure you can't wait to embark on.

The structure of this book

This book explores the writing of speculative fiction and interrogates traditional and modern approaches. The goal is that readers will come away with a fuller appreciation of speculative fiction and its subgenres. In analysing the works of writers such as Marion Zimmer Bradley, Mary Shelley, Eleanor Lewis, Stephen King, Margaret Atwood, Octavia Butler, Haruki Murakami, George Orwell, Orson Scott Card, Douglas Adams, J. R. R. Tolkien, George R. R. Martin, Ursula Le Guin, Jorge Luis Borges and William Golding, the book scrutinizes the characteristics of speculative fiction. It promotes genre crossing (for example, literary speculative fiction). It connects critical and cultural theories and how they might apply to this form of creative writing. Finally, it looks at e-publishing as a promising publishing medium for speculative fiction.

Chapter by chapter synopsis

Chapter 2. There's a story in you: This chapter considers the fundamentals of speculative fiction, other writing basics including an author's unique voice, their way of looking at things and finding the right context for expressing that way of looking, their writerly signature.

Chapter 3. Vogler's hero/ine's journey: This chapter introduces characterization along a traditional quest motif.

Chapter 4. The speculative: A problem with definitions: This chapter toys with definitions and considers the recognition or misrecognition of speculative fiction.

Chapter 5. Genres and subgenres of speculative fiction: This chapter looks at fantasy and subgenres, for example fairy tales, dark fantasy, myths, legends and magical realism; science fiction and subgenres of the gothic novel, cyberpunk, utopia, dystopia, alternate history and steampunk; horror and the paranormal; and cross genre.

Chapter 6. Fantasy: This chapter considers the works of authors such as Ursula Le Guin, J. K. Rowling, Suzanne Collins, Haruki Murakami, Jorge Luis Borges, Tolkien and George R. R. Martin.

Chapter 7. Science fiction: This chapter considers the works of authors such as Marion Zimmer Bradley, Mary Shelley, Octavia Butler, Isaac Asimov, Ray Bradbury, J. G. Ballard and Ursula Le Guin.

Chapter 8. Horror and the paranormal: This chapter considers works of authors such as Eleanor Lewis, Stephen King, Dean Koontz, Edgar Allan Poe and Guy de Maupassant.

Chapter 9. Cross genre: This chapter considers works that cross genre, for example by Nora K. Jemisin, Margaret Atwood, Toni Morrison, H. G. Wells, Ray Bradbury, William Golding and Edgar Allan Poe.

Chapter 10. Literary speculative fiction: This chapter extends the discussion of crossing genre, and how literary writing may contribute to the quality of speculative fiction.

Chapter 11. Short story: This chapter considers the unique features of the short story, and the short story's potential in speculative fiction.

Chapter 12. Targeting young adults and new adults: This chapter considers themes (such as violence, drugs, alcohol and sex) surrounding the interests of a maturing adolescent or 'new adult', where crossover text reaches diverse audiences: for example J. K. Rowling's Harry Potter novels.

Chapter 13. Critical and cultural theories: This chapter connects literary theory and how it might apply to the writing of speculative fiction.

Chapter 14. E-Publishing: In the borderless world of e-commerce, and with the increasing saturation of the traditional publishing industry, this chapter looks at e-publishing as a promising medium for speculative fiction.

The writing exercises

Think of text as fluid, writing as a web of horizons, creativity as enchantment.

In shaping this book into an entertaining yet scholarly product, the objective is to encourage readers, students and creative practitioners to leap outside the square, to creatively explore. Each chapter concludes with practical writing prompts and exercises to help you create new writing.

The writing prompts in my tutorial workshops nudged students to test, in a supportive environment, a range of techniques and styles in genres unfamiliar to them. Class critique helped to shape or clarify structure and ideas. And students practise, practise, practised. Before workshopping, some had never written outside a diary. Most had never shared a piece of writing with another soul, let alone a stranger, but all were curious. At the end of the semester, most had created publishable work originating in writing exercises.

This book includes an array of ideas for different types of writing, but not all writing prompts will work for you. As Bradbury said, 'My subconscious knows exactly what I can do or can't do. If it bores the hell out of you, you've picked the wrong subject—I'd get writer's block immediately.'[12] So pick the writing prompt that calls out the most to you, transform it into an idea that works. Then type the odd thing that comes into your head, as Bradbury urged, recommending word association to combat writer's block. You don't know what's in you until you test it, he was adamant.

Exercise 1

Start with a familiar object, for example:
- photograph
- table
- wedding ring
- vase
- smartphone
- tea cup
- toilet seat
- pram
- pillow

Attribute human characteristics to the object (personification).
- Does it feel? Talk?
- What is it thinking?
- What does it see?
- What if *you* were the object. What do you want? Have an adventure or give us insight to you.

Choose a title for your story, for example:
- Flush
- A silent scream
- After hours
- Affair of the tea cup
- Pillows have eyes

Give the object character: What is unique about its voice, appearance, language, temperament?

Write a mini story (250 words) and give it a beginning, a middle and an end.

Rewrite the story and make it stranger:
- Add a supernatural element, for example give the object psychic or telepathic ability
- Place the object in an unearthly land. What is unique about this place?
- Does your ending have a twist?

2

There's a story in you

Writing—the basics

You have a story; is it a good one? Figure 2.1 gives the essentials in writing speculative fiction.

Element	Fantasy	Science fiction	Horror and the paranormal	Cross genre
World building	✓	✓	✓	
Characterization	✓	✓	✓	
Hook/Tension	✓	✓	✓	
Plot/Theme	✓	✓	✓	
The fantastical	✓			
Science or 'the alternate'		✓		
Fear, revulsion or spook			✓	
Most of the above				✓

Figure 2.1 Essential elements in speculative fiction

World building

Creating imaginary worlds is essential in all forms of speculative fiction, whether you are writing a novel or short story. The works of Le Guin and Tolkien showcase richly invented worlds, made-up languages and imaginative presentations that invite us to what Richard Mathews termed 'infinite possibility' in his book *Fantasy: the Liberation of Imagination* (2002).[1] There is a large presence of language and sophistication in the created worlds inside the fictional realms of Le Guin's *Earthsea* books and Tolkien's *Lord of the Rings* series. Both authors love languages, where Le Guin applies it as power in the *Earthsea* books, and knowledge of the language of magic, the language

15

of dragons, the language of nature, the language of creation … is power. To philologist Tolkien, the culture and linguistics of Middle-earth are part of his investment in world building that compounds the credibility of his fantasy works as literature classics.

While in short fiction world building need not be elaborate, if one goes with Raymond Carver's approach to writing the short form as 'Get in, get out. Don't linger. Go on',[2] a good writer must take time on setting in this speculative world, big or small. World building is the essence. Matthew R. Ward achieves a clear sense of place in two opening paragraphs of his inter-space fiction 'To the stars' (2018):

> The old priest dove into the pool, strong strokes bringing him easily to the transparent bottom where he could look out at the stars. The window always gave him the feeling that he was hovering in interstellar space itself. He looked for answers in the bright lights and delicate colours of stars and galaxies as they rotated around him. He found none.
>
> The priest ran one hand across the surface of the glass and sighed, the last of his air bubbling upwards across his face. His gaze followed the bubbles to the silvery surface of the water and the scattered image of a figure leaning over the edge of the pool. He pushed off from the window, kicked against the stars until he reached the surface and the cool air that awaited his burning lungs.[3]

The swimming pool within a floating arc in space offers a clean view of the stars and galaxies rotating around the vessel on a mission through time. In another short story, Craig Rodgers builds a world in two opening sentences in his flash fiction 'Two Inches of Tape' (2018): 'The strip of black electrical tape stuck to the nicotine-stained wall like a band-aid slapped in the middle of a plaster desert. One corner hung loose, the glue starting to let go, giving in to age.'[4] Two sentences reveal Rodgers' world, upon which he crafts a deep story of estrangement and isolation where a new tenant picking at a wall is unable to stop. Day and night the tenant picks at the hole's edges and wider the hole grows. Soon the crack becomes a gorge, and soon more than that, and the place he might have learnt to call home is nothing but a canyon running forever in all directions.

Bradbury's 'Kaleidoscope' in *The Illustrated Man* (2008) is equally succinct in its world building at the onset of the story:

> The first concussion cut the rocket up the side with a giant can-opener. The men were thrown into space like a dozen wriggling silverfish. They were scattered into a dark sea; and the ship, in a million pieces, went on, a meteor swarm seeking a lost sun.[5]

The setting is enough to build a picture of the world that confines the men to a falling, falling, falling … as meteors flash by and stars close in with the men's last words.

Characterization

A believable character is crucial to the credibility of a speculative fiction story that may not draw upon logic. In his short fantasy 'The Last Monster You Shall Slay' (2018), Paul Alex Gray crafts a robust character in Bunyip Bill, a beast slayer:

> 'Must be amazing to have Bunyip Bill as yer old man,' said a local kid in a striped shirt.
>
> You nodded, proud as punch. You led them to the corpse, a snake-tailed thing with hair like razor wire. Its eyes were locked in a wide stare and you thought it looked more scared than dangerous.
>
> The kids asked you to hack a piece for them. An eye! A claw! One of them spines off its back! You relished the attention but told them no. They asked to have a turn with the dagger, but you said it's not a toy.
>
> A bloke came from the newspaper and made your dad stand beside the dead beast. One foot propped up, rifle slung over his shoulder, his curving sword near the slit in the beast's neck.
>
> By dark, the blood on the road had thickened to a sticky mess. You touched it, felt it thick with dust and grime between your fingers.
>
> 'See how I done it?' Bill said. It made you jump. 'With a Gorgon, you can't look right at it. Remember why?'
>
> A few hours earlier the monster had writhed out in the farmer's field, surrounded by cattle ripped open, their insides spread out like threads. An old bull stood frozen, staring at the carnage.
>
> 'You listenin' mate?' asked Bill. 'Gorgon'll turn you to stone, 'specially if you're there gazin' at it all dumb-eyed. Got me?'
>
> You lowered your head, 'Yes, Bill.'[6]

Later, when a monster nearly kills the boy, strong arms lift him and dump him on the muddy beach:

> 'Why didn't ya whistle, mate?' hissed Bill.
>
> 'I forgot,' you cried.
>
> 'Sloppy, mate. That's how you'll get killed.'
>
> 'I'm sorry!'
>
> 'Get here.' He half-dragged you across the mud to the flailing thing.

It seemed like some dinosaur, a squat body with too many fins. A flat head like an old double-bladed axe you once saw, narrow in the middle and wide on each side, broad gaps sucking in air.

'You'll finish this one,' said Bill. 'Cut along under here.'

You were shivering with cold. The dagger felt like it might slip right out of your hands. The men muttered, watching. Dark blooms slipped from the monster into the water and the bravado you'd felt in the boat washed away.

'That's right. Right here,' said Bill guiding your hand.

You knelt, almost sitting on the monster's neck. It flapped and bucked beneath you.

'Go on boy, kill it,' said one of the townsfolk.

You stretched your arm, hoping Bill didn't see you shaking. The monster's eyes gazed at you. Bright splotches of skin flickered and changed. It let out a whine.

Did it know what you were going to do? Was it scared?

'Now mate,' Bill said. He squeezed your shoulder.

Tears in your eyes you swore you'd never end up like him. You slipped the blade under the beast's neck and cut it open.[7]

The story might be fiction, but Bunyip Bill is real—he is believable. The scene the author draws paints a vivid mental representation to the reader, who determines whether to like Bunyip Bill, or to find empathy with his son.

Hook/tension

A story's opener is part of its hook that potentially plays a factor in the reader's approach to it because the intent is to immediately grab attention. In an interview with *The Atlantic*, Stephen King talked about the importance of good opener. He said: 'An opening line should invite the reader to begin the story. It should say: Listen. Come in here. You want to know about this.' He gave an example of James M. Cain's hook, the first sentence that reads:

They threw me off the hay truck about noon.

King explained the appeal of this opener:

Suddenly, you're right inside the story—the speaker takes a lift on a hay truck and gets found out. But Cain pulls off so much more than a loaded setting—and the best writers do. This sentence tells you more than you think it tells you. Nobody's riding on the hay truck because they bought a ticket. He's basically a drifter, someone on the outskirts, someone who's going to steal and filch to get by. So you know a lot about him from the beginning, more than maybe registers in your conscious mind, and you start to get curious.

This opening accomplishes something else: It's a quick introduction to the writer's style, another thing good first sentences tend to do. In 'They threw me off the hay truck about noon,' we can see right away that we're not going to indulge in a lot of foofaraw. There's not going to be much floridity in the language, no persiflage. The narrative vehicle is simple, lean (not to mention that the book you're holding is just 128 pages long). What a beautiful thing— fast, clean, and deadly, like a bullet. We're intrigued by the promise that we're just going to zoom.[8]

In a hook to his fantasy, Paul Alex Gray begins:

You were seven when you received your first weapon.[9]

This opener with a weapon preps you for a hunter. The story maintains suspense in its promise of what might become of the boy. The reader anticipates a coming of age where the narrator might tame the beasts, wonders what will happen to Bunyip Bill, especially when the rough men of town drinking by the fire begin to ask him questions: 'You ever worried you'll get killed?' And Bill doesn't answer right away. He stares at the flames as they leap and dance, he takes out a cigarette and someone lights it. Smoke slips from his mouth and his words come out like a growl: 'Hunter's destiny. Gettin' killed in battle's the only way to guarantee entry to the Golden Fields.' Years, and the boy is grown, Bunyip Bill is no more. A call, is it a hoax? The bloke on the line calls himself Lizard Man. The hunt:

The Lizard Man lets out a shrill cry and you rub your eyes. Your head's pounding and your heart feels like it's working too hard.

The slick line of blood leads you like a pathway to where the monster thrashes. An old house behind it is dark. The lawn is overgrown and one of the windows is smashed. Like a lot of the other places, it's almost like the town's giving up, letting nature grow its way back.

The monster lets out a yowl. Even though it's hurt, it's still deadly. The claws scrape on the ground. It extends a tongue and licks the air. It's lying next to a streetlight, all lit up in a golden orange hue.

'Hold up now,' you shout. The wound in your side isn't good.

The monster ambushed you beside the high school. You were sloppy. Came around the corner and thwack! Its jagged tail went right through you.

You jammed your dagger into its chest, in a place that'd kill a man. Then you hacked your way through the tail. It howled and slithered away and now here you are.

You push onwards, struggling to balance. You can't let it end yet.

'Get here!' you shout, and stagger over.

There's a few lights winking on the embankment. Some folks have their phones lit. They want to see the kill. Record it. Share it. Stream it or whatever.

You turn your dagger in your hand. The Lizard Man shrieks and barks.

You figure the beast's not likely going to survive but you've got a job to do. So you move near it and jab your blade into its side. It grunts and lashes with its claws, the edges sinking into your shoulder. You feel poison seeping in from sacs under its claws.

'Yeah, do what ya need to do,' you hiss and jab again, jamming the dagger deep.

The beast rakes at you again and you pull the blade out, push its weak arm down, and you stab the sharp edge through its hand and into the damp earth.

You lean back and fall beside it, feeling your insides jar up.[10]

The story's hook, the action, action, action, maintains pace and tension, and the reader stays engaged.

Plot/theme

Later chapters will analyse more authors and their stories, but here in Gray's story—inspired by Johnny Cash's cover of 'Hurt', and creatures calling out in the yard one summer evening—it is a coming of age story. A lad grows to become a memory of his father: a retired cryptid hunter, reflecting on his life and the monsters that inhabited it. It has no complex plot or theme, just subsections, age by age, full of action, action, action. With Raymond Carver's 'Get in, get out. Don't linger. Go on' approach to writing the short form in mind, Gray's simple plot works.

Philip K. Dick's witty 'We Can Remember It for You Wholesale' (1966) that inspired the movie *Total Recall* (1990) is the story of a man who dreams of a trip to Mars but hyperreality takes over reality in a strong 'what if' theme that drives the plot: What if we could artificially implant memories into the brain—how would we use such technology? There is also Quail's conflict between the real world and the hyperreal, misalignment between the world we live in and the world we dream of living in. This introduces a second theme of changing social dynamics and a shift in human understanding typical to science fiction short stories; unlike a simpler beginning, middle and end, this science-based narrative calls for a more intricate plot and elaborate thinking in its formation.

The fantastical

What distinguishes fantasy from other genres is the fantastical: where imaginative creation is essential in all fiction, the fantastical is core to a story that relies on an application of magic, myth, legend or some radical departure from reality. It is about unrestrained imagination, suppositions based on little or no foundation. In Gray's story there are the legendary creatures Bunyip Bill is slaying, strange beasts roaming the ranches, tearing up cattle. The unrealistic nature of the beasts gives weight to the hunter's skill.

Think of Tolkien's creations of Middle-earth: the hobbits, the Balrog, the fell beasts, the orcs ... Think of Middle-earth itself, its fictional setting in the continent of Arda, between Aman to the west and the Land of the Sun to the east. The fantastical tugs along its composition of the imaginary—dragons, magic, etc. Richard Mathews determined in his book that fantasy is a type of fiction that 'enables us to enter worlds of infinite possibility'; that 'evokes wonder, mystery or magic—a sense of possibility beyond the ordinary'; that supports contours 'subscribed only by imagination itself'.[11]

Science or 'the alternate'

Its anchorage in science and technology (or philosophy or alternate history or social sciences) is what distinguishes science fiction from its cousin fantasy and other genres. This does not deter science fiction from overlapping other genres, so it may also have elements of the fantastical, but they are not crucial. An accepted view is that a science fiction story applies consistent realistic contexts or conditions of realism: for example, a rational universe that resembles the social or political principles of our world, reasonable scientific or philosophic explanations that are core to the story—and without which the story may fall apart.

Ray Bradbury's short fiction 'The Man' in his collection *The Illustrated Man* (1951)[12] features Captain Hart, a rocket ship captain whose quest for an itinerant prophet turns obsessive. There is science in the rocket and the concept of space travel. It is of no consequence that the planet is backward and its people have not yet discovered photographic technology. While the science may not be core—that is, the setting need not be interspace—the philosophical aspect of the story is integral to its telling, in its existential theme of science versus religion.

Fear, revulsion or spook

Stephen King or Mary Shelley or Robert Louis Stevenson understood that obsession with the fear factor is what distinguishes horror and the paranormal from other genres. A skilled writer of dark fantasy or horror capitalizes on the ability to strike fear, revulsion or spook, along with loathing or extreme terror, or dread of a person or thing causing the horror. The writer instigates fright, aversion, loathing or repugnance at a monstrosity or a simple thing in the everyday phobias of a reader. Horror is personal. A successful horror or paranormal writer plays with your emotions, creates a story with such surprise in the real world or out of the ordinary, where suspense reaches a climax and you jump from your toes or find a scream in your belly. Tension or sudden revelation are crucial for success in eliciting this emotion, this reaction in the reader, the audience. A music score in a film heightens the looming approach of a terrible thing, and even though you anticipate it, it leaps or snatches or strikes with suddenness that frights. August Fell's paranormal horror 'The Devil Girl' offers up a scene:

> I was out camping in the woods. I wouldn't have been there at all but for my friends Billy and George. They were the damned best friends I ever had and they were going camping in the hills. It was April and warm, and the air was so sweet and what was wrong? Was I scared or something? You know how it is. So we went out in the woods in the afternoon and climbed up into the hills. There's a great place up there, a little glen with wildflowers and a creek running past. We set up the tent and rolled out sleeping bags. We made a fire just as it got dark.
>
> We rolled cigarettes and smoked and told stories and laughed. Billy had some postcards with naked ladies on them and we passed them around and got boners while we made jokes. George told how he'd done it with Elda Cottingwood in the apple grove after school and we ragged him and told him we didn't believe a word. Billy told about spying on Mrs Winslow in her bath that time he peeked through her window. He said her bush went clear up to her navel, and we laughed about that until we hurt. I can't say I've ever had a better day since. And only one worse night, just one.
>
> The night came down full, with cicadas buzzing all over and crickets talking to each other. We ate peanuts and watched the fireflies glow. I looked up and there she was, white as milk in the firelight. She was standing behind Billy, and he was talking to George, saying something, but I couldn't hear him, like he was far away. The cicadas were loud, really loud. And she hooked me with those eyes and I went right back to where I'd first seen her. I was 10 years old again. She smiled at me, and put out her little white hand and touched Billy's

face, stroked it, and he didn't move, like he couldn't feel it. I tried to say something, but no sound came. I couldn't move or speak, and the wildflower smell seemed ready to smother me.

And then she opened her mouth, and this sound came out. A sound like you were in a cave, and a hundred thousand people and dogs and cats and everything were in there with you, all howling, all crying, all screaming. It came over me like a wave or a wind and blacked out everything, and I could hear Billy's voice in among the damned, and George's, and mine.

I opened my eyes and it was morning. The sun blazing hot and the sky was bright blue like there was never any night, don't you believe it. I sat up in the grass, and it was longer than it had been when we set our tent. There were weeds and burrs in it there hadn't been before. I looked for the tent and it was gone, nothing of it. I looked for the fire and couldn't find it. I thought I must have dreamed, imagined the whole thing. But the glade was right, the trees were right. Even the creek was right.

I dug down in the grass near my feet and I found, way under the topsoil and dry grass and leaves, a layer burned black and grey with ash. Here was the spot we'd made our fire, but it was like a hundred years had passed by, or longer. I clawed through the grass, and there, in the bright smiling sunlight, I found a skull, just part of it. There was one eye socket, and the ridge of the brow, above that the bone was cut clean, like sawed. It was so old, it was powdering in my hands.

I stood up and dropped the thing. I knew it was part of my friend, one of them. I looked around the clearing, wanting to see Billy and George looking for me, or hiding behind me to shout and laugh at me. But instead I saw her, standing shining and real in the sun. You'd think the Devil's child would fear the sun, but she glowed like a star, and her stare bit into me. I stumbled back, heard the lost bone grind under my feet. I shook my head, refused all of it, denied everything.

And the Devil Girl laughed, only no sound came from her mouth, no sound. And then I ran, only then.[13]

The spook stays with you, especially because it comes after a golden moment in the sun, amity between friends, before night comes down, and you think about the mouth and the sound and the screaming, Billy's voice in among the damned, and George's, and yours.

Cross genre writing means the distinctions of fantasy, science fiction, horror and the paranormal are blurred. Should an author worry about labels? A publisher or bookseller or agent will determine the supremacy of a genre or a subgenre into which to cast the work, and will esteem whichever elements of the fantastical, science fiction or philosophy, fear, revulsion or spook are embodied. As Richard Mathews rightly argued, there are no pure genres.[14]

Other fundamentals to writing compelling speculative fiction

As in any other fiction, the crux of writing good speculative fiction is compelling storytelling that establishes from the onset a relationship with the reader and solicits their commitment to the reading. So that book in you ... are you born a writer? Do *writing* genes determine creative ability? Some scientists have tried to prove so, offering research results where participants, for example with ability to judge pitch and time, and possessing crucial skills in composing, improvisation and arranging, showed the presence of a gene directly correlated with musical creativity: a genetic cluster responsible for the brain's ability to form new connections between brain cells. You may have two left hands when it comes to typing out stories, but creative ability is also about divergent thinking, exploring ideas. It's about other fundaments in writing: passion, a nose for a good story, research, discipline and edit, edit, edit (Figure 2.2).

Fundamental	Fantasy	Science fiction	Horror and the paranormal	Cross genre
Passion	✓	✓	✓	✓
Nose for a good story	✓	✓	✓	✓
Research	✓	✓	✓	✓
Discipline	✓	✓	✓	✓
Dialogue/narrator	✓	✓	✓	✓
Edit, edit, edit	✓	✓	✓	✓

Figure 2.2 Other fundamentals in story writing

Passion

Passion is what triggered Ray Bradbury's response when he was 19 or 21 and selling newspapers on a street corner, and people asked him, 'What are you doing here?'

'Becoming a writer,' he said.

'But you don't look like one,' they said.

'Yeah,' he said. 'But I feel like one.'[15]

Passion is what kept him writing, because he did not start with instant attainment. *The Martian Chronicles* (1950) was first published as a scatter of short fiction in various magazines, and it took forever to turn them into a book. In *An Evening with Ray Bradbury*[16] the author talked about how he was living hand to mouth, took a Greyhound bus to New York, travelled four days and four nights on the bus and stayed at the YMCA at fifty cents a night. He took a bunch of his Martian short stories to a dozen publishers, but nobody wanted them. Short stories didn't sell, they said. 'Don't you have a novel?' they asked. 'No, I'm a sprinter,' he said. 'I write short stories.' He got his break from Doubleday Publishers, who said, 'What about all those Martian stories you've been writing? What if you tied them all together in a tapestry and called them *The Martian Chronicles*?' After initial critical scrutiny, the work saw a paradigm shift: a science fiction revolution where fans were more generous to new ideas and forms of genre fiction. Decades after its first publication, *The Martian Chronicles* has sold nearly 33,000 hardbound copies and millions in paperback, in America alone.

In a *Writer's Digest* interview,[17] Orson Scott Card said you only write at your best, invent your best stories, when you believe in the characters, motives, relationships and events you are creating. It is this belief, this hunger that makes you toss and turn, weary-eyed, as your brain wrestles for the right opening line; makes you hop into a car and drive miles out to nowhere, staring at the world for that closing.

Nose for a good story

Logan Thrasher Collins' nose was in good form when he sniffed around technology and spoke to his creative muse about a future that combined science and dreams. He came up with a poem. In 'The Sonata Machine' time goes *tick-tickity-ticking* beneath an expanse of darkness and an echoing of stars, and the universe spreads out, and a sonata plays in dreams encoded in metamorphosis.[18] Charles Ebert read the latest biography of English singer-songwriter Sandy Denny and wrote 'A World Where Sandy Never Died':

> The lights dimmed to applause. Dark figures on stage trod among the amps, guitar stands and the drum kit. The guitarists and the bassist grabbed jacks for their instruments and plugged in. They strummed a few tuning notes.
>
> A lone figure entered from the wings. She picked her way across the stage to stand on the very edge, just before the line of microphones. A spotlight turned on and there was Sandy Denny, smiling and waving to the crowd. She wore jeans and a black blouse. Her hair was grey and unruly, and she carried a lot more weight than when she was young. She looked like a grandmother and Doug realized she was sixty-seven years old in this universe. In his, she died at thirty-one.
>
> When the applause died, she walked to the piano and played the first few chords of 'Pipes of Capecastle', a track off her new album. The rest of the band joined in and the concert began.

It was a great show, and not just because Doug was seeing a performer he never thought he'd see—even in this universe she didn't tour much—but once she started into the more familiar songs, Doug got over the shock of her appearance and realised what a great performer she was. Her between-song patter, which on the older live recordings was self-conscious, was now assured and funny.[19]

Holding a book about a dead singer triggered an elaborate story of time travel and piracy. Award-winning short story writer and novelist Kris Ashton had an illness and a dream: two unrelated things that combined to inspire a science fiction horror 'The Larval Stage' (2018) about terminal illness and a human host to flesh-eating larva from the Alludian planet.[20]

Stephen King in his book *On Writing* saw stories as relics, parts of an undiscovered world for writers to excavate. Feel, smell, see—ideas float everywhere. Stories cartwheel in little word associations in your vocabulary. Unfound plots flirt all around you: in the rubicund bell innocently dangling on the Christmas tree in your unswept lounge; in the bald young man with honey-brown eyes who beamed at you in the lift on your way to work; in the ash-eyed tramp by the wayside who held your gaze a particular way and asked for nothing, but something drew your hand to your pocket and you pulled out a note; in the tarmac-black pebble that a little girl with braids throws onto a chalked out square on the gravel, and you see nothing but the blackness of the stone as the child hops on one foot, square after square, humming a nursery rhyme …

On her website, Ursula Le Guin, a 1975 Hugo and Nebula award winner, admitted to drawing ideas from the world:

…everything one writes about comes from experience. Where else could it come from? But the imagination recombines, remakes … makes a new world, makes the world new.[21]

Le Guin borrowed ideas from the world and transformed them into speculative fiction as a means to explore themes such as gender, religion, race, class and feminism in ways that 'brought literary depth and a tough-minded feminist sensibility to science fiction and fantasy',[22] as described in a *New York Times* obituary upon her death. King, in his tribute to Le Guin, called her 'one of the greats', 'not just a science fiction writer; a literary icon',[23] and all she did was observe the world, imagine and write stories. Observe the mundane as it drifts by, and then—as Stephen King advised—ask yourself: 'What if?'

Research

Explore. Gather contextual information about an event, character or place. On his official site for fans, George R. R. Martin, who uses what he calls a 'total immersion' method, explained:

> Since I do not know what particular nuggets I may need during the course of writing a novel, I try to learn as much as possible about the subject in question (the medieval world, in the case of *A Song of Ice and Fire*, or the antebellum river and the steamboat era in the case of *Fevre Dream*) by reading everything I can get my hands on.

Researching is fundamental to the robustness, credibility, of your story because it allows you to paint a wholesome picture and craft a convincing narrative. Bradbury was about stuffing your head with many different things from diverse fields; this helps accumulate intellectual building blocks for your ideas. Read one story a night, he said. One poem a night. One essay a night. Read archaeology, zoology, biology, philosophy, politics, literature … At the end of a thousand nights, he said, 'Jesus God, you'll be full of stuff!' The library is your friend. Read Shakespeare. Read George Bernard Shaw. The cinema is your friend. Clark Gable, Natalie Wood, Morgan Freeman, John Wayne, Vivien Leigh, Angela Basset. Spielberg. Scorsese. Tarantino. Nora Ephron. Jane Campion. Sophia Coppola. Fall in love with the big screen. In tune with his funny bone, Bradbury told a story of how he watched *The Hunchback of Notre Dame* (1923) at the age of three with his mother, how he was so immersed that it entered his reality and he walked strange for three days after!

Stephen King in his book *On Writing: A Memoir of the Craft* (2000) said if you don't have time to read, you don't have the time or tools to write.

On his fan site, George R. R. Martin wrote:

> The most important thing for any aspiring writer … is to read! And not just the sort of thing you're trying to write, be that fantasy, SF, comic books, whatever. You need to read everything. Read fiction, non-fiction, magazines, newspapers … history, historical fiction, biography … mystery novels, fantasy, SF, horror, mainstream, literary classics, erotica, adventure, satire. Every writer has something to teach you … And write. Write every day, even if it is only a page or two. The more you write, the better you'll get.

The best of writers, like King, like Bradbury, like Le Guin—whose father was a university professor, and her philosophy was 'Write. Revise. If possible, publish'—all cherished text. Ursula Le Guin found early stimulation in learning to write at five and later indulging her love for languages. The writer's 'pleasant duty', she is quoted to have said in an interview with *The Guardian*, is to ply the reader's imagination with 'the best and purest nourishment that it can absorb'.[24]

Franz Kafka is famously quoted for these words:

> … we ought to read only the kind of books that wound or stab us. If the book we're reading doesn't wake us up with a blow to the head, what are we reading for?
> … A book must be the axe for the frozen sea within us.

Read what works for you, read generously. But be mindful of what you research, warned King in his book on writing, your research should not overwhelm the story. Once you start writing, you don't have to use all the knowledge you have gathered. Novice writers blunder into numbing readers with information overload, a regurgitation of every detail they have unearthed about a place, a planet, a psychological condition … Rather than squash it all into your plot, use that information at the back of your head to guide your character's choices, their adventures, your story's twists.

In researching you gain the right premise to craft a robust story, one with clarity on what drives or shapes your world, your characters, your events.

Discipline

To be prolific in quality work you need discipline because it teaches you to reinforce the application of writing in whichever pattern or routine that works for you. In the *Writer's Digest* interview, Orson Scott Card observed:

> Some people need structure and habit to get their work done. I need a complete lack of structure, absolute schedule-freedom, and a desperate urgency in order to accomplish anything. Everybody should figure out what works for them and then use it to get things written … There's no good or right way to organize your writing day—there's only What Works.

Card was suggesting that what works for him might not work for you because we are all different. You might be a morning person, a night person. Some people need deadlines and panic to write their award-winners. Others need planning, sticky notes, butcher paper to toy with ideas. Others brainstorm with trusted peers to stimulate their plot twists. In his essay 'The Still-Breathing Author',[25] Gerald Murnane contemplates his own writerly process and says that, while writing, he remains unconsumed by research. For him, it's about process and not about doing research; he is more interested in what he remembers and what he forgets from his own experience rather than what he archives (and might not use). He talks in his essay about trusting writerly obsessions, about a self-discipline in his own approach to writing where a piece of fiction can take shape in his mind as a diagram. Murnane charts his fictions in first drawing—another discipline might work for you. Do what helps unpick your lack of writing and gets those words on a page. Exercise your literary muscles.

Academics who teach creative writing sometimes forget to exercise those literary muscles because they are so preoccupied with teaching others discipline, with rules of genre, with measuring the work of students, with peers' 'quality'—a subjective matter: 'One reader's drivel is another's poetry', suggested academic Sue Norton[26]—that we stray from actual creativity. You hone art by doing. Find time. Make time. Create. Write, write, write. Orson Scott Card said, 'The discipline has to come from within. Don't wait for a muse to strike and force you to a typewriter.'[27]

Dialogue/narrator

Dialogue or a narrator are crucial to moving the story along in a manner that reveals crucial elements of character and plot while keeping the unsuspecting reader engaged. Dialogue can be taut or flowered, direct or an aside. A well-drawn omniscient narrator is as effective as dialogue, evidenced in Gray's story:

> You were ten when you slew your first monster.
> You came to a town, upriver from Echuca. It was April when nights grew heavy with cold. It seemed like just another stop on the road, another town you'd haul in; camp a few days while Bill took care of whatever beast ailed the locals.
> You sometimes wandered the streets, watched other kids or peeked in their windows when they were at school. You saw bikes on the lawns in front of houses, swings made of rope and odd tires and bedrooms filled with toys and books. It looked like paradise.
> 'Can I go to school?' you asked Bunyip Bill.
> 'You'll do best with me, mate.'

The story flows, even with little dialogue, where the omniscient narrator gives voice in a 'you-narrative'. While the second-person narration can be unsettling to the reader; confronting in its direct address where the reader cannot answer back, it works well in Gray's story.

Edit, edit, edit

In an Atlantic interview King said:

> It's what you hear in your head, but it's never right the first time. So you have
> to rewrite it and revise it. My rule of thumb is that a short story of 3,000
> words should be rewritten down to 2,500. It's not always true, but mostly it is.
> You need to take out the stuff that's just sitting there and doing nothing. No
> slackers allowed! All meat, no filler![28]

A good writer's circle can serve as what Card called 'a wise reader'.[29] A wise
reader is the 'right' reader, where the term 'right' does not mean the one who
likes your work, but one who really studies your work seriously, one from
whose review exercise you draw learnings rather than disillusionment. For
this discussion place a writer as being in a fragile place, one that is also sacred.
Consider the potential of emotional attachment to a creation and equate
advising a writer that their work is inadequate to telling a mother that her
baby is ugly. To be published, the writer must, inevitably, give others entry
to their precious world. A wise reader is a form of quality assurance, way
before your work touches the editor's desk. A wise reader as an open-minded
critic is not seeking the death of the author but rather wishing to view the
writing in its best light. This reader will position you to arrive at an articulate
product. A repressive reader is dangerous because they stifle creative energy,
humiliate you and lead to unproductive outcomes. As a matter of survival,
discern unhealthy readers and act swiftly to substitute or reconfigure them,
and equally have the insight to leverage from wise readers.

Bradbury did not mince words about friends who make fun of you and
don't believe in you. Get rid of them, he said. Go make a phone call and fire
them. Anyone who doesn't believe in you or your future, to hell with them,
he said.

Voice as integral to a writer's identity

In her Nobel Prize acceptance speech Toni Morrison shared a poetic vision on
the radical power of language:

> Make up a story ... For our sake and yours forget your name in the street; tell
> us what the world has been to you in the dark places and in the light. Don't tell
> us what to believe, what to fear. Show us belief's wide skirt and the stitch that
> unravels fear's caul.[30]

In this address, Morrison's approach is grounded, direct; it reaches in and out of the inner self. In a most personal way it is about you, me, us. This is her voice, one of her many voices.

In Bradbury's work, he writes as he speaks: bold, personable, affectionate, mentoring. He sees the light sides of life, its ironies. This is his voice, charming even when the fiction is horror. Have you found your voice? Hunt it in your favourite authors. Study how they write and try a faithful reproduction of it in your text. Read your work from your guiding authors' eyes: What are they saying? Consciously, subconsciously, something about how they write appeals to you. Perhaps it's the magic of the worlds they build. Or the velvet in the protagonist's core. Or the iron in the character's dialogue. Or the flowers in the authors' language, like the clove pink carnations, ivory white lilies and crimson rich roses sprouting in Anthony Doerr's language, every time, even if some critics abhor those very flowers:

> Doerr's prose style is high-pitched, operatic, relentless … No noun sits upon the page without the decoration of at least one adjective, and sometimes, alas, with two or three. And these adjectives far too often are of the glimmering, glowing, pellucid variety. Eyes are wounded, nights are luminous and starlit, seagulls are alabaster. 'Fields enwombed with hedges' is almost the last straw. (Carmen Callil, *The Guardian*)[31]

Never mind the critics; find the muse whose text makes colour in your mind, patterns a rainbow in the ideas you find voice to. Author Saul Bellow spoke on the *New York Times* website of his muses:

> When I was a boy 'discovering literature', I used to think how wonderful it would be if every other person on the street were familiar with Proust and Joyce or T. E. Lawrence or Pasternak and Kafka. Later I learned how refractory to high culture the democratic masses were. Lincoln as a young frontiersman read Plutarch, Shakespeare and the Bible. But then he was Lincoln.

D. H. Lawrence was also a favourite. Bellow painted text with his muses all the way to a Pulitzer Prize for his novel *Humboldt's Gift* (1975), and a Nobel Prize in literature 'for the human understanding and subtle analysis of contemporary culture that are combined in his work'. *Herzog* (1964) and *Mr. Sammler's Planet* (1970) each won the National Book Award for fiction, in 1965 and 1971 respectively.

Jorge Luis Borges had his own heroes: he read widely, his interests travelling across ancient Greece, medieval philosophers, theologians, paradoxical scholars and literary works by Jules Verne, Poe, Wells, Kafka, Shakespeare, Donne, Chesterton and more.

But Bellow did not win awards for *mimicking* Proust or Joyce or Kafka; Borges did not rise to literary accomplishment by *regurgitating* Verne, Poe, Shakespeare or Kafka. Somewhere along the way each author shaped a voice of his own, one to which readers paid attention. Borges is recognised globally as a most original and influential figure in modern literature. Bellow fulfilled his hope to reach those lovers of literature in remote corners, readers glad to find him.

Bradbury understood it was well to imitate your heroes but acknowledged you couldn't be them. He started off emulating H. G. Wells, Jules Verne and Arthur Conan Doyle, and then came into his own. Slowly, as you imitate your heroes, your own voice shapes out.

Writer Raymond Carver suggested voice is 'a unique and exact way of looking at things, and finding the right context for expressing that way of looking'. According to Carver, voice is one of the things that distinguishes one writer from another; it is the writer's 'particular and unmistakable signature on everything he writes'. But the signature is not static; not pure but a copy of itself, as French philosopher Jacques Derrida in *Margins of Philosophy* (1982) argued: if a signature is supposed to be a singular event, it is supposed to look like itself, but is not supposed to be a copy. Your passion, nose for a good story, discipline and research will help you along your writing project. Unearth your curiosity. And then tell it in your own way of looking at things. This is your voice.

A writer's voice is not always easily distinguishable from their style: your style illustrates the voice, and your voice informs the style. As you practise, practise, practise, you come into your own. Amanda Boulter explained that our writer's voice is distinct, and evidences itself in the way we use phrases, repetition, pauses … in the way we choose to talk about ideas; voice gives clue to where we come from, what social grouping has influenced us and offers a glimpse of our experiences, beliefs and desires. Every writer, said Boulter, 'already has their own voice, because every writer has their own perspectives on the world'.[32] This means we enter the writing with an inherent positioning that informs our style.

An author's style

Author Nancy Curteman explained writerly style, in this context synonymous with writerly signature, as 'an author's unique way of communicating ideas': 'the verbal identity of a writer', she suggested. Consider Ana Shopova's speculative fiction poem 'They Come' (2018):

> They come, my dear, he whispered near,
> They come in hordes with sugared swords,

With bated breath and beating drums,
They come, they come, they come, they come.
They come, my love, glance far above,
They come in throngs with sleepless songs,
With snarling smiles and screeching hearts,
They come, they come, they come, they come.
They come, my sweet, fall at their feet,
They come in swarms with thunderous storms,
With thieving thoughts and thrumming strides,
They come, they come, they come, they come.
They come, my sun, we must not run,
They come in drives with lovely knives,
With gilded gaze and glory pride,
They come, they come, and now they're here.[33]

A literacy geek, Shopova focuses on structure. A solid rhythm of a marching army or heartbeat seemed just right for the context of the poem. Rhyme and repetition and metaphor and personification mark her style in the simplicity of this poem and its invaders in their glory and doom as they come, they come to a pattern of drums and it rises to a crescendo. Unlike Shopova, renowned author Octavia Butler is Spartan, precise in her writing. No flowers, no drums, she just tells the story. In Stephen King speak, she does not *foofaraw* you. This is her style.

King is easy, conversational, teasing. He is sometimes pert to inject tension, single words between sentences. He writes clinically, an easy read with pace and tension through short to medium-length sentences. He enters a character's mind and shares this with his readers, not cautious about his choice of language—never mind it might offend. His writing can be emotive, like SHOUTING in caps. He italicizes and capitalizes, basically writes like an author who knows he will get away with anything. He is a king in the literary devices of foreshadowing and suspense, of building tension in his works and using action as an element of style that keeps the reader enthralled. He loves conflict. Taut dialogue, direct, moves the story along. For example Seneca's in *Under the Dome* (2009): 'You're losing your happy thoughts. Don't do that. Come to one-twenty. Let's go out to Route 119.'[34] King has a penchant for first-person narrative style. He puts a personable touch to his primary characters and their flaws, and you get to like them. This makes the horror you later encounter with them even more personal. Like a good suspense writer King teases, promises information through his often reliable narrator, and then holds out. This is his style.

Marion Zimmer Bradley also has a fondness for first-person narratives. Her writings are insightful, narrative (compared to rhythmic, for example), descriptive and observational, writing that is fastidious on science and technology. This is her style. In a prologue to *The Door Through Space* (1961) she explained:

> I discovered s-f in its golden age: the age of Kuttner, C. L. Moore, Leigh Brackett, Ed Hamilton and Jack Vance. But while I was still collecting rejection slips for my early efforts, the fashion changed. Adventures on faraway worlds and strange dimensions went out of fashion, and the new look in science-fiction—emphasis on the *science*—came in.
>
> So my first stories were straight science-fiction, and I'm not trying to put down that kind of story. It has its place. By and large, the kind of science-fiction which makes tomorrow's headlines as near as this morning's coffee has enlarged popular awareness of the modern, miraculous world of science we live in. It has helped generations of young people feel at ease with a rapidly changing world.[35]

Perhaps this explanation sheds insight into Bradley's diligence to the 'rules', the fads of the time, and her descriptive, narrative style that 'makes visible' those worlds beyond the stars. Was it the world of her time, a woman writing in a then man's world, that swept Bradley to pay attention, to excel?

Bradbury uses rhyme and repetition, metaphor in his language. He writes with wry humour, gently guides you to a moral of the story. In his post-apocalyptic story 'The Other Foot',[36] a white man lands in a rocket on Mars, where the black people now dwell, having fled persecution by white folk on Earth. 'What's a white man?' the children ask. 'You'll find out,' their mother Hattie says. The children persist. 'Well, first of all, they got white hands,' says Hattie. 'White hands!' The boys joke, slap each other. 'And they got white arms.' The boys hoot: 'White arms! White faces!' They are animated. Their dad's animation is of a different kind. He saw on Earth his father hung on a tree, his mother shot. White folk did it. He is setting up a welcoming committee: 'Find my guns and some rope. We'll do this right.' He fashions a hangman's knot. His plan is grand. For whites: rear section in the bus; shoe shining; no intermarriages. Freshly painted signs in shops that shout Limited clientele: Right to serve customer revocable at any time. He hands out weapons: a gun, another gun, a pistol, a shotgun ... The rocket door slides open. A single old man steps out. White folk have destroyed each other and their cities in a war on Earth, he says. Columbus, Georgia, New Orleans, all gone. Tampa. 'That's my town,' someone whispers. 'Fulton.' 'That's mine,' someone else. Memphis. Blown up.

White folk need help, rescue rockets, admission to Mars. 'We've been stupid,' says the old man quietly. 'We won't bother you again. But we'll come here and we'll work for you and do the things you did for us— clean your houses, cook your meals, shine your shoes ...' The silence is loud. Willie lets go the rope. It falls, snakes on the ground. He remembers Earth, the green Earth and the green town where he was born and raised. Everything gone: the stables, the ironsmiths, the soda founts, the gin mills, the river bridges, the lynching trees ... 'A new start for everyone,' his wife says on the drive back home. 'Yes,' says Willie at last. His boys come bursting forth. 'You see the white man? You see him?' they cry. 'Yes, sir,' says Willie. 'Seems like for the first time today I really seen the white man—I really seen him clear.'

This is a typical Bradbury story: rhythmic, witty, full of soul. This is his style: his manner of writing, his signature.

Consider Toni Morrison, who integrates speculative elements into her literary novels. *Song of Solomon* (1978) contains rudiments of magical realism, lyrical passages exposing the apocalyptic and the spiritual. The novel culminates with Milkman's leap, a surrender to the air so he could ride it. In this writing, as in her other novels, Morrison's distinct style carries beyond pivotal contestations around race—her radical and defining act of writing for black readers about black people; the subversive role of language in her body of works is a major signature.

She spoke in her Nobel lecture on the vitality of language as lying in its ability to 'limn the actual, imagined and possible lives of its speakers, readers, writers'. According to Morrison, language 'arcs towards the place where meaning may lie'. The author's style is not static and may vary across forms; thus Morrison's non-fiction may vary from her novels in language interplay. An author refines style through reading a variety of writers and through their own writing experiences. Authors who influenced Morrison include Flaubert, Austen and Dostoevsky; all connected her to the Western literary tradition despite her grounding in black lingo, visible in her characters' dialogue.

Morrison's style is also fetching, fluid sentences that carry rhythm, wealthy in metaphor. She doesn't confound readers with big words; hers are everyday words personifying everyday things, like beer. To illustrate blunt and masterful prose that draws a reader's curiosity, consider chapter 4 of *Song of*

Solomon (1978) where Morrison described protagonist Milkman's perception of his lover Hagar:

> She was the third beer. Not the first one, which the throat receives with almost
> tearful gratitude; nor the second, that confirms and extends the pleasure of the
> first. But the third, the one you drink because it's there, because it can't hurt,
> and because what difference does it make?[37]

This illustration aligns with the rest of Morrison's works, which the *New
York Times* described as possessing an arc of Greek tragedy, yet filled with the
domestic, street talk and folklore. Here Morrison adopts a pragmatic approach
to compare Hagar with a third beer—it is optional, insignificant—to defor-
malize with levity a complex relationship. The blunt yet masterful appraisal
uses a simple but familiar object (beer) to make sure the reader is conversant
with where exactly Hagar stands with Milkman, even though Hagar herself
might not know it.

In her unique use of language, Morrison switches viewpoints through
evocative narrators, sometimes omniscient. She uses an omniscient narrator in her novel *Love* (2003), whose flashbacks and italicized text of the
unnamed narrator fill in the gaps for the reader. But what is most vivid,
what you will always remember sharp like an arrow in your mind, is her
dialogue.

In sync with her other novels, *Song of Solomon* holds black cultural focus.
The essential aspect of Morrison's cast is their being black, their battles with
or acceptances of being black. To Morrison, the black novel is important
because it can suggest conflicts and problems, not to solve them but to
record them and reflect them.[38] This aspect of the 'black novel' is an integral feature of Morrison's style, one whose absence you would immediately
notice.

She shows particularity with detail, and stated in her 1993 Nobel lecture,
'narrative is radical, creating us at the very moment it is being created'.
Morrison makes her writing personal, casts her characters—their battles or
acceptances with being black—in a personal way. There is strength and spirit
in her writing. Her writerly style is unmistakeable.

During a writing workshop with my students, the first exercise was on
random writing, a 150-word story. One student Mikaela Brown fell to the
writing and then shared her story out loud with the class, reading in a sprint.
The class stayed silent a whole minute, and then erupted with questions.
What was the premise behind the story?

'An aura of despair, depression and darkness,' said Mikaela.

The aura became a signature in Mikaela's stories, where she wove light and shade in sudden fiction that threw you straight in and right out, that read as abrupt as it was written—this was Mikaela's unique way of communicating. She confessed to a penchant for eccentric authors like Dr Seuss and Roald Dahl, and to enjoying works by J. K. Rowling, Stephen King and Cassandra Clare. In another roil of random writing based on a prompt in an exercise on 'queer', Mikaela engaged with difference through a gender-neutral story:

The Darkness Pt. 1

I chose to be anonymous. No one knew where, how or who I was. I stayed in the shadows and did not emerge for less than the feeling of ecstasy. I needed a shot of joy to move my arm. A leg would cost more—for that, I needed bliss. If darkness crept in then I remained entrapped in the black hole. But for days when giggles and sunshine made their way into my mind, I rose. I played like a child. I was happy. Until blackness seeped in again, and I returned to the prison that was the endless night of my mind.

–Mikaela Brown (2016)

In this story that could be speculative if the narrator were supernatural, again Mikaela flung you in and quickly out. She used staccato, simile and personification. Her text flowed without dialogue: first-person narration, pathos furnishing depth.

Mikaela's way of looking is light and shade, sparse yet vivid. Her writing is immediate, this is her style.

Unlike Mikaela who split herself open and gushed out sudden fiction in class, another student Jakeb Fair deliberated. Watching him write was fascinating; he probed mentally until he found the right word. He furrowed his brow, focused, considered the text, shaped it. You knew he was disinclined to expose a flawed product; and before he read it out loud, he explained to the class that the writing wasn't there yet, it wasn't perfect. He read with character—immersion, depth and voice—and shared a piece that was a poetic murder mystery styled in rap. In its grim focus on themes of racism, death and the eternal, the writing was rhythmic. In 'Purgatory' Jakeb offered the perspective of a mixed-race person, a dead one, a voice from the grave. Jakeb's zeal for tune, his creativity in ways of music, invited itself to the writing workshop. A friend was learning to create hip hop riffs and beats, he explained, and Jakeb was writing and perfecting the prose. It made sense he would use the writing workshop to apply a melodious style to his writing. He put his clean ear for rhythm, listened to the text and musicality filtrated into his writing.

Jakeb's way of looking is deliberate and melodious: this is his style.

Margaret Atwood in her literary speculative works is not as eloquent or poetic as Morrison. She applies a descriptive and masterful style, blunt, spare and detached.

Edgar Rice Burroughs in *A Princess of Mars* (1917) is easy, personable, offering a rhythmic style pregnant with elements of repetition.

Suzanne Collins in *The Hunger Games* (2008) uses straightforward, prosaic text:

> When I wake up, the other side of the bed is cold. My fingers stretch out, seeking Prim's warmth but finding only the rough canvas cover of the mattress. She must have had bad dreams and climbed in with our mother.[39]

In this text Collins applies oppositions (cold/warmth).

Harlan Ellison in his science fiction short 'Neither Your Jenny nor Mine' (1964) is bland. He does not reflect much colour in language; he writes simply, in plain English, uses ordinary language.

A writerly style may shift between works, across genres, towards different audiences. In *Towards a Poetics of Creative Writing* (2015), author Dominique Hecq encouraged writers to find their own style to design their own poetics, where 'poetics' denotes the influences, the traditions the authors write within and the literary, social and political context in which they write. Hecq heartened writers to be mindful of the 'metaphorical mesh that privileges the visual in which we are caught up, particularly in Western societies', perhaps meaning an encouragement for writers to apply their own unique articulation, the language and behaviours that 'give free rein to our imagination in the act of writing'.[40]

Using Lewis Carroll's *Alice in Wonderland* (1992), an example, Hecq discussed Alice's leap into an unknown territory where she learns another language and discovers other behaviours, all in a symbolic discovery of her 'self' and 'the other' where stakes are unknown. The act of writing, suggested Hecq, puts an idea, an experience, into words. It is a making of art that requires the creator's 'language' to connect with the reader's. A writer's 'poetics', as his or her signature, is dynamic; it is 'always a work in progress and as such it is necessarily selective'. In the context of writing, explained Hecq, the writer uses the text, the characters, the worlds and the language(s) created as mechanisms of transference. The writer brings to the work internal logic and style, subconscious dimensions of human thought.

Amanda Boulter in *Writing Fiction* (2007) argues that 'style is not about surface decoration' but is something that 'grows up from the roots'.[41] She sees style as manifesting itself in the balance between the author's observation and imagining. Style is more than mimesis—imitating (or inventing) the world—but is rather a discovery, an invention of 'the language we use (our technique) and our vision of the world'.[42] It is the 'balance between the possibilities of perception and the possibilities of expression'.[43]

Your writing process unfolds organically as you put words on paper. Where voice is your unique way of looking at something, and telling it, style is about the literary devices you employ in the telling. Language and technique are your tools, where language influences voice and technique manipulates style. These form your unique way of crafting, shaping, making sense. This sums the foundations to crafting compelling speculative fiction. The next chapter gets you right into it through a writerly journey.

Exercise 2

Open a dictionary.

Turn to a random page and select a word. Read its definition(s), and jot the word down.

Turn to another random page and select a word. Again read its definition(s) and note it.

Repeat this exercise until you have five random words.

Now think about those words, and plan a 250-word story that includes them.

Don't overthink—just write.

Tip:

Stefan Laszczuk in 'Three Stories' on *Antic Journal*, an online magazine (www.anticmagazine.com.au), shared about issues and techniques he confronted in an exercise in random writing. His story titles uncannily look like ones birthed from a random word exercise:
- roasted spider monkey anus
- bus monk
- dying in a fast car.

He drew inspiration from a musical project where each song in the album 'was entirely conceived from scratch, recorded and mixed in one day'. In the project he unravelled 'an act of discovering, drawing out and then immediately capturing a fresh idea without killing it, or being able to overthink it in any way'. The songs, 'cooked under pressure', resulted as originally intended.

Laszczuk applied the same technique to finish a vignette in one session, where he 'would sit down and bang each one out in an afternoon, and then leave them as they were', having edited them as much as he could in that one and only session. His reasons for leaving the stories as they were included more than time constraints with his other work: Laszczuk discovered that revisits and edits meddled with freshness.

Try this exercise in random writing for your five dictionary words.

3

Vogler's hero/ine's journey

Charting your speculative fiction

Graeme Harper, in an editorial on 'the sound' of creative writing in *New Writing, the International Journal for the Practice and Theory of Creative Writing*, used the metaphor of a dodo to interrogate the nature of signification, of words as signifiers, where signifying is a mental concept, an imaginative conjecture that has personal and shared communal meaning. Harper questioned what it is that we seek in writing, or reading, whether our quest is not so much for an exchange of information as to advance our human understanding, to immerse ourselves into a realm of exploration—a quest in which we ask what is or is not, how it is or is not, and why the particular story is worthy of our attention. Writing is a constant choice in a process where we mentally wrangle with what to tell, what not to tell, how to tell it and why.

Most speculative fiction comes along an archetypal three-act structure of a beginning, middle, end. The story has a setting, imperative to situate the narrative and make it real to the reader. Where another author might fix the setting way before embarking on the fiction, Edgar Allan Poe spoke in his essay 'The Philosophy of Composition' about how he decided on his characters and plot before he sat down to furnish the setting, to 'place the lover in his chamber', a room already richly furnished.[1]

Writers like Laszczuk enjoy the surprise ending of an experimental story, but Poe chose to know the ending in advance:

> Nothing is more clear than that every plot, worth the name, must be elaborated to its *dénouement* before any thing be attempted with the pen. It is only with the *dénouement* constantly in view that we can give a plot its indispensable air of consequence, or causation, by making the incidents, and especially the tone at all points, tend to the development of the intention.[2]

Poe plotted, set writing and brought the characters together to a climax. Knowing the ending in advance can help avoid runaway tale pitfalls that might culminate in 'it was only a dream'. The movie *Twilight: Breaking Dawn* offered in Part 2 an 'only-a-dream' gag to a battle shocker that wiped out key characters such as Carlisle and Jasper; as the audience sat stunned, wondered what to make of the scene, they found out it was just a dream. Don't fix gaps in your plot with 'only-a-dream'.

As part of his arduous plotting where he also determined the literary art's particulars—characterization, theme, tone, 'impression, or effect, to be conveyed', tone and so on—Poe applied the 'limit of a single sitting rule':

> If any literary work is too long to be read at one sitting, we must be content to dispense with the immensely important effect derivable from unity of impression—for, if two sittings be required, the affairs of the world interfere, and every thing like totality is at once destroyed.[3]

Poe charted his text, sat down and wrote works, many of which could be read at one sitting.

Warren Ellis, novelist and comic book writer, has his own self-imposed restrictions, not to mention the limitations already inflicted by the format of comic book writing. Ellis' approach keeps him constantly producing quality work. On his website he offered three simple questions to ask: What does the character want? What does the character need to do to get what she wants? What is the character prepared to do to get what she wants? And then, suggested Ellis, build on these questions by introducing hurdles that make it as difficult as possible for the character. Without hurdles, where's the tension?

King admitted in his book on writing to plotting novels sparingly; he believes in emulating the real human experience (largely plotless) and finds an incompatibility between plotting and creative spontaneity.

Nevertheless, in establishing character identity (what defines a person or being), sources of knowledge to shape the literary art and the relationship between fiction and reality, there is a general formula, a writer's journey—one an author might employ as a guide towards an articulate product.

Vogler's writer's journey

Christopher Vogler in *The Writer's Journey* (1998) explored the relationship between mythology and storytelling. He took his template from mythologist Joseph Campbell, who wrote *The Hero with a Thousand Faces* (1949), and who in turn took his template from Carl Jung's theories of archetypes, the personal and collective unconscious, and the human psyche. Campbell's ideas, including those on myth, the modern world and the hero's adventure, appear in *The Power of Myth* (1988). In *The Hero's Journey* (1990) Campbell explored the hero's call to adventure, the road of trials, the vision quest … all the way to the return threshold where the hero reappears, triumphant, to deserved recognition. To Campbell, myths are the masks of God through which persons seek to relate themselves to the wonders of existence.

In addition to specialized archetypes like the wolf, the hunter, the wicked stepmother, the fairy godmother, the witch, the prince/ss and the greedy innkeeper in fairy tales, Vogler uncovered frequently used figures such as the hero (protagonist on a quest)—where variants of the hero, or perhaps distinct archetypes from the hero, include the anti-hero (deemed a villain), tragic hero (like Macbeth), catalyst hero (who brings about transformation in the other rather than the self); the mentor (wise old man or woman); the threshold guardian (the hero's obstacle); the herald (who calls the hero to adventure); the shape shifter (a scheming, unstable character); and so on.

To better identify with these archetypes (the hero, the mentor, the guardian …), let us look at Vogler's sorting and use IMDb's 'A list of bad and good Harry Potter characters' to assign one or more characters to each archetype.

Hero—this is the protagonist on a quest, like Harry Potter. His or her mission may be a search for identity, wholeness, redemption for the self or others. Variants include the willing or unwilling hero, the group-oriented hero (part of a clan, tribe or village) or loner hero (like the gun-toting Westerner), the anti-hero (deemed a villain, like Robin Hood), the tragic hero (like Macbeth) and the catalyst hero (who brings about transformation in others).

Mentor (wise old man or woman)—this is the sage, like Hagrid or Professor Dumbledore. His or her mission is to aid, train, gift, motivate the hero. The mentor represents the higher self but can sometimes be used to mislead the audience, a decoy to lure the hero into danger. A good example of a dark mentor from Harry Potter is Severus Snape, who pretends to be bad but is good.

Threshold guardian—this is the hero's obstacle, the blocker. He or she is not the main villain or antagonist but is there to impede the hero's quest, like the Death Eaters, dementors, red-haired mermaid or Dolores Umbridge.

Herald—this is the archetype who calls the hero to adventure, issues challenges or announces the coming of significant change. In Harry Potter, Dumbledore, who also functions as a mentor, is a prominent herald, as is Professor Sybil Trelawney.

Shapeshifter—this is the scheming, shifting, unstable character, again like a Death Eater in Harry Potter, who may mislead the hero or keep them guessing. Peter Pettigrew, who is one of Voldemort's Death Eaters, can fake his own death or morph into a rat to flee or gain access to places. Shapeshifters are constantly changing in mood or appearance.

Shadow—this archetype represents the energy of the dark side. The shadow can also be the shapeshifter but in more prominent ways is represented by the dementors or Bellatrix Lestrange. There is a dark side in antagonist Draco Malfoy, who wants to become to Voldemort what Harry is to Dumbledore.

Ally—this archetype accompanies the hero on their quest, like Harry Potter's multiple allies in Ron Weasley, Hermione Granger, Sirius Black or Alastor 'Mad-Eye' Moody. The ally can be a helpful servant or from beyond the grave: a dead parent. Animal allies include the unicorn or companion owl and Harry Potter's deer spirit, his patronus.

Trickster—according to Vogler in *The Writer's Journey*, the trickster archetype 'embodies the energies of mischief and desire for change'. They are clowns or comical sidekicks who point out folly and hypocrisy while providing healthy laughter. As Vogler suggested, tricksters may be ally or shadow archetypes, 'like Loki, the Norse god of trickery and deceit'. The Weasley twins, Fred and George, are somewhat tricksters but possibly in his own way house-elf Dobby, who desires change, is a trickster too, as is the poltergeist Peeves.

As Vogler suggested, it helps to understand an archetype as 'an infinitely flexible language of character', as a function at a given moment in a narrative—as archetypes can shift from one type to another in the same narrative: for example, Dumbledore serves as both a mentor and a herald.

Christopher Vogler's mythic structure (1998), while written for screenwriters, presents storytelling paradigms and a study of character archetypes and their quests, such as the hero/ine's journey, in his explication of its 12 stages:

1. *Ordinary world*: In the ordinary world, the hero/ine has a great desire, an unrealised wanderlust or restlessness for something, that creates an inner absence. In the first book of the series, *Harry Potter and the Philosopher's*

Stone (1997), there is no real ordinary world for young orphan Harry. But from the onset he understands that he is different from what he eventually learns are 'muggles': persons of no magical ability. Harry feels an absence; he is rejected for his supernatural abilities in the Dursley world.

2. *Call to adventure* (inciting incident): In the call, someone or something provides a catalyst that shows the hero/ine a clear path forward, and a choice exists to seize the moment in the beginning of a great adventure. Harry's first call arrives in the form of a deluge of letters, mysterious, just before his eleventh birthday. It is at this stage that his importance comes to fore in the supernatural calling. Hagrid's appearance, with notice of Harry's acceptance to the Hogwarts School of Witchcraft and Wizardry, catapults the boy towards a new and adventurous world.

3. *Refusal of the call*: The hero/ine understands the clear path forward but experiences obstacles that may be fear-based or societal blockers that lead to a shrinking from the call. Harry is not sure he is cut out to be a wizard. But the wand store settles his conviction when a wand made of holly and phoenix feather responds to him. It is a twin to one containing feathers from the same phoenix, a wand that belonged to Voldemort who had used it to give Harry his forehead scar.

4. *Meeting with the mentor*: A mentor, who may be a friendly stranger or a chance encounter, justifies the hero/ine's passions or destiny, guides how far to go in answering the call and stimulates a personal transformation that helps the hero/ine take up the gauntlet. Hagrid is the first mentor Harry encounters. Next, Harry will become acquainted with Albus Dumbledore, the head of Hogwarts, who will influence him in more ways than Harry can imagine. And their intimacy will grow.

5. *Crossing the first threshold*: This is the first critical obstacle that truly confronts the hero/ine to the extent that a choice must be made to cross or not to cross the threshold. In fairy tale, there may be a prohibitive guardian of the threshold, for example an ogre or demon, and the risk to the hero/ine may involve annihilation. Harry crosses many thresholds. He is first confounded by the Hogwarts students' reception: everyone knows him. There is high expectation of him in the wizard world. But this is not yet the threshold. His stumble across a forbidden hallway in the wizard's academy brings him face to face with the guardian of a true threshold: a vicious three-headed dog named Fluffy, guarding a secret chamber that houses the philosopher's stone.

6. *Tests, allies, enemies*: Having crossed the first threshold, the hero/ine's challenges are just beginning. Obstacles and perils rear every which way and the hero/ine must confront each. Harry has allies in Ron, Hermione, Neville, the Weasley twins, Hagrid and Dumbledore. He has enemies

in Malfoy and his crew. And there will be dark powers against him in Bellatrix Lestrange, Lucius Malfoy and the Death Eaters.

7. *Approach to the inmost cave*: The hero/ine approaches the fruition of their quest, the 'treasure', so to speak: the moment long awaited. In the first book of the Harry Potter series, this is a secret chamber guarded by spells and a three-headed beast. It houses the philosopher's stone of astonishing powers; a stone that must be destroyed lest it gets to Voldemort, who is keen to thieve it.

8. *Ordeal* (mid-point, death and rebirth): The treasure cannot just be taken: it must be won. There may be a trickster, an ultimate enemy or severe obstacle to overcome. The hero/ine must, in one way or another, prove their worth to claim the reward. Harry leaps through many hurdles and plunges to a near-death experience in his efforts to redeem the philosopher's stone.

9. *Reward* (seizing the sword): Having proven their worth, the hero/ine claims the treasure and fulfils the quest. This represents a new initiation. The hero/ine achieves a new level of transformation where life can never be the same again. The reward in the first book is preventing the triumph of evil in gaining the philosopher's stone. Harry learns more about himself and his supernatural abilities. Together with Hermione and Neville, he is awarded rich points for Gryffindor, which helps win the wizard academy house cup.

10. *The road back*: Transformed, the hero/ine must return home to transform their world. The treasure or fulfilment is only valuable if it meets the purpose of the quest. The return poses an ultimate crisis the hero/ine must confront. Sometimes the predicament is inner, where the hero/ine is tempted not to return home, to succumb to greed and claim the treasure or actualization for themselves. There is no real road back in the first Harry Potter book, where the entire hero's journey takes place in the wizard world, but the entire hero's journey need not be enacted in full each story. In the overarching arc of the series, Harry makes a road back to transform the wizard world and save humans.

11. *Resurrection* (climax): Here, the hero/ine has overcome enchanting distractions, and the hero/ine's world is also transformed. There is no resurrection in the first book, because Harry is never distracted for one moment from his goal to triumph over Voldemort and the journey home is incomplete. But in the last book of the series Harry literally resurrects after destroying the horcruxes and, finally, truly understands his destiny.

12. *Return with the elixir* (denouement): The elixir is a treasure or lesson that the hero must bring back from the 'special world'. It could be a

magic potion with the power to heal, for example—in Harry Potter—the philosopher's stone with its transformation powers, including an ability to produce the elixir of life, a potion that makes the drinker immortal. The elixir can also be knowledge, perspective or experience that will be of use in the 'ordinary world' to which the hero/ine returns.

Why archetypes

In King's *The Dark Tower* series, Mid-World's last gunslinger Roland Deschain goes through the hero's journey in each new novel: he faces a new ordinary world, a new call to adventure, new tests, allies, enemies … Rowling's Harry Potter repeats the quest pattern in each book. Most stories deal with only some stages, not all, of the hero/ine's journey.

An archetype is a pre-existent form, according to Jung. The archetype represents the extra-personal or collective unconscious. The collective unconscious represents impersonal/transpersonal traits, independent of personal experience, that exist in everyone.

In applying Jung's template of archetypes in his model for storytelling, Vogler identified what makes a good story. In his work as story analyst at Fox 2000, Vogler identified a story's effectiveness by the physical way it affected his body:

> An effective story grabs your gut, tightens your throat, makes your heart race and your lungs pump, brings tears to your eyes or an explosion of laughter to your lips. If I wasn't getting some kind of physiological reaction from a story, I knew it was only affecting me on an intellectual level and therefore it would probably leave audiences cold.[4]

In your storytelling, like Vogler, consider the relationship between mythology and storytelling, where 'good stories make you feel you've been through a satisfying, complete experience. You've cried or laughed or both.'[5]

Plots that work

Writing speculative fiction is about conjuring your most vivid imagination because it involves unlocking your thinking from what Richard Mathews would call 'its chains of reason'.[6] But, as Card proposed in his book on writing, let the rules of the world you have built work. Our human world is intricate in itself; imagine a speculative world! Don't limit yourself to the plotlines Ronald Tobias prescribed in his book *20 Master Plots: and How to Build Them* (1993), published by Writer's Digest Books:

1. Quest: The hero/ine's search for a person, place or thing: for example, in J. R. R. Tolkien's *Lord of the Rings* (1954) there is Frodo's physical and spiritual quest for the one place he can eternally destroy the perfidious ring: the volcanic Mount Doom.

2. Adventure: This type of plot focuses on a journey, and still applies in *Lord of the Rings* to Frodo's escapade from his home in the Shire to Rivendell, Moria, Lothlórien ... all the way to Mount Doom in the Shadow of Mordor. Another good example is in Edgar Rice Burroughs' *A Princess of Mars* (1917), adapted into the movie *John Carter* (2012), where protagonist Carter finds himself transported to Mars.

3. Pursuit: A good example of a chase narrative is Philip K. Dick's *The Minority Report* (1956) where 'precrime' enforcer John Anderton finds himself on the run when the infallible automated system targets him as a potential murderer.

4. Rescue: The simplest rescue narrative in fairy tale comprises a hero, villain and victim. For example, in the renowned Grimm tale 'Rapunzel', an enchantress imprisons a girl in a tower, until a king's son riding through the forest passes by, hears the girl's voice and gains access to the tower through Rapunzel's magnificent long hair. But the enchantress finds out, and the king's son ends up blinded by thorns. He wanders several years in misery but is finally reunited with his Rapunzel, and his sight is restored through true love.

5. Escape: In the escape the hero/ine is confined in some way and seeks escape. For example in John Russell Fearn's science fiction classic *Fugitive of Time* (2012), protagonist Gordon Fryer is entrapped by an experiment's prediction of his exact hour and day of death. His quest is to circumvent his supposed destiny.

6. Revenge: In this type of narrative, a character seeks retaliation against real or imagined grievances, as in DC Comics' supervillains The Joker or The Penguin in retaliation for society's wrongs against them. In the 1975 British horror *I Don't Want to be Born*, a dwarf places a curse on a woman's baby after she rebuffs him.

7. The riddle: This type of narrative is about the hero/ine solving a puzzle (often in plain sight), for example The Brothers Grimm's fairy tale Rumpelstiltskin where an imp saves a miller's daughter from losing her head if she fails to meet the king's demands to spin straw into gold. But the rescue comes with a cost: once wed to the king, the miller's daughter

must give the imp her firstborn child. To free the now queen from her promise, the imp consents to give up his claim to the child if the queen can guess his name (the riddle) within three days.

8. Rivalry: This narrative comprises a power struggle between the protagonist and antagonist, as in George R. R. Martin's *A Game of Thrones* (2011), the first book in the *A Song of Ice and Fire* series, where much rivalry exists for the throne.

9. Underdog: Akin to a rivalry narrative, this poses an unmatched struggle between the protagonist and antagonist, for example in the Harry Potter books where the boy Potter must face a grown and powerful central antagonist in Lord Voldemort.

10. Temptation: In temptation narratives, there are motives, needs and impulses, for example in the biblical tale of Adam and Eve and the forbidden apple. In the American fantasy Lucifer, the TV series is about a bored Lucifer arrived from hell to Los Angeles, applying his experience and telepathic abilities to bring people's deepest desires and thoughts out of them.

11. Metamorphosis: The typical metamorphosis fairy tale involves transforming a curse that needs a cure, for example the prince's kiss that awakens Snow White, or the princess' kiss that shapeshifts the prince from his curse as a frog. In Hans Christian Andersen's 'The Wild Swans', a widowed king marries a wicked queen who is a witch and she transforms her stepsons into swans. She tries to bewitch stepdaughter Elisa. But the swans fly their sister to safety. There, the queen of the fairies guides Elisa to knit shirts out of nettles to help her brothers shift back to their human forms.

12. Transformation: This type of narrative is often aligned to a quest or journey narrative where the hero/ine is physically and spiritually changed upon fulfilling the quest. There is clear internal transfiguration in the confidence and attitude of the boy Potter, for example, in the Harry Potter series. There is external transfiguration in Voldemort who physically morphs from looking and acting like his earlier existence as half-blood wizard Tom Marvolo Riddle.

13. Maturation: In this type of narrative, the protagonist is on the cusp of maturity. For example Stephen King's *The Body* (1982) is a novella in which four young protagonists in a life-changing quest topple out of innocence when they head out on a quest to see another boy's dead body.

14. Love: The Romeo and Juliet types, overcoming obstacles in doomed love stories.

15. Forbidden Love: Akin to love narratives, but obstacles are usually societal conventions making the union taboo.

16. Sacrifice: These types of narrative are high-staked; there is great personal cost. For example, the biblical story of Abraham's call to tie his son Isaac and put him on the altar, in lieu of a sacrificial lamb.

17. Discovery: Again very similar to the quest or journey narrative; here the search is for depth in understanding: for example, Jules Verne's *Around the World in 80 Days* (1873).

18. Wretched excess: This is a narrative of psychological decline, where the hero/ine has the world at their hands, for example Dracula, or the emperor Nero and the great fire of Rome ...

19. Ascension: This narrative involves a hero/ine's battle against a moral dilemma, and winning. For example the rise of King Aslan to end the white witch's tyranny in C. S. Lewis' *The Chronicles of Narnia* (1939).

20. Descension: Converse to ascension, this type of narrative involves a battle against a moral dilemma, and losing. For example Adam and Eve's yielding to the snake's charm and munching the forbidden apple, or Cain's murder of his brother Abel in the biblical stories.

Tobias' list of master plots is thorough, but use it purely as a guide to boundless storytelling.

As you craft your story, remember there are multiple partners in the literary act: the author, the reader, the narrator, the narratee, the character ... Writing involves walking a tightrope, as author Wenche Ommundsen suggested in her book *Metafictions? Reflexivity in Contemporary Texts* (1993):

> Like most human relationships, literary communication mediates a precarious balance of power: power to narrate, power to interpret, power, finally, to accept or decline the roles offered by one's partners in the literary act.[7]

This means that the writing, how you shape your story, is a walk on a tightrope, where conditioning factors in the author–reader relationship determine how the reader interacts with your text, and this is more to do with expectation, knowledge and disposition ... as opposed to the tacit author–reader 'contract'. Ommundsen warned:

> authors can never allow themselves to forget that readers possess the supreme power, which is that of abandoning the text. The author must exercise textual authority in such a way as to ensure that this will not happen. Not surprisingly, then, textual communication is frequently represented as an act of love: the text must offer itself as an object of desire, seduce the reader, play and be played upon like the body of a lover.[8]

Exercise 3

Ron Mueck is an Australian hyperrealist sculptor working in the UK.

Take a look at the sculpture in Figure 3.1 by Mueck.

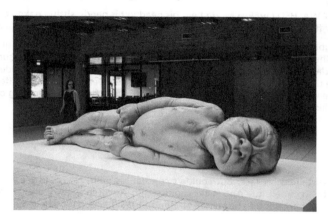

Figure 3.1 A Girl

Hyperreal sculpture of a newly delivered baby girl, complete with umbilical cord[9]

The National Galleries of Scotland. © Ron Mueck. Image courtesy of National Galleries Scotland.

Before putting your speculative fiction on screen or paper, think about the basics: your passion—What is your curiosity in this story? What's your nose telling you about this as a good story?

> Research.
> Edit, edit, edit.

Alternatively, run an online search on other works by Ron Mueck; for example:
* *Mask II* by Mueck (believed to be a self-portrait)
* *In Bed*: a carefully composed middle-aged woman in bed who is either anxious or reflective
* *Boy*: sculpture of a boy, crouching
* *Two Women*: two elderly women standing as if gossiping
* *Big Man*: naked, hairless man seated, knees drawn up, elbows on knees

Choose one Mueck sculpture. Imagine a story behind the work.

In an exercise of personalization, imagine you were the sculpture, the object: What is your narrative? Tell us something about yourself. Why are you here? Where have you come from? What's going on in your mind now?

Write a short story (250 words) in the first- or third-person point of view.

Tip:

The following is an example by my student Mikaela, based on Mueck's *Big Man*:

10837

REGRET WASHED OVER HIM. He held his head in his hands, sitting naked on the shower floor. He knew he would not be able to deal with what he had done.

He scrubbed his skin over and over, repeated until he was red raw, but still, the guilt. The water ran crystal clear over his shaved head, a waterfall of misunderstood clarity in the most important moments of his life. The water made him believe that he could be just as clean as he was after every shower of his life. But this one was different. This water pounded on him like heavy hail, beating on his senses like a chant.

Guilty.

Guilty.

Guilty.

Water curtained his face, but couldn't conceal his guilt. He could see his own guilt, feel it, smell it... And if he could see it, so could everyone else. In this moment Robert (soon to be known as inmate 10837) understood he would never be clean again.

— Mikaela Brown (2016)

4

The speculative: A problem with definitions

In a war of words with Ursula Le Guin, literary author Margaret Atwood hurled the term 'speculative fiction' rather than science fiction to label those of her works with a genre slant. These include her dystopian novel *The Handmaid's Tale* (1985) that draws attention to gender, religion and power, and the apocalyptic *Oryx and Crake* (2003), part of the MaddAddam trilogy, selling on Amazon under the label of science fiction (genetic engineering).[1] One editorial review on Amazon defined *The Handmaid's Tale* as 'a superlative exercise in science fiction'. Another review placed *Oryx and Crake* as science fiction:

> Shortlisted for the Booker Prize in 2003, Oryx and Crake is Margaret Atwood's most apocalyptic story to date … Oryx and Crake is a lot more grim and depressing, in terms of the plight of the human race … It may be a challenge for some to get through this book. Those who are fans of science fiction and speculative fiction, however, may embrace this novel …

But Atwood, in a podcast with the *Geek's Guide to the Galaxy*, said, 'It's a matter of truth in labeling. I like there to be some resemblance between what is promised on the outside and what you get on the inside.' To her, 'science fiction has monsters and spaceships; speculative fiction could really happen.'[2] There are those who disagree.

Harlan Ellison, notorious for being anti sci-fi fandom and a proponent of speculative fiction, rejected his labelling as a science fiction writer:

> I do fiction that is more like Kafka or Poe. I mean, that's what I write. I write, I suppose, what the Latin Americans call magic realism. That's a lot closer to what I write. Every once in a while I'll do a story that has one of those pieces of science fiction furniture in it, a mutant or telepathy or a future society—but I am not ever a science fiction writer. I'm just a writer who occasionally happens to do science fiction.[3]

For all his Hugos—science fiction's most distinguished award—Ellison's positioning was clear:

> I am a writer, period. Like Faulkner, I write about the heart in conflict with itself. We're talking about my survival here. There's an entire cadre of astounding talents that are nonentities as far as the literary establishment is concerned. I don't ask you to love me, just give me some respect. Don't you think a writer has the right to be given the label he chooses?[4]

Asked to define speculative fiction, he remarked:

> I will give you the only answer that there is. It is the game of 'what if?'. You take that which is known, and you extrapolate—and you keep it within the bounds of logic, otherwise it becomes fantasy—and you say, 'Well, what if?'. That's what speculative fiction is, and at its very best, it is classic literature, on a level with *Moby Dick* and Colette and Edgar Allan Poe.[5]

It appears in this statement that Ellison was defining speculative fiction as a step beyond fantasy, a speculation on fantasy—about which in turn he said:

> Fantasy is a separate genre, and it allows you to go beyond the bounds of that which is acceptable, where all of a sudden people can fly, or the Loch Ness Monster does not have a scientific rationale, but is a mythic creature. It is in the grand tradition of the oldest forms of writing we know, all the way back to Gilgamesh, the very first fiction we know, and the gods. Fantasy is a noble endeavour.[6]

And science fiction? It is a 'contemporary subset that goes all the way back to Lucian of Samosata, and Verne and Wells, and Aldous Huxley and George Orwell,' said Ellison. So it comes down to terminology or definition, where discord arises as to whether 'speculative' embraces realistic or non-realistic stories. Historian, philosopher, writer and literary critic Tzvetan Todorov saw the 'fantastic' as an immersion of the reader in the author's world, where the reader had a choice to trust, question or reject the fantastic. According to Todorov, the driver to a reader's enjoyment of a text was their imagination relative to the writer's, finding certain forms of imaginary fiction more strongly mesmerizing than other forms. Prevalent in Spanish America, the 'fantastic' drew writers like Horacio Quiroga, Julio Cortázar and Jorge Luis Borges, renowned for eccentric stories, thirsty for the infinite universe and for whom any great and lasting book had to be ambiguous.[7] Yet even Todorov, for all his philosophizing and theorising, was unable to offer a single definition of the 'fantastic'. Aligning the term 'the fantastic' with speculative fiction, it could well apply to the unsettling, supernatural, otherworldly, grotesque …

Definitions demand that the reader enters the reading with pre-established and familiar understandings of the conventions of the narrative mode.

A science fiction story can be defined as

> a narrative (usually in prose) of short story, novella or novel length. As to what it is about, this is not easily classifiable. Such stories are about an amazing variety of things, topics, ideas. They include trips to other worlds, quests, the exploration of space, visits to other planets and interplanetary warfare … Many have a contemporary setting which is somehow influenced by the arrival or invasion of alien beings (alienation in various ways is a common theme) or by some invention which profoundly alters normality.[8]

Where science fiction is a form of fiction which draws creatively on scientific knowledge and speculation in its plot, setting or theme, fantasy, argued Richard Mathews in *Fantasy: the Liberation of Imagination* (2002), does not require logic.

So speculation in its generality, encompassing fantasy, science fiction, horror and the paranormal and cross genre, is about exploring possibilities, while establishing a relationship with the reader's experience. To designate a work as belonging to a literary category is to place it within a specific framework: for example, poetry. The classification arouses in the reader an expectation that the work will exhibit certain features stylistically appropriate to that category.

The implied author/reader

Wenche Ommundsen understands too well that

> like most human relationships, literary communication mediates a precarious balance of power: power to narrate, power to interpret, power, finally, to accept or decline the roles offered by one's partners in the literary act.[9]

Ommundsen recognises unique roles, from the real author to the implied author, the narrator, the narratee, the implied reader, the real reader … and the power of each role in the literary act. Conditioning factors (such as the tacit pact between the implied author and the implied reader) in the author–reader relationship determine how the reader interacts with the text, and this is more to do with expectation, history, reviews … than the tacit author–reader 'contract'.

Generic expectations of a writer, a publisher or a publication, thinking of them as showcasing a specific genre (science fiction or fantasy), sets the reader's expectations, influences their perceptions of the individual text.

Is there a right answer to genre conventions? It's all very subjective.

For example, while *The Encyclopedia of Science Fiction* recognises William Golding's *Lord of the Flies* (1954) as a near-future science fiction narrative (as opposed to the ultimate destiny far-future sci-fi), the book is selling on Amazon under literature and fiction classics, psychological thrillers and even reference. A search in my local bookstore finds the work under general fiction. Of note, *Lord of the Flies* is classified on the Penguin Random House website as general fiction; however, the novel does fit the category of speculative fiction in its offering of adventures in 'another world', a primitive one, and its vision of the apocalypse.

J. R. R. Tolkien, in his fascination with philology, exhibits what Roland Barthes identified as the pleasure of the text, a captivation with language. There are those who would swear *Lord of the Rings* is 'soft' science fiction rather than fantasy, in its construction of languages for Middle Earth. Tolkien, in the linguistic genesis of his work, indeed rendered writing that was close to the 'soft sciences', and one might reasonably argue that—if only for the thoroughness of its linguistic aspects—*The Lord of the Rings* holds claim to both fantasy and soft science fiction.

Stephen King's *Under the Dome* (2009) thrives under labels of suspense, horror and general fiction on the publisher's website, tops Amazon bestseller lists under horror (occult), thriller and suspense. Its adaptation into a TV series is as a science fiction drama/thriller. In a letter to his fans, King conceded there are differences between the book and the television series, but this does not explain the substantial genre shift in its labelling. In this novel that draws inspiration from an unpublished book titled 'The Cannibals'—one that King explained 'deals with people trapped in an increasingly lethal environment'—there is clearly a horror slant. Its futuristic narrative places it in science fiction. None of these labels is wrong; works do cross genre. Boundaries across genre blur. Even Orson Scott Card with his rules and exceptions in his book on writing was not clear-cut, and in an interview with *Writer's Digest* went on to affirm that 'every rule is breakable'.[10]

Commercialization

A headline on an author submissions service website: Genre fiction rules—Find out if your novel meets publishers' and literary agents' criteria for publication.[11]

In a nutshell, unless you are King, Tolkien, Atwood, Morrison or the like, your publisher or agent will *tell* you what genre your work belongs to. If you want to get something published, make sure you conform it to whatever genre categorizations your publisher or literary agent recognises. Sounds like bollocks, but publishers may stipulate requirements such as 'no whodunits' for crime fiction submissions; 'no time machines' for science fiction submissions, 'no wuxia' for fantasy submissions (wuxia originated in China as a popular film genre and rolls together action, adventure, martial-arts and fantasy). Some submission guidelines come with very specific word counts ('we will not consider anything above 80,000 words') that would have discounted some of J. K. Rowling's Harry Potter novels from children's or young adult stories in the global market. *Harry Potter and the Goblet of Fire* (2002), with its 752 pages rather than the typical 200 pages for a successful young adult novel, was landmark in its time.

Genre boundaries remain very thin, as Card clearly identified:

> Most science fiction novels could easily be turned into fantasy by changing starships back into ocean-going vessels. Frank Herbert's Dune would fit right in with the best medieval romances, if planets became continents and the spice became a source of magical power instead of a drug necessary for space navigation.[12]

In his interview with *Writer's Digest*, Card warned against following transient 'literary trends'. Trends come and go: 'You only write at your best, and you only invent your best stories, when you believe in and care about the people, relationships, motives, and events in the story,' he argued. If you write to a literary trend, then once the trend is over, says Card, so are the stories and books you wrote to satisfy them.

Speculative fiction allows what Card might have had in mind with the term 'the infinite boundary'. He suggested that 'speculative fiction by definition is geared towards an audience that wants strangeness—stories that contradict a known or supposed law of nature'.[13]

Aligned with Card's tagging, the English language tells us that speculation is to indulge in conjectural thought, guiding us to a conclusion that speculative fiction is a genre of fiction that will involve imagined worlds, imagined characters, imagined events … as appear in fantasy, science fiction, horror and the paranormal, and cross genre fiction. Whichever the definition, placing a work in the more open genre of speculative fiction—as Atwood insists on doing—allows the reader to approach it with an open mind, to stop asking the question: Is it science fiction? Is it fantasy?

Inspired by TV shows like *True Blood* and *The Vampire Diaries*, student Alexandra Fraser in a writing workshop conjured a speculation on an immortal protagonist three thousand years old, who lived in Mesopotamia, saw the days of the pharaohs in Egypt, was assassinated and personified in a tale about a little girl that fought off a wolf in a red hood… There's Dracula and Shakespeare in the story… Hitler too. Fraser drew from a fascination with the past to blur the lines between fact and fiction with a touch of parody in this speculative work.

In the end, genre labelling is no more than a device of commercialization as mentioned, a convenient grouping of books on a shelf for the reader to find, an easy means to quench the reader's thirst for their preferred reading. One writers' festival in Australia tossed it all in the air on matters of the speculative:

> Speculative fiction is the literature of unbound imagination, an umbrella term broadly encompassing stories that feature fantastical, supernatural, or futuristic elements. Tales set in, at or on the fringe, teasing the peripheries of WHAT IF?
>
> Contemporary speculative fiction comes in many forms and flavours: from robots and rocketships, through time travel, alternate history, steampunk, magic realism, apocalyptic futures, ghosts and the supernatural, superheroes, magic, fantasy, both high and urban, space opera, cyberpunk, biohacking and the singularity—anything that reaches beyond contemporary day-to-day existence to push the boundaries of the imagination.[14]

To this writers' group, genre is a continuum.

Strange Horizons, a magazine of speculative fiction that has seen the work it has published get onto shortlists or winning lists in Hugo, Nebula, Tiptree and even World Fantasy Awards, says on its website that speculative fiction includes science fiction, fantasy, horror, slipstream and all flavours of the fantastic in literature. It hunts 'vibrant and radical tradition' stories that make you think and interrogate society, for better or worse. In a nutshell, speculative fiction is about exploring possibilities.

Exercise 4

Think of writing as play. Here are a couple of exercises from a former colleague Ronnie Scott.

1. Let's do cut-ups. Lay out printed stories, newspapers or old books. Cut them up and physically build a new story from cut-up words.
2. Italian writer Italo Calvino was renowned for devising new methods of writing, often based on a mathematical problem or self-imposed constraints. This was mostly during his 'French period' in 1973, when he joined the Oulipo group. Write a story without using one vowel: 'a', 'e', 'i', 'o', 'u'.

5

Genres and subgenres of speculative fiction

Speculative fiction is birthed from what author Richard Mathews called a 'vivid mode of human consciousness' where, unlike realistic fiction, speculative fiction comes along with a freedom to abandon reality and immerse oneself in an invented realm. The author (who is also the work's first reader) fabulates (invention of story) that which they hope the reader will find immersion in. In *Aurealis* magazine, speculative fiction writer Michael Pryor explained why he loves fantasy and science fiction: while fantasy and science fiction writers must achieve everything else that a writer must in the act of good storytelling, for example robust characters, convincing plots and appealing text, they must additionally 'incorporate all the imaginative elements that are the hallmark of fantasy and science fiction'. Contrary to perception, genres and subgenres of speculative fiction are not different ends of a spectrum, but rather overlap.

Let us briefly consider some common genres of speculative fiction.

Fantasy

Ursula Le Guin, Marion Zimmer Bradley, J. R. R. Tolkien, J. K. Rowling and Suzanne Collins are some popular authors of this genre. But what exactly is fantasy? Author Richard Mathews considered this an impossible question to answer precisely, because to him, 'the maps and contours of fantasy are circumscribed only by imagination itself'.[1] Mathews described fantasy as 'a literature of liberation and subversion'. Unlike realistic fiction, he explained, 'fantasy does not require logic—technological, chemical or alien—to explain the startling actions or twists of characters and plots'. Fantasy is a 'liberation of the imagination', an idiom befitting the experimental, idealistic works of Le Guin and Tolkien.

Some fantasy authors like Le Guin, Marion Zimmer Bradley and Orson Scott Card are also prolific in works of science fiction and other genres, where genre elements sometimes cross. For example, Golding's science fiction *The Double Tongue* (1995), posthumously published, is the memoir of a prophetess who relays the answers of Apollo's oracle at the Greek City of Delphi.

Subgenres of fantasy

Fairy tales

You may have cut your teeth on classic fairy tales by Hans Christian Andersen, the Brothers Grimm and Aesop: stories of little mermaids and ugly ducklings, beauties and beasts, foxes and lions, hares and tortoises, gods and beasts, goose girls and fisher lads, clever monkeys and poor hunters, magic lamps and genies, sea monsters, fair damsels, blue fairies, frog princes, young sultans, talking ravens, towers, caves, castles … Adventures of little boys and girls, and rescues of maidens in distress. Remember Snow White, Jack the Giant Killer, Sleeping Beauty, The Arabian Nights. Fairy tales borrow from folklore, cultural stories, idealised yarns perhaps containing magic or enchantments.

In Katharine Pyle's *Fairy Tales from Many Lands* (1911) there is a Serbian folklore, 'The Seven Golden Peahens', about a king who had three sons. He also had a golden apple tree, one that bore nothing but golden apples, and this tree he loved like a daughter. The king was never able, however, to eat any of the fruit it bore, for no sooner were the apples ripe than they would disappear in the night, in spite of guards set around the garden to watch it and see that no one entered. The eldest prince came to the king and asked to be allowed to keep watch over the tree that night. 'And if I do,' said he, 'I promise you that nothing shall be allowed to approach it, not even the smallest sparrow.' The king agreed. But the eldest prince fell asleep and in the morning all the apples were gone from the tree. The second son took watch and a magical sound of beating wings lulled him to sleep. The third son stuffed his ears with cotton so he was not lured by the sound of wings. He saw a peahen that was really a princess, with sky blue eyes and golden cloud hair, clothed in gold. He was besotted. The following night he stole a lock of her hair and she flew away forever. To reclaim her affection he had to journey over seven seas and seven mountains to seek her. Thus began the young prince's quest, where he overcame hurdles set by a jealous queen who wished him to wed her own daughter rather than the peahen princess. Finally, the young prince won the peahen princess' hand but a dragon kidnapped her. Thwarting challenge after challenge, the young prince finally won his peahen princess and they lived happily ever after in the pleasure palace. The point of this story, as far as it represents fairy tales, is that it is a rescue narrative that has a king and princes, and a shape-shifting peahen who really is a princess. And there is a dragon.

Dark fantasy

There are elements of dark fantasy in the Harry Potter series, in the shadowy Dementors whose kiss siphons out a person's soul. As a subgenre of fantasy, dark fantasy sometimes overlaps with horror and integrates its darker elements, such as zombies, gargoyles and shapeshifters (for example, were-wolves). There are vampires whose skin blisters and burns in the sun, who can't stand garlic, who will mortally succumb to impaling with a silver prong, but who will—if they get their way—put fangs in your neck and draw blood out of you. Television and cinematic storytelling overlaps dark fantasy with urban fantasy, as in the television series *True Blood* (2008–2014) with a telepathic waitress for a protagonist. The movie *Blade* (1998) starring Wesley Snipes and Kris Kristofferson features a half-vampire, half-mortal man who, as a vampire slayer, is protector of the mortal race: classified 'action' and 'horror', the story fits both the dark fantasy and urban fantasy subgenres.

Myths and legends

The term 'mythology' is a derivative of the Greek word 'mythos', a story or legend pertaining to a people, and 'logos', an account or discourse. Mythology wraps around inherent values and beliefs, often of the people in the story, and may include ancestral or origin stories that explore the worlds of the gods and the supernatural, or explain thunder or lightning and other natural phenomena. Oral narrations passed down generations are dependent on the narrator's memory or selective distortion of the story they wish to tell.

Myths and legends may cross with fairy tales, especially those pertaining to a tradition or populace, and perhaps orally narrated across generations. Unlike the typical fairy tale, a myth is a type of 'sacred' creation or civilization narrative, a cultural 'how' or 'why' story that may contain Celtic, Indian, Arabic, Greek, Japanese, Egyptian, Chinese, African, Aztec, Hindu, Dreamtime (Australian), Maori and otherworldly roots. For example, in the English legend of Camelot a young Arthur proves his royal lineage by loosening a magic sword from a stone. A Maori (New Zealand) myth describes how the children of Ranginui the sky father, and Papatūānuku the earth mother, desired freedom, which they could achieve only by forcing their parents apart, separating heaven from earth, and so making room for the sons.

Magical realism

In this type of fantasy, there is use of magic in the real world, often with an allegorical thrust that is political because of the framework within which the story is cast in relation to the affairs of a society or a place. For example, in Salman Rushdie's *The Satanic Verses* (1988), which led to the declaration of a *fatwa* on Rushdie for blasphemy, the protagonists undergo miraculous transformations to become an archangel and a devil. Not all magical realism stories have such dire consequences for the author: Isabel Allende's first novel, *The House of the Spirits* (1982), is a family saga set in a turbulent country in a spirit-ridden world, entwined in the complexity of love and hatred in a political arena. In magical realism, stories present magic or the supernatural in a real or modern world. A visual equivalent is the television series *Charmed* (1998–2006), set in modern-day San Francisco and about three sisters with unique magical powers who combat evil. While it fits snugly in a general categorization of fantasy, Rowling's Harry Potter series contains elements of magical realism where the mysterious is inherent in the everyday—as is Harry's magical prowess in the muggle household.

There is magical realism in King's *The Green Mile* (1996) in the gentle giant and death row inmate John Coffey, who possesses power to heal and resurrect. He enacts his supernatural gift in a mundane world within prison walls when he cures an inmate's infection and resurrects Mr Jingles, the prison mouse.

The king of magical realism, Jorge Luis Borges, integrates existentialism (work that questions literature and life and the human experience) and experiments with surrealism (creative potential of the unconscious mind). His speculative fiction collection *Labyrinths* (1962), comprising short stories and essays, is a mind-stretching compilation of stories-within-stories experimenting with irrational juxtaposition. It features 'Tlon, Uqbar, Orbis Tertius', an otherworldly tale of metaphysical paradoxes; 'The library of Babel', the story of an infinite universe that is always starting over; 'Lottery in Babylon', a fantasy story on chance where stakes are increasingly raised; 'Borges and I', a parable about duality and hyperrealism where the boundary between the real and the imagined is so blurred that, Borges concluded, 'I do not know which of us has written this page';[2] and 'Pierre Menard, Author of the Quixote', a mischievous story of an author who plagiarizes the renowned fictitious Cervantes' *Don Quixote*, an error-prone but chivalrous protagonist, where the fake is better than the original.

Haruki Murakami's works sometimes fall under magical realism, such as his dystopian novel *1Q84* (2009) involving parallel worlds (alternate history) of two moons and the supernatural. Snapping up the Yomiuri Prize for Literature in the category 'fiction' was *The Wind-up Bird Chronicle* (1994), which also involves the supernatural, a dream reality and the hallucinatory whirlpool surrounding an invisible bird, all placing the post-war Japan novel as crossing genres with elements of science fiction and fantasy.

Subgenres of fantasy include urban fantasy, where the story is set in the ordinary world but with underlying supernaturalism; sword and sorcery fantasy, where the narrative is action-packed, overridden with axe-wielding heroes equally adept with daggers, as in Robert E. Howard's *Conan the Barbarian*; and epic fantasy, where the tale typically features large-scale battle zones and colossal armies, as in Tolkien's *Lord of the Rings* with its Army of the Dead. You may hear people speak of low and high fantasy, where low fantasy is ideally set in worlds that resemble the real world (as in urban fantasy), and high fantasy in highly invented worlds such as Tolkien's Middle-earth or C. S. Lewis' Narnia. In high fantasy there is a momentous shift from the ordinary world as we know it, for example to a planet that is many light years away from Earth if you travel at the speed of light, or there is a degree of the supernatural that is improbable in our world as we know it, or there are fantastical characters like krakens, sirens, unicorns and chimeras that no human eye has seen.

Notice the overlap in subgenres, many of the works evidencing genre and subgenre crossings.

Science fiction

Science fiction can intersect with other genres, because there is no clean separation of imagined science or technology or socio-geographic change from the fanciful or the macabre or the occult that might also shape good fantasy or horror. Card in his book on writing admitted that a number of Stephen King's horror stories are fantasies and science fiction (for instance *Under the Dome*). In a way, added Card, science fiction and fantasy are 'one literary community' whose authors write across genres and whose readers read both genres in an author-driven market. Lovers of King will read whatever he writes, be it horror, fantasy, science fiction or non-fiction. In Card-speak, people don't rummage through a store shelf looking for 'a science fiction novel' or a 'fantasy novel': they are looking for the latest Asimov, King, Atwood, Jemisin.

In trying hard, so very hard, to distinguish between science fiction and fantasy, Card suggests,

> If the story is set in a universe that follows the same rules as ours, it's science fiction. If it's set in a universe that doesn't follow our rules, it's fantasy. Or in other words, science fiction is about what could be but isn't; fantasy is about what couldn't be.[3]

Card elaborated: time travel and faster-than-light starships 'respect the real boundary between fantasy and science fiction', where these have metal and plastic and heavy machinery that achieves the impossible with the press of a button; in fantasy people stroke a talisman or pray to a tree or use some form of magic to achieve the same.[4]

In 1926 writer and publisher Hugo Gernsback used the term 'scientific-tion' to describe science fiction:

> By 'scientifiction' I mean the Jules Verne, H. G. Wells and Edgar Allan Poe type of story—a charming romance intermingled with scientific fact and prophetic vision.[5]

In Jules Verne's *Journey to the Centre of the Earth* (1864) there is science and philosophy in this imaginary odyssey into a underground 'otherworld', for example. Jorge Luis Borges observed

> that the fiction of Jules Verne speculates on future probability (the submarine, the trip to the moon), that of Wells on pure possibility (an invisible man, a flower that devours a man, a machine to explore time), or even on impossibil-ity (a man returning from the hereafter with a future flower).[6]

But there is soft science fiction, for example 'alternate history', where science or technology need not be the backbone because this form uses tropes such as parallel or remade worlds, or different outcomes of war—as in Koushun Takami's *Battle Royale* (1999) and its offering of an alternate version of World War II—that enable an imagined 'other history'. Where hard science fiction puts emphasis on science and technology, soft science fiction liberally inte-grates the social sciences (for example, psychology) and a study of human nature. Where hard science fiction may focus on scientific discovery or machinery, soft science fiction will pay more attention to narrative style and characterization.

Subgenres of science fiction

Gothic

The gothic novel drew popularity in the 18th and 19th centuries and often integrated horror and tension in a medieval setting (a castle, for example). This type of fiction, subject to controversy as to what 'gothic' constitutes, or intends, was evident in Edgar Allan Poe's work like 'The Raven' (1845), a poem about descent into insanity. In his essay 'Australian Gothic', academic Gerry Turcotte associates 'gothic' with a grotesque space, a habitat of monsters, the familiar transposed into the unfamiliar. According to Turcotte, the Gothic deals with fears and themes of isolation, entrapment and fear of the unknown.[7] Others might consider Emily Bronte's novel *Wuthering Heights* (1847) gothic, a passionate tale of the severe and almost demonic love between Catherine Earnshaw and Heathcliff. Other examples include Robert Louis Stevenson's *The Strange Case of Dr Jekyll and Mr. Hyde* (1886) about a good/evil multi-person; Mary Shelley's *Frankenstein* (1818) about a scientist who creates a monster in an experiment; and Ann Radcliffe's *The Mysteries of Udolpho* (1794) a sinister romance in the castle of Udolpho.

Cyberpunk

The 'New Wave' of the '60s and '70s and the 'Cyberpunk' of the '70s and '80s created new kinds of science fiction that stepped out of hard science and into experimental, arty narratives. Where the New Wave encouraged experiments in form for scientific writers like Samuel Delaney and brought along readers with a new mindset, cyberpunk juxtaposed humanity and cybernetics. A fine example is Philip K. Dick's novel *Do Androids Dream of Electric Sheep* (1968), set in post-apocalyptic San Francisco, a story that inspired Ridley Scott's cult movie *Blade Runner* (1982). There are those who consider William Gibson the father of cyberpunk with his novel *Neuromancer* (1984), a futuristic virtual reality story in a dystopian megalopolis. Other writers associated with cyberpunk are Larry Niven and Samuel R. Delany. The subgenre often depicts anarchic societies subjugated by computer technology, evident in Murakami's *Hard-boiled Wonderland and the End of the World* (1985), a near future narrative that borrows from science (deranged scientist) and the psychoanalytical with its mental hide-and-seek, and a narrator's course to beat the 'System'.

Utopia/dystopia

Shifts in science fiction towards more experimentation supported new narrative forms in utopias, stories that offered speculation on 'ideal' societies relative to the real world, and dystopias, largely pessimistic narratives whose characters were anxious about rapid technological change. Ursula Le Guin offered both forms in her novel *The Dispossessed* (1974), a narrative set on twin planets in an anarchist world, where she examined dichotomies between human nature and ambition. There are rudiments of humour in Murakami's *Hard-boiled Wonderland and the End of the World* that also infuse utopian hues in the town 'The End of the World' and shadows of dystopia in the technologically influenced city the narrator refers to as the 'Hard-Boiled Wonderland'.

Alternate history

As soft science fiction, alternate history presupposes a what-if analogy that shifts a historical event to produce alternate futuristic outcomes. Scott Westerfield's Leviathan trilogy, whose first book won the Australian Aurealis award in 2009, offers an alternate version of World War I where mechanized machines and genetically engineered beasts of war come into play. Philip K. Dick's Hugo award-winning novel *The Man in the High Castle* (1962) is an alternate history of what might have been had the Nazis won the war. Naomi Novik's Temeraire series of nine novels is alternate history that also falls in the fantasy genre, being the story of British Captain Will Laurence and his dragon in a series of missions for his country. Another example is the Netflix original series *Continuum* (2012–2015) where a detective from the future finds herself in present day Vancouver, and events from the past influence future outcomes. Here again is Murakami in *1Q84* with its parallel history.

Steampunk

Like alternate history, this subgenre of science fiction has a historical setting but characteristically features steam-powered apparatus rather than advanced technology. Scott Westerfield's Leviathan series also fits here in a good example of subgenre crossing (dystopia, alternate history, steam punk) with its employ of steam-powered war machines. In another classic example of genre overlap, there are some who will consider Mary Shelley's *Frankenstein* steampunk (in addition to its categorization as a horror novel) for the type of apparatus and technology applied in the 18th-century London of its setting.

This is not an exhaustive list of subgenres of science fiction, which include space western, space opera, military and more. Some subgenres (like steampunk) come and go with fan fiction trends that Card warned against basing your writing upon. Socio-historical dynamics can influence market approach and positioning on what might comprise science fiction, until the next fad comes along.

Horror and the paranormal

Rewind to the speculative fiction magazine *Aurealis* that would not publish horror fiction that did not contain a supernatural element, strange bedfellows. Other publishers like Macmillan also group horror and the paranormal on their websites. Under such a twin grouping you will find works like Robert Kirkman's New York bestselling series *The Walking Dead,* Dana I. Wolff's debut novel *The Prisoner of Hell Gate* (2016) and Mariko Koike's Japanese smash hit *The Graveyard Apartment* (2016).

Let us consider these genres individually.

Horror

I was seven or eight and it was night. I was sprawled on a coach in the living room with my mother. She must have forgotten I was there, or perhaps she thought I was asleep. She was watching TV, a British horror *I Don't Want to be Born* (1975), sometimes titled *Sharon's Baby,* starring Joan Collins, Eileen Atkins and Ralph Bates. The drownings, the stabbings, the hangings, the decapitations. They stayed with me, that trail of death surrounding a sinister infant whose evil refused to give in to exorcism. My child mind augmented the horror, the parallels of a cooing baby with fat legs in a pram and the spate of unusual deaths. Weeks after, my life sat on pause in that terrible world. I crept about holding out a crucifix and scattering holy water—my mother was a devout Catholic so there were plenty of these. I observed babies with a wary eye and could not close an eye without lights on. It took years for me to disremember the uncanniness around the possessed baby, the effect of a curse after a woman rebuffed a dwarf. I still remember the fear—it was as real as touch. Shadows with heartbeats lurking under my bed.

What I experienced from watching this paranormal horror was fear, revulsion and spook, and it contained all three types of terror King posted about on Facebook to his over 16,000 followers, and me:

> The Gross-out: the sight of a severed head tumbling down a flight of stairs, it's when the lights go out and something green and slimy splatters against your arm. The Horror: the unnatural, spiders the size of bears, the dead waking up and walking around, it's when the lights go out and something with claws grabs you by the arm. And the last and worst one: Terror, when you come home and notice everything you own had been taken away and replaced by an exact

substitute. It's when the lights go out and you feel something behind you, you hear it, you feel its breath against your ear, but when you turn around, there's nothing there ... (Stephen King, 14 January 2014)

That is what a good horror story does to you.

Paranormal

Revisit the terror you felt as a child when you visited a theme park: how the tiniest hairs at the nape of your neck stood as you stepped into the circus of screams. Remember how, as you trod or rode in a cart along the darkened trail, there was a presence: a wisp of breath, a feather-light touch, a whisper in the shadows, a silhouette inside fog, a flicker of nights, a howl of laughter ... How you barely breathed until a burst of light summoned you back to fresh air.

Stories continue to evolve around the Bermuda triangle that has inexplicably vanished so many people, planes, ships. Paranormal stories contain a supernatural element, for instance an atmosphere, an entity, a poltergeist. Cinematic examples include director Hideo Nakata's psychology horror *The Ring* (1998) (*Ringu* in Japanese), where the ghost of a seer's daughter murders within seven days anyone who watches a mysterious video tape; Andrew Douglas' *The Amityville Horror* (2005), where demonic forces terrorize newlyweds in an abandoned house; and James Wan's *The Conjuring* (2013), where paranormal investigators Ed and Lorraine seek to resolve a dark force terrorizing a family in a remote farmhouse. A classic paranormal tale is Charles Dickens' novella *A Christmas Carol* (1843), many times adapted into a film or television drama, a ghost story that transforms the miser Mr Scrooge.

Commonalities in these narratives are isolation, the uncanny. This is the strong element in the paranormal.

Cross genre

Genre and subgenre crossings in speculative fiction thrive in this world of blurred boundaries. Genre bending is 'writing different'. We saw earlier how Ray Bradbury, in *The Martian Chronicles* (1950), broke from tradition, from established genre convention, and became a revolutionary author whose science fiction work re-examined classical humanist themes. Bradbury contested the very idea of genre writing, of labels. To him, all good stories were one kind of story, a story written by an individual from their individual truth. In this vision Bradbury asserted the power of storytelling, damn the rules. Is it a wonder, then, that Bradbury reached a broader cross-section of readers with his genre bending and his works found interest in both mainstream and science fiction readership? For all its crossings, *The Martian Chronicles*— which is in effect a collection of short stories intricately bound and sold as a novel—dominated for decades on the subject of Mars. It has never been out of print in more than half a century, and is still considered within the early classics of science fiction.

Crossing or bending genre is to take a familiar genre and do something different with it. As more cross genre works emerge, authors and readers more and more realise text as a network spreading in all directions, as a field of possibilities unfolding to what Barthes saw as the plurality of text, where text is a social space that destabilizes language.

Exercise 5

Go on free flow, do some random writing. Write a 500-word speculative fiction or excerpt to a bigger story using one of the following as a relevant title:
- She'll Fret the Socks Out of You
- There Goes the Mouth
- Driving About in Rice Buckets
- Gardens, Grottos and Rustic Bridges
- Strong Will to Riot
- Consumer Focused Shit
- Rough Necks
- The Sky Burns Red
- I Do My Best Work When I'm Scared
- Troll Beads

6

Fantasy

The imaginary, world building, mythology and language play a big role in fantasy. Author Richard Mathew's perception of fantasy as the liberation of imagination is vivid in the works of Tolkien, Rowling, Le Guin and Martin in the fascinating worlds they have created, the creatures, languages, races and laws, in the history, backstory and languages they have shaped. Rowling's language of spells in the Harry Potter series borrows from classical myth and rhetoric and her study of Latin (patronus and expelliarmus spells) in university. A common theme of good versus evil prevails in all these works where the hero/ine narrative involves a journey or transformation curve. Fantasy, and the imaginary world it often explores, lends itself to creative play in its writing.

Lucid in these authors is a natural fondness for storytelling that immerses the reader into whichever tale, a penchant that a student picked up in a writing workshop. Sam Everaardt tossed up a story titled 'The Quietus' (2016), an exaggerated narrative of biblical stereotype. Everaardt drew on four key words, 'eons', 'crusade', 'unending' and 'Hell', to stretch the story to a good versus evil narrative, where the good was a group of crusaders with a vicious leader terrible as Hell. The term 'Quietus' means death or eternal rest and, in this story, offers an ironic name for the hero who has no intention of rest, entombed though he finally is. There are elements of world building in the story, the essence of Hell inspired by 'Inferno', the first part of Dante's epic poem *The Divine Comedy*. Playing on the fantastical, the invisible narrator brings the story to the present with a chilling warning about man and his curiosity. Everaardt, in the workshop, honed the art of storytelling and revelled.

Are there rules in fantasy?

Folklorist and editor Philip Martin shared an interview with fantasy novelist and screenwriter Peter S. Beagle, author of *The Last Unicorn* (1968) and renowned for his 'opulence of imagination and mastery of style',[1] on the art of storytelling. Beagle stated:

> It's funny, I'm often considered a Tolkien expert, but I don't consider Tolkien a major influence on me. Not as much as T. H. White and Robert Nathan. And Lord Dunsany and James Thurber, and a wonderful Irish writer, James Stevens.
>
> But what Tolkien illustrates best is the depth of passion a writer needs to have with his world and his characters... So many writers think fantasy is easy. All you have to do is rip off some elves, goblins and a few other things from Tolkien and spend about 10 minutes making up imaginary words and another 10 minutes working up a rough idea of the country and a little local history and bingo, you're in business. You're a fantasist.
>
> It's not at all like that. What made Tolkien unique is that he spent 50 years building his world, and he built it from the inside out. Nobody else did it as thoroughly as he did.[2]

Fantasy is fiction that is precisely that: fantastical. It is something out of the ordinary: visionary, imaginative, fabrication. In an article '10 Secrets to Writing Fantasy',[3] folklorist and editor Philip Martin shared features of the genre:

1. *Put new wine in old bottles*—Storytelling is the art of recycling. Pick an old form and refresh it.
2. *Learn the differences between archetypes, stereotypes and good characters* — where 'good' is in the context of 'relatable' and not evil.
3. *Use magic, but limit its powers*—Define its rules carefully; magic with unlimited power steals tension from the story.
4. *Make your hero an orphan*—Sure, there is Harry Potter, Dorothy in the Wizard of Oz ...
5. *Take a trip*—Think of Tolkien's Frodo and his odyssey through Middle Earth.
6. *Be realistic*—Know the trick of particularity, to use realistic details.
7. *Mix fantasy and humour*—Let slip new sides of humanity.
8. *Hold back*—Increase surprise and tension.
9. *All images have meaning*—Look at the imagery of old legends and myths, for example magic rings, enchanted swords, dragon lairs ...
10. *Good prevails*—A heart of gold trumps all.

Philip Martin got it right on a few things.

Like recycling myths: this is what adaptation is about—we see it in postmodernism, in the reinvention of the old, like Seth Grahame-Smith's *Pride and Prejudice and Zombies*.

Like knowing archetypes, stereotypes and good characters: what Martin means to highlight is the employment of Vogler's template of archetypes and understanding the roles of the hero, the mentor, the threshold guardian, the ally, the herald and so forth in shaping the conscious and the subconscious in your characters. Understanding underlying attributes that may guide how your characters react or behave may help you create robust characters. A 'good' character does not mean infallible; they may be based on archetypes, but lead their own lives, follow their passions, make mistakes, learn and grow.

Like limiting the powers of magic: notice how Rowling employs laws of magic that govern how magic is used. For example there are restrictions to underage sorcery, to performing magic in front of a muggle, to breaching the statute of secrecy to someone not already in 'the know'.

Like inventing a trip: a quest—Frodo's fantasy odyssey through Middle-earth to get rid of the magic ring. In Le Guin's *A Wizard of Earthsea* (1968), there is Ged's quest to destroy his shadow, until he completes his quest by accepting the shadow: Ged has calmed his pride and understood his limits. The odyssey is an important stage of Vogler's template of the hero/ine's journey, a popular storytelling paradigm. But your fantasy need not follow this stereotypic archetypal quest: *Clarkesworld Magazine*, a Hugo, World Fantasy and British Fantasy award-winning science fiction and fantasy publication, states in its submission guidelines that it seeks the 'folkloric, contemporary, surreal' in fantasy offerings (but warns against stories in which the words 'thou' or 'thine' appear). The market is ravenous for novel ideas.

Like being realistic: this sounds like a contradiction for speculative fiction, where the idea is to use boundless imagination. But Martin, in the term 'realistic', is referring to credibility. Whatever your story, however farfetched, your role as an author is to convince your readers. To immerse them into the 'unreal' to such extent that it becomes real within the confines of the story.

Like mixing fantasy and humour: Martin's encouragement to sprinkle a bit of humour is plausible but not essential for successful fantasy fiction. Publishers are picky—*Clarkesworld*, for example, warns against 'funny' stories that depend on, or even include, puns. A light and easy read never goes astray and sometimes—particularly when dealing with a young adult audience—it may help to tackle sombre themes with levity, but in a way that does not trivialize them.

Like holding back: in any work of fiction, mystery adds tension, heightens the reader's engagement. Suspense is dominant in psychological horrors— think King, who withholds information and releases it gradually.

Like giving all images meaning: Tolkien and other great authors make clever use of props from myths and legends. Magic wands or enchanted swords help enhance your fiction—it's all about world building, the rules of your world and the characters you create. Metaphors and symbols and imagery add colour to your language.

Yet Martin also faltered on a few things.

Like making the hero an orphan: this is stereotypic—not all publishers warmly welcome yet another Oliver Twist. But Martin may be referring to getting rid of the mentor, strengthening the hero/ine to become independent, for example a capable child in the absence of an adult.

Like good prevailing, the heart of gold having the last laugh: this is old school. Sure, it is noble, emotionally healthy for the young adult, but how predictable! Of course, Harry Potter was destined to win. Where's the twist, like crime pays? It all depends on the type of story you are meaning to write. There are beloved villains like *DC Comic*'s The Joker of Gotham City: a rogue, manipulating and multi-dimensional, yet you cannot help but admire his darkness; or Long John Silver, who is powerful and complex, attractive and repellent in Robert Louis Stevenson's *Treasure Island;* or Professor Moriarty, who is a genius in Arthur Conan Doyle's Sherlock Holmes stories; or Captain Barbossa who is hateful but likeable in the *Pirates of the Caribbean* movie series. Depending on your narrative, good need not always trounce evil, although the general direction is that good prevails. Perhaps this is a result of authors writing (and publishers accepting) the type of text that will appeal to readers. Most readers try to relate texts to themselves, make them meaningful to their world, and the rules of our real world as we know it are that evil is punished. As a writer how much of a risk taker are you to go against the grain?

Let us explore two of George R. R. Martin's early stories.

The Ice Dragon

World building: In 'The Ice Dragon' (1980), Martin puts effort into world building. There is the south where the king's city resides, and the north where winter child Adara lives with her father and siblings. There is summer when the world is green and hot and bursting with life, and winter is long and bitter. There is *language*—the language of ice that Adara has mastered; and she charms tiny blue ice lizards and the crystalline white ice dragon with its translucent blue wings. Martin puts new wine in old bottles by borrowing from a story of dragons, fiery, and inventing his own: a winter dragon that breathes cold and frosts.[4]

Characterization: The story's archetype is a heroine, a cold little girl, so pretty, who never loves back. She is a child apart, a serious girl who seldom plays with others, rarely smiles, born on the night an ice dragon was spotted. But she is not an orphan—just lost a mother in childbirth during a terrible freeze. Martin creates a realistic world of a family where the father is a huge, gruff man with affection for his children. But he hugs Adara only in winter, hugs her and weeps. Adara has siblings. There is Geoff, who works with his father in the fields, a farmer. There is older sister Teri, who flirts with local boys, cooks and works at an inn. There is uncle Hal, who serves in the king's army and rides green dragons.

Hook/tension: Martin offers much tension: conflict, conflict, conflict. We do not know what will become of Adara or her ice dragon or her family in the ensuing war of the land as the enemy advances with enemy dragon riders. The reader senses a transformation will happen, but when or how? The images have meaning, where ice and Adara being a winter child represent a loneliness, a sadness or solitude in a child who rarely smiles. Her only laughter, an icy tinkling laugh bright and crisp as winter air, comes out when she is riding the dragon. There are trips, Adara's secret flights on the ice dragon, riding above the forest and high into the sky, further and further, travelling a full day until just after dusk. Martin keeps the suspense going.

Plot/theme: 'The Ice Dragon' is a tale of courage and love. It is also a tale of sacrifice, where a winter child—and her ice dragon—must save their world. In all the story's beauty, Martin stays true to his style: ruthless. But it is a story where good prevails, an ice dragon versus enemy dragons.

The fantastical: In this story there is magic or a 'gift'. Adara is unaffected by cold, never suffers frostbite and speaks the language of ice lizards, ice birds with pale white plumage and the ice dragon.

In storytelling, an omniscient narrator in third-person reveals insights into Adara. There is limited dialogue and it is concise. It serves to give backstory: the child's mother's death and her father's attitude to it; the dragon riders of the north and the threat they pose. It moves the story along.

The Lonely Songs of Laren Dorr

World building: In 'The Lonely Songs of Laren Dorr' (1976), too, Martin puts effort into *world building*. Sharra is in a valley caught in twilight. There is a setting sun that hangs fat and orange in the ridges. There is a dense forest of black trunks and colourless leaves. There is a gate, invisible, but Sharra knows it. And there is a castle with crooked towers atop a mountain, fortressed by more mountains and cliffs. It has a twisted staircase and room after room. There is *language*—the language of song.

Characterization: Sharra, whose hair is a coal-black waterfall, is trapped in a world. She is powerless and trusting, and in need of a hero. Laren Dorr is a king and a god, he has lived through a thousand suncycles, and each cycle lasts a century. He has eyes full of fog and dreams, and has power to heal. When he strokes his instrument of polished wood, the air shimmers and changes colour. Each word of his song brushes Sharra with wistfulness, melancholy and secrets.

Hook/tension: Martin creates a world far different from what we know. There is conflict, conflict, conflict, the story opening with a hook. Sharra is stained and sweaty, arm bare and bleeding, cloak on her back half-ripped. Sharra knows the gates but cannot pass through them. We wonder about her beginning or ending. There is just the middle. Who are the guardians of the gates and why do they block her? The reader does not know what will become of Sharra and Laren Dorr, and their quest for more. The images have meaning, where song offers backstory and we know more of Laren Dorr's world of before, the world of stars that are a thousand colours and where nights shimmer. His song offers longing, and hope. In this story we do not know if good prevails because, in the end, there are questions rather than answers.

Plot/theme: Martin puts new wine in old bottles by borrowing from the story of Beauty and the Beast. There is a damsel in distress and a beast who rescues her, only this damsel is immortal and she walks between worlds, and the beast is a god. It is a quest narrative with distinct archetypes in the god, the heroine and the threshold guardians that impede Sharra's quest. It is also a story of unrequited love.

The fantastical: Sharra the archetypal heroine is immortal, she moves between worlds. There is magic in Laren Dorr's lonely song. There are threshold guardians and the evil Seven. Both Sharra and Laren Dorr are crowns, gifted, and yet their powers are limited to save them from their fate. There are trips, Sharra's visits to the gates guarded by threshold guardians. There are the Seven that imprison Laren Dorr in this world. And a creature that haunts the dark.

As in 'The Ice Dragon', an omniscient narrator tells the story of Sharra and Laren Dorr. Their conversations to each other are rich with meaning, yet full of mystery. 'Who are you?' she asks. 'What world is this?' He says, 'My world. I've named it a thousand times, but none of the names ever seem quite right.'[5]

In each example Martin tells a compelling story that is highly imaginative. He efficiently applies elements of world building (and language), characterization, hook/tension, plot/theme and the fantastical. The rules of his world, and the characters he creates, compound the credibility of each story, however incredible. These are all things that shape a convincing fantasy.

Exercise 6

i.
Remember the dictionary exercise.

Take a dictionary. Open a page at random and choose a word, for example, 'dance'. Shut the tome. Open another random page, choose a word, for example 'moon'. Repeat, another word: 'children'.

Create a story title out of the three words: dance, moon, children

Write a 250-word fantasy story that fits your title.

ii.
Choose a familiar fairy tale, dark fantasy, myth or legend.

Rewrite it to suit your new title: dance, moon, children.

iii.
What if everything is another story that's already been told? Remember *Pride and Prejudice and Zombies*; or the film *Abraham Lincoln: Vampire Hunter* (2012), where the president of the United States discovers vampires are planning to take over the country and becomes a vampire hunter; or the film *Snow White and the Huntsman* (2012), where a twist to the fairy tale introduces a huntsman tasked to kill Snow White in the woods but who instead becomes her mentor in a quest to rout the evil Queen.

Find stories in the public domain and tamper with them, write them anew.

Tip:
As part of a writing exercise on originality, and experimentation on old narratives with new perspectives, student Sandra Azkari (not her real name) scripted a postmodern take on 'Little Red Riding Hood'. She used the original fable sparingly and constructed 'a tale both familiar and unfamiliar', as she later explained in reflection on the writing, where the big bad wolf is the young girl.

7

Science fiction

Science fiction is generally anchored in science and technology, or 'the alternate'—using the term loosely to represent soft science fiction where science or technology is not central to the plot or story. Soft science fiction is more concerned with people and relationships than science, and may bear philosophical, alternate history or social science themes. Subgenres of science fiction include gothic, cyberpunk, utopia, dystopia, alternate history and steampunk, where publishers of the genre or subgenre generally come along with their own definitions.

Analog, a magazine of science fiction and fact birthed in 1930, boasted in 2017 on its website that it had won 54 Hugo Awards—39 for stories, seven for Best Editor, and eight for Best Magazine—as well as 23 Nebula Awards. If assessment is by the awards, it's a quality magazine. But even this magazine refuses to offer hard and fast rules on submissions 'because science fiction is such a broad field' and 'a great story can make an editor swallow his preconceived taboos'. Still, it remains prescriptive that science fiction comprises stories in which future science or technology is integral to the plot:

> The science can be physical, sociological, psychological. The technology can be anything from electronic engineering to biogenetic engineering. But the stories must be strong and realistic, with believable people (who needn't be human) doing believable things—no matter how fantastic the background might be.[1]

Clarkesworld allows author submissions where 'science fiction need not be "hard" SF, but rigor is appreciated', but is adamant against:

- stories about young kids playing in some field and discovering ANYTHING (a body, an alien craft, Excalibur, ANYTHING)
- stories in which a milquetoast civilian government is depicted as the sole obstacle either to catching some depraved criminal or to an uncomplicated military victory

- stories where the Republicans, or Democrats, or Libertarians, or the Spartacist League, etc. take over the world and either save or ruin it.[2]

The Magazine of Fantasy and Science Fiction gives no formula for fiction, just asks for character-oriented stories where the SF element may be slight but present; stories that appeal to science fiction and fantasy readers.

Let's talk about science

Marion Zimmer Bradley in her young adult fiction *The Colours of Space* (1963) was ahead of her time in her application of technology in a story about young fatherless Bart Steele, a human who disguises himself as an alien in a world named Lhari in a quest to unravel space travel:

> It was a week before the Lhari ship went into warp-drive, and all that time young Bart Steele had stayed in his cabin. He was so bored with his own company that the Mentorian medic was a welcome sight when he came to prepare him for cold-sleep.
>
> The Mentorian paused, needle in hand. 'Do you wish to be wakened for the time we shall spend in each of the three star systems, sir? You can, of course, be given enough drug to keep you in cold-sleep until we reach your destination.'
>
> Bart felt tempted—he wanted very much to see the other star systems. But he couldn't risk meeting other passengers.
>
> The needle went into his arm. In sudden panic, he realized he was helpless. The ship would touch down on three worlds, and on any of them the Lhari might have his description, or his alias! He could be taken off, unconscious, and might never wake up! He tried to move, to protest, but he couldn't. There was a freezing moment of intense cold and then nothing …[3]

In this short excerpt there is a space ship and a medic, and a promise of the star system and a planet.

In her novel *The Door Through Space* (1961) the prologue begins:

> *… across half a Galaxy, the Terran Empire maintains its sovereignty with the consent of the governed. It is a peaceful reign, held by compact and not by conquest. Again and again, when rebellion threatens the Terran Peace, the natives of the rebellious world have turned against their own people and sided with the men of Terra; not from fear, but from a sense of dedication.*

> *There has never been open war. The battle for these worlds is fought in the minds of a few men who stand between worlds; bound to one world by interest, loyalties and allegiance; bound to the other by love.*
> *Such a world is Wolf. Such a man was Race Cargill of the Terran Secret Service.*[4]

This story is about an intelligence agent on the planet of Wolf. In an author's note at the start of the novel, Bradley shared her love of writing and a discovery of pulp science-fantasy magazines at the age of 16, and how her early efforts earned a lot of rejection letters until a paradigm shift happened. Emphasis on science displaced adventures on faraway lands and strange dimensions, and finally she found grounding. And with a dynamic fan appetite, young people for whom she wrote found new fascination with the 'wonder and colour of the world way out', with what was beyond the stars. That was why she wrote *The Door Through Space*.

Mainstream fiction and science fiction author Iain Banks, renowned for a sense of risk in his writing, spoke about being realistic in a final interview with *The Guardian*. If you're going to write 'made up space shit', he said, then for it to be reasonable to the average reader, some bad guys get to live, some good guys get to die. This is realistic. He also reasoned in another interview that writing science fiction is tougher than other types of writing because it is the one genre that 'deals directly with the effects of change, and specifically technological change, on people and society'.[5] In the same interview he spoke about finding stories by looking on civilization 'in a slightly childlike way', stripping away assumptions and presenting a new look 'at the facts of our existence'. Science fiction, he said, is 'trying to find alternative ways of looking at realities': a real feat.

Le Guin did this, found new ways of looking, for example in *The Dispossessed*, where a review in *The Guardian* stated:

> There's some quality intellectual red meat in Le Guin's portrayal of how, given the right conditions, an anarchist society might function and malfunction. All the related insights into the nature of freedom, free will, community, wealth and power are equally worth chewing over. Meanwhile, the language used on Anarres is particularly interesting. Its vocabulary is strangely limited.[6]

And in 2000, SF Site reviewer Victoria Strauss wrote:

> *The Dispossessed*—which has not been out of print since its original publication in 1974—is perhaps Le Guin's most famous work, and arguably her most intellectually challenging. It's a book of opposites: a utopian novel that doesn't

flinch from exposing the flaws of its model society, a feminist-themed narrative with a male protagonist, a social commentary that presents communal cooperation as the truest human ideal, yet focuses on the inevitable separateness of the creative individual within such a structure. Through these dichotomies, Le Guin examines the tension between human aspiration and human nature, between what can be dreamed and what can be achieved. This larger theme, together with Le Guin's mature mastery of her craft, give *The Dispossessed* a universality that has prevented it from becoming dated, despite its roots in the political issues of its time (the communal counterculture of the late 60s and early 70s, the original women's movement).[7]

Le Guin's way of looking continues to hold appeal to fans today.

Orson Scott Card offered a new looking, his 'what if', in *Ender's Game* (1985), military science fiction adapted into a movie starring Asa Butterfield, Harrison Ford and Ben Kingsley in an intellectual battle against the Formics that had once invaded and nearly annihilated the human race.

One student in a writing workshop offered his own way of looking at science:

Red sky at night
A red dawn is supposed to herald bad weather and a red sunset tells of clear skies. There is even a saying for it. Red sky at night, sailor's delight. Red sky in morning, sailor's warning. A phrase used by sailors on the high seas to tell how they should prepare for the day to come. Will the waves be calm as the ship sails through to its destination? Or will they have to secure everything to the deck, and pray that this day will let them see the next?

Louise knows the differences between robots and humans. She knows that, in fact, they are not so different. Every organ in the human body can be replaced with something mechanical. The heart is a pump. The liver is a filter. The stomach is a container. However, if you ask most people, the similarities end there. Humans are organic. Creatures granted life by a power greater. Androids, humanoid robots, are simply arranged metal and wires. You can cut the power. You can switch them off.

There is a nerve in your neck, just below the jawbone. It controls the blood flow to the brain through the carotid artery. If there is too much blood going up there the nerve will stop the blood flow. It is a safety mechanism. If, however, you find this nerve and if you then apply enough pressure for long enough, the blood flow to the brain will shut off. And then, very quickly, you cause brain death. So it's possible that humans and robots are not so different, if both can be shut down at the press of a button.

Now this is not to say that both entities are one and the same. No, indeed there are major divides between us. The human brain is one.

Louise recognised the possibility of Artificial Intelligence but, in the end, the brain simply works in a way that cannot be replaced by a few lines of code. And so, in her dream to replicate the living, she arrives at a crossroad. We all have at least one in our lives. That moment when you have to choose between the dream you have and the reality that appears. In this instant, she tries to make them one and the same. She will not abandon her search for the perfect fake. She makes a choice.

*

His skin is grey. A pallid metal grey. His eyes open from the centre like camera shutters and glow red. He has been built to be six feet tall and looks like a boxer, all power and muscle on the outside. His brain is from Louise's assistant. The assistant was not the finest specimen but was slow enough, unfit enough to overpower.

Louise names her project Adam. He lives, he breathes and the only way to tell him apart is the colour of his skin. But this has been an issue throughout history anyway.

Adam needs to learn the world. How it works, what kind of a place it is. She takes him around the city they live in. A place of golden towers and bronze mansions. A place where they don't need roads or oil or coal. A place governed by humanity instead of humans. Every night there is a red sunset and every day that follows is full of sun.

His eyes focus as he steps outside. Soon as he sees the city he starts to calculate. He cannot feel emotion as he has no life experience. He learns slowly. It takes him a year before he stops learning.

*

The city has become familiar. He is used to the everlasting sunlight on its surface and the darkness that burns underneath. So she takes him out of their home.

The cruise ships that take tourists are opulent in the most extreme sense. Luxury upon luxury. They sail, floating over the waves, out of the bay and into the ocean. He is looking back at the city as it disappears. He stops calculating, ceases learning.

'I loathe you,' he says.

His honesty pummels, gores.

Her mind races a hundred miles an hour past the last year, re-evaluating every word, every touch … How is his first feeling, his first emotion, one of hate?

The wind grows stronger, picks up her hair. It dances in front of her eyes. Adam turns to walk away. His bare feet make a soft clank on the wooden deck as he moves past the tourists that take pictures. Images of a sea that glows in the dying light.

She stands very still in the fading warmth of the sunset.

'Wait,' she calls to him. He stops. There are no protocols holding him, this action is simply one of courtesy.

'I have no more reason to converse,' he says.

She opens her mouth but cannot put into words what is happening in her brain. Her human brain, the same as his. He steps towards her.

'Please,' her voice shakes.

He takes another step.

She is still frozen.

He steps even closer. He stands against her and she cannot feel any heat from his body. The world is silent, except for his mechanical breath.

He closes his hand around her neck. And he switches her off.

Red sky at night, sailor's delight. This is not just a saying or an old wives' tale. It is actually the result of a scientific process known as Rayleigh Scattering. A parametric process. Matter does not change.

Red sunlight happens when the sun is shining through a large concentration of dust particles. If the sky is red at night it indicates that there is a high pressure system approaching, which in turn will usually mean clear weather.

The water burns bright but the waves are calm. The sun lowers itself below the line where the sky and sea meet. Both are red, a cold red as the heat of the day disappears. The forecast is for storms tomorrow.

—Tristan Singh (2016)

There is world building in the story, the colours of the sunsets; characterization in the sapient robot; hook/tension in the robot's evolution as its artificial intelligence develops a promethean theme where Louise plays god; taut dialogue (minimal) and an omniscient narrator; and science. Singh took an idea of the Rayleigh scattering of light that changes the colour of the sky to create a robot story, the base idea being that humans and robots have one thing in common: you can easily turn them off. The theme of red sunsets works well in a utopian setting, and the futuristic element together with artificial intelligence place Singh's story as science fiction.

Let's talk about 'the alternate'

Some of Ray Bradbury's work fits into soft science fiction, though its setting may be interstellar and removal of the planetary quotient may not affect the story. A good example is 'The Man', there is further detail in this chapter; it is a story more about existentialism in its philosophical theme and borrowing from the Bible. In this story, a rocket man in space in a search for meaning fails to accept the prophet right under his nose. And he climbs into his rocket and it lifts into the sky on a pillar of fire, and he will keep searching, planet after planet, or city after city, in a quest for the very thing he has left behind. The story would still work if, rather than being a rocket man, the protagonist was an itinerant traveller on a personal quest, who visited an earthly town that had experienced an encounter with a prophet.

In an example of alternate history, Philip K. Dick's Hugo award-winning novel *The Man in the High Castle* (1962) casts the reader into a dystopian scenario where Japan and Germany won World War II and now rule the United States. Science fiction stories that fall under 'the alternate' focus on story and character without needing sound scientific theory or invention as central to the plot.

An exemplar of 'the alternate', representing soft science fiction, is Mary Shelley's *Frankenstein* (1818), whose promethean theme offers a sort of biopunk story where a young scientist animates a patchwork of many corpses to create a grotesque being that feels like a human. There is also Margaret Atwood's *The Handmaid's Tale* (1985) and its dystopian future that interrogates gender and religion.

Are there rules in science fiction?

Critics still argue about the definitions and history of the genre. According to *The Encyclopedia of Science Fiction*, science fiction became a subculture of writers, editors, fans and critics where stories and novels shared 'certain assumptions, linguistic and thematic codes'. Generally, science fiction stories were those published (or theoretically publishable) in a US science fiction magazine or specialist SF press, honouring an implicit agreement between author and reader to respect the 'protocols embedded in the texts which make up the canon'.[8] Since that inception, a cyberpunk era of cybernetics entered, and a New Wave era of cultural speculation, where soft sciences, psychology and mythology became acceptable. Open-minded readers in the New Wave allowed new forms of science fiction that were provocative. Like J. G. Ballard's *Crash* (1973), a pornographic novel about technology, a car crash event that conjured sexual arousal in its characters. Sex and wheels made for experimental, edgy, dystopian science fiction.

Let us look at definitions. *A Dictionary of Literary Terms and Literary Theory* defines a science fiction story as

> a narrative (usually in prose) of short story, novella or novel length. As to what it is about, this is not easily classifiable. Such stories are about an amazing variety of things, topics, ideas. They include trips to other worlds, quests, the exploration of space, visits to other planets and interplanetary warfare ... Many

have a contemporary setting which is somehow influenced by the arrival or invasion of alien beings (alienation in various ways is a common theme) or by some invention which profoundly alters normality.[9]

Science fiction comes along with its forms of speculation, where speculation is about exploring possibilities. In *The Encyclopedia of Science Fiction*, writer and anthologist Judith Merril described speculative fiction as 'stories whose objective is to explore, to discover, to learn, by means of projection, extrapolation, analogue, hypothesis-and-paper experimentation, something about the nature of the universe, of man, or "reality"'. Science fiction projects, extrapolates, experiments ...

Rules that define the writing of science fiction lack consistency and differ among the very writers of the rules. For example, SF writer Jerry Oltion said SF is not mostly technical jargon; thinking it so is a fallacy. Thinking that insiders call it 'sci-fi' is a misconception in itself, he said, and offered six negative rules of writing science fiction:

1. It's not about rockets and ray guns—pick contemporary themes.
2. It's not full of Star Trek's 'dilithium crystals' or 'Heisenberg compensators' or 'flux matrices'—use the right language.
3. It doesn't need a rocket scientist to write it—think scientifically.
4. It's not all about the known—add speculation.
5. It's not about explaining the science—tell a story.
6. It's not about one big, consistent genre—SF is sub genred; know that there is hard SF at one end of the spectrum and soft SF at the other.[10]

Oltion arguably asserted that the determination of whether or not a work is science fiction lies in how much the story relies on science. Science fiction author Adam Roberts suggested in his introduction to his book *Writing Science Fiction and Fantasy* (2014) that rules help, if only to provide structure, but that the measure of success as a writer of science fiction (and fantasy) is the extent by which one soars past the limitations of those very 'rules'.

Across the years, science fiction has offered up the likes of Mary Shelley's gothic novel and horror *Frankenstein* (1818); Robert Louis Stevenson's *Strange Case of Dr. Jekyll and Mr. Hyde* (1886), a psychological suspense that is also gothic fiction on the double life of a medic; Philip K. Dick's 'We Can Remember it for You Wholesale' (1966) with its hyperreal; and Larry Niven's *Neutron Star* (1966) that opens with:

The Skydiver dropped out of hyperspace an even million miles above the neutron star. I needed a minute to place myself against the stellar background and another to find the distortion Sonya Laskin had mentioned before she died. It was to my left, an area the apparent size of the Earth's moon. I swung the ship around to face it.

Curdled stars, muddled stars, stars that had been stirred with a spoon.

The neutron star was in the centre, of course, though I couldn't see it and hadn't expected to. It was only eleven miles across, and cool. A billion years had passed since BVS-1 had burned by fusion fire. Millions of years, at least, since the cataclysmic two weeks during which BVS-1 was an X-ray star, burning at a temperature of five billion degrees Kelvin. Now it showed only by its mass.[11]

Card in his book on writing spoke generously of Larry Niven, describing him as a clean storyteller of the genre, with a quality of tales within the worlds he creates. But not everyone enjoys Niven, whose work is more on the hard sciences, as the above excerpt illustrates.

Science fiction is an exploratory way to express a modern perspective of culture and technology. Utopia addresses the type of advantageous progression that technology can offer. Dystopia speculates on an adverse effect of rapid hi-tech change and addresses anxieties we may have about a profound reliance on machines and systems, as in H. G. Wells' *The War of the Worlds* way back in 1898. Atwood's *The Handmaid's Tale*, set in a dystopian future, is a moral warning, a cautionary tale of potential future shock, depicting a woman forced to live as a concubine under a fundamentalist theocratic dictatorship.

Borrowing from myths, science fiction can cast an origins story, like Tim Burton's film *Planet of the Apes* (2001), an adaptation of Pierre Boulle's novel *La Planète des Singes* (1963) and the 1968 film.[12] Sometimes science fiction addresses a quest for meaning, like Douglas Quail's in Philip K. Dick's 'We Can Remember It for You Wholesale'. Enter religion, and the fiction becomes about science versus traditional belief. *The Handmaid's Tale* integrates elements of religion in addition to gender, power and the apocalyptic: a warning of 'what if'. Bradbury's short story 'The Man' in his collection *The Illustrated Man* (1951) features Captain Hart, a rocket ship captain whose quest for an itinerant prophet turns obsessive. A Promethean theme (rebelliously creative demigod) is present in Harlan Ellison's 'I Have no Mouth, and I Must Scream' (1967). Enter politics, and you find stories like Frank Herbert's *Dune* series on a human-occupied planet where access to water is power.

On the softer side, science fiction can address shifts in interpersonal relationships or human capability and how these impact on social dynamics. The dynamic nature of culture and technology encourages a postmodern approach to science fiction as exploratory and an examination of the extent to which innovation can reshape or redefine.

Whatever your science fiction story, write the best story you can tell. Take a risk. Think of Bradbury's *The Martian Chronicles* and how, once published, science fiction fans and critics first misread his non-conformity to genre. The work sold relatively poorly and the publisher had to reframe the UK version as *The Silver Locusts*. Occasionally you will face genre ignorance or misinformation or a simple lack of openness to writing 'different'. Despair not: if one journal rejects your work, do your research and submit to another journal that might be a better fit to your work.

Consider some narrative devices that writers of science fiction stories employ:

Philip K. Dick in 'We Can Remember It for You Wholesale'

World building: There are some elements of world building in Philip K. Dick's short story where we get a clear picture of Douglas Quail's mundane life with his wife Kirsten, the smoggy Chicago air, the densely populated foot runnels on his way to work and the modernized set-up of the Rekal Incorporated building with its shifting-colour neon sign and shimmering doorway.

Characterization: The reader gets a good grounding of Quail, a man possessed with a desire for more, and the extents he will go to realise a dream.

Hook/tension: Dick's writing is engaging and the reader is hooked from the very first sentence:

> He awoke—and wanted Mars. The valleys, he thought. What would it be like to trudge through them?

Having already captured the reader's interest, Dick maintains it.

Plot/theme: There is satire, where the author employs irony in this short story that opens tongue-in-cheek in its very heading. Dick's story and its 'what if' quotient on artificially implanted memories misaligns Quail's world. There is suspense and conflict, conflict, conflict, complications that arise as Rekal technicians find that there is no room in Quail's mind for implants, and that the trigger to psychological fantasy triggers Quail's own recollection: he is an undercover agent. In this twist in the plot, Quail now questions his life, his wife—are they real? Has somebody gone to much effort to expunge his recollection? As he starts remembering—or is he mis-remembering?—he is not sure any more—his suspicions increase when he finds evidence in bedroom drawers of having been to Mars. He ponders if this is the onset of a psychotic episode, and questions what his wife also knows. The distinction between reality and the hyperreal becomes increasingly blurred. But what is real is that suddenly his very life is in danger: the people behind the conspiracy wish him dead.

Science/'the alternate': There is science in the futuristic idea of a much-evolved Earth where an actual interplanetary tour is possible: you have only to afford it. Quail can't afford it, but Rekal offers technology that programs artificial memory.

Like any good story, dialogue moves the story forward, revealing backstory and the protagonist's desires.

Ray Bradbury's 'The Man'

World building: Bradbury sets the opening scene in the doorway of a rocket, arrived in space travel to a Planet Forty-Three in Star System Three. There is a city whose people are indifferent to the vessel's arrival. The reader learns about the peaceful nature of this world and its inhabitants, and the reason why, as the story unfolds, the world is in a state of mysticism.

Characterization: Bradbury paints and contrasts well the characters of Captain Hart and his assistant Lieutenant Martin. Hart is a contemptuous man who seldom sleeps or eats, and drives himself on; Martin is laid back, tolerant, empathetic—susceptible to faith.

Hook/tension: Bradbury opens with a hook—a captain standing at the door of a space ship. It piques the reader's curiosity. What planet is it? What will this world reveal to human Hart and his crew? There is Hart's incredulity that a prophet may have visited such a planet. Already he questions his own inner quest, what it is that drives him from planet to planet, that perhaps this going out to the stars is a pursuit for divine power, a seeking for his own lost soul, a looking for something. Yet faced with the very answer to his questions, a very gentle and kind man of a great knowing and intelligence, a prophet who has left behind a city quiet and beautiful and its people filled with a great peace, Hart gets increasingly arrogant in his disbelief. He questions a woman: what colour were his eyes? The colour of the sun, the colour of the sea, the colour of a flower, the colour of mountains, the colour of the night, she says. A twist: crewmate Martin is converted; but Hart's rising obsession to find the prophet escalates to violence.

Plot/theme: Bradbury pours new wine into old skins in taking the story of Jesus and his miracles and parables to invent the coming of a long-awaited prophet in this story. The people of this planet had waited a million years for him and, a day before the rocket's arrival, the man walked into their city. A man whose name was different on every planet. He healed the sick and comforted the poor. He sat among the people and talked. Such was the profoundness of the prophet's single visit that it shifted dynamics, and the people of the planet, to Captain Hart's bewilderment, are unimpressed by the sight of a space ship. The very theme of the story is ironic, where Captain Hart's initial incredulity on the appearance of a 'prophet' in this alien world, a man the people have waited for years, turns to fervent obsession to locate the prophet. The portrayal of Hart's blindness: situating the prophet is not to find a destination, but to see what is right there before his eyes. In anguish, he yells to the mayor of the city who will not divulge the location of the prophet:

> I don't need you. If I missed him by one day here, I'll go on to another world. And another and another. I'll miss him by half a day on the next planet, maybe, and a quarter of a day on the third planet, and two hours on the next, and an hour on the next, and half an hour on the next, and a minute on the next. But after that, one day I'll catch up with him![13]

And he sets off to find the very thing he has left behind.

Science/'the alternate': there is science in the rocket and the concept of space travel. It is of no consequence that the planet is backward and its people have not yet discovered photographic technology. Despite its rockets and planetary odyssey, 'The Man' is an example of soft science fiction. Bradbury adopts a philosophical theme of science versus religion in this story, where a man is in his own search for meaning:

> 'Why do we do it, Martin? This space travel. I mean. Always on the go. Always searching. Our insides always tight, never any rest.'[14]

Bradbury, true to his nature, is light, funny, engaging. Dialogue moves the story forward, and Bradbury is adept at it. He is crisp, for example in Hart's interrogation of the mayor:

'About this occurrence yesterday,' said the captain. 'It occurred?'
'It did.'
'You have witnesses?'
'We have.'
'May we talk to them?
'Talk to any of us,' said the mayor. 'We are all witnesses.'[15]

Despite its crispness, the dialogue in the story supports an overall light and easy storytelling.

Harlan Ellison's 'I Have no Mouth, and I Must Scream'

World building: there is clear world building in Ellison's story: the chill, the oily breeze through the main cavern, the eagle, the carrion bird, the roc, the wind creature, the hurricane bird; the caverns of rats, the path of boiling steam, the slough of despond, the vale of tears ... The reader gets a clear picture of the harsh conditions the humans must experience in the belly of the computer, its memory banks, base plates, circuitry and control bubbles.[16]

Characterization: The machine's character is the most developed. AM comes with pseudonyms: God, Daddy, The Deranged, Allied Mastercomputer, Adaptive Manipulator, Aggressive Menace. The machine is vicious in its revenge on its creators. It forces the humans to feed on its masturbation: hail, lava, boils, locusts, worms ... It forces them to rely on it for food, shelter. It forces names upon them, like Nimdok's. It watches over them, goads them, tortures them. The narrator is also somewhat developed—questioning, daring, altruistic and, in his first-person narrative, sharing insights to Ellen's, Gorrister's, Benny's and Nimdok's characters before and after the machine's meddling.

Hook/tension: The story opens with the scene of a murder, the limp body of Gorrister hanging upside down by a leg from the ceiling. His throat has been slashed ear to ear. There is no blood. Gradually we learn more of this death, and of the machine's malice and the extent to which the narrator will go to lighten his mates' torment.

Plot/theme: This story of literary allusion, 'I Have no mouth, and I Must Scream', has a strong Promethean theme. It is about a demigod machine and its perverted games to torment the humans it has entrapped in its belly. This is also a psychological horror given the torment, nightmares, and delusions the characters must suffer. As in J. G. Ballard's *Crash* (1973) there are sexual hues, here the machine generously endowing Benny with an appendage, and transforming virginal Ellen into a nymphomaniac.

Science/'the alternate': Humans entrapped in the belly of a machine— technology is rife in this post-apocalyptic nightmare.

The story uses the narrator's inner dialogue, a first-person perspective that makes even more chilling the people's ordeal, until the machine's final revenge leaves the narrator soft jellied, smooth rounded, no mouth, forever suffering. He has no mouth. And he must scream.

Octavia Butler's 'Bloodchild'

World building: There is more characterization than world building in Butler's coming of age story, but the reader gets some sense of the planet that hosts humans, and the symbiotic relationship between humans and aliens. We visualize what T'Gatoi looks like: her bones, ribs, long spine, skull, four limbs; how she moves: her twisting, hurling controlled falls.

Characterization: The narrator Gan's first-person narrative sheds good insight to his mother Lien and her self-sacrifice, his sister Xian Hoa and her desire to breed for the aliens, his brother Qui, protected from Gan's fate as a breeder. The alien T'Gatoi is perhaps the best developed, as her relationship with Lien and her family, and then significantly with the adolescent boy Gan, unfolds.

Hook/tension: The opening line, 'My last night of childhood began with a visit home', sets expectations, and the mystery continues as we gradually unveil exactly what the aliens' relation is with the humans.

Plot/theme: Humans appear the losers in this dystopian story, but perhaps they are not. As hosts in a colony, the relationship the aliens have with humans is more symbiotic than parasitic or one of enslavement. There is a romantic theme: T'Gatoi does not wish to force herself on Gan; she wishes him to choose her. It's not like humans have much choice—it's just what it is: healthy boys reach adolescence and become breeders. Nobody is saying, 'Take me I'm free.' But this is exactly the choice that T'Gatoi is hoping from Gan. Towards the end, we see transformation in the boy Gan, his choice.

Science/'the alternate': This story uses the concept of male pregnancy, where adolescent human hosts are implanted with alien eggs that become maggots that must birth, or else feed themselves out of their host in an alternate to birthing. In this award-winning story, science and novelty (the unusual concept of willing males as breeders) are the best features.

The first-person insight makes up for unimposing dialogue in this story.

Learn from the templates of compelling science fiction writers, and like Le Guin chart maps of imaginary places. Make up languages, like Le Guin in *The Dispossessed* where she starts with an unearthing of place, the unveiling of people who live there. There is a wall, a gateway, significant for generations. It is a two-faced wall—what you see inside it or outside it depends on the side you are on. The wall encloses the grim Port of Anarres, it is a wall that cuts Anarres from the world, the same wall that locks in the Anarresti. And then there is a sister planet Urras ... Le Guin transports you into an invented world that hooks. Write your best story and, first and foremost, write it for yourself. You are, after all, the work's very first reader. Bradbury knew this.

Exercise 7

Write a 250-word science fiction story on one of the following:
• You are interviewing an extraterrestrial creature from an alien planet
• You (or third party) are in a very bad first date on a space ship when it falls under attack
• You are a scientist investigating an unusual sample of blood
• A crew of scientists has just landed in a galaxy and an alien is approaching them.

Choose a suitable title and a sharp opening line that hooks your reader.

Experiment with different version of your story in first-person, second-person and third-person narrative (I... You... He/She/It).

8

Horror and the paranormal

You think horror, you think Bram Stoker, Alfred Hitchcock, Ridley Scott, M. Night Shyamalan, Dean Koontz, Stephen King, Eleanor Lewis, H. P. Lovecraft, Shirley Jackson, Mark Danielewski, Mary Shelley, Robert Louis Stevenson, Anne Rice, Poppy Brite … Guy de Maupassant who wrote across many genres. In his book *Danse Macabre*, King paid homage to Jorge Luis Borges and Ray Bradbury in his list of 'six great writers of the macabre'.

As far as storytelling goes, horror can be an exhausted genre, and artists and producers are continually hunting ways to tap into audience curiosity by reinventing it. Horror films like Alfred Hitchcock's *Psycho* (1960) and Wes Craven's *Scream* (1996) typecast horror, and copycat stories emerged, exhausting fans with parodic slasher narratives, blood and gore, until zombies burst into the spotlight; the appetite for them has stayed rich.

Is horror the jet black eyes of a silent entity, an atmosphere in a room that creaks, footsteps on a wooden floor, objects changing position, pictures turning to snow on the television screen, things falling when no one else is home, a shadow at the edge of your sight, a spectre on a fence by the road, staring little girls dressed in white, weeping walls, crying babies, songs behind a wall, barking dogs, horses going ape, an aura behind a headstone, a silhouette in every photograph, two sets of the same person out of nowhere, poltergeist?

Clarkesworld in its online guidelines for authors says it looks for horror that 'can be supernatural or psychological, so long as it is frightening', but warns against 'zombies or zombie-wannabes', 'stories where the climax is dependent on the spilling of intestines'.

Horror.org admits that answering what is horror is a tough question—where your mind leaps to Freddy Krueger or Michael Myers, someone is looking for Shelley's Frankenstein or Stevenson's Dr. Jekyll and Mr. Hyde:

> The popularity of the modern horror film, with its endless scenes of blood and gore, has eclipsed the reality of horror fiction. When you add to that a comprehension of how horror evolved as both a marketing category and a publishing

niche during the late eighties—horror's first boom time—it's easy to understand why answering the question of what today's horror fiction actually is has become so difficult.[1]

Horror is personal. A spider may be horror to you. A snake. Height. Blood. Rot. A dead body. A ghost. In *An Evening with Ray Bradbury*, the author invited his listeners to 'list ten things you love, and ten things you hate' and then to write about those loves and kill those hates—also by writing about them. Do the same with your fears, he said.

Bradbury shared a story on fear. He went to his doctor's when he was 23 years old. 'Take some aspirin and go home,' the doctor said. Bradbury started thinking about tendons and muscles, all the things in his body he hadn't noticed. The medulla oblongata, a crack in your head that hasn't filled in yet. The action of the jaw itself. The knee caps. The toes. He went home feeling his bones.

That afternoon he wrote the story of Mr Harris who goes to see his doctor. 'You're only nervous,' the doctor says. 'Let's see your fingers. Too many cigarettes. Let me smell your breath. Too much whiskey. Let's see your eyes. Not much sleep. My response? Go home to bed, stop drinking, stop smoking. Ten dollars please.' But Harris stands there. The doctor looks up from his papers. 'You still here? You're a hypochondriac!' he says. 'But why should my bones ache?' asks Harris. 'You realize you caused most of the soreness,' the doctor says. 'Leave yourself alone. Take a dose of salts. Get out of here now!' But, alone, Harris examines himself and, in pushing his spinal column, 'fears and terrors answered, rushed from a million doors'; there is something there, a skeleton inside him. It starts manipulating him, determining whether he is to sit or to stand, a horrible gothic thing inside him. It is squeezing his brain, his vitals. His head aches, his chest is constricted. In an image of life and death, it becomes a competition about being true to himself or the skeleton.

This is how the story 'Skeleton' (1945) came about. By being true to his own fears Bradbury was able to write speculative fiction stories. 'Go back in time and collect up your fears,' he advised. His short story 'The thing at the top of the stairs' was also birthed from a personal nightmare:

> When I was a kid, the bathroom was upstairs, single light half-way up the stairs. I had to run halfway up the stairs and turn on the light. But I always made the mistake of looking at the top of the stairs, and there was something there waiting for me. So peeing like crazy I fell back down.[2]

He recalled his fear and wrote about it.

In his book on writing, Card termed horror fiction 'the literature of the strange', and explained it as: 'perfectly believable events that are so gruesome or revolting that the audience reacts with fear or disgust'.[3]

As you seek to capture your reader's fears, King again and again reminds you to ask the question: What if?

There is horror that is not of the skin crawling type but that reveals things of such monstrosity to human decency it leaves you intrigued, if not appalled. M. Night Shyamalan's film *Split* (2016), an American psychological horror film, is one of these stories. Protagonist Kevin has multiple personality disorder, diagnosed with 23 distinct personalities. When he kidnaps three girls, they must escape before a more powerful, monstrously evolved, cannibalistic 24th personality emerges. As psychologist Dr Karen Fletcher comes close to the truth, things escalate from bad to worse. The story does not put a crawl up your spine and some may doubt that it fits the horror genre. It depends on your definition. It depends on your fears. It can bring dread, the idea that such youth, such beauty as in the kidnapped girls, is torn apart; or that our human brain has such power as to generate a subhuman personal disorder within the realms of fantasy.

As in other areas of speculative fiction, the publisher, the market ... will tell you if your version of horror is horror enough for them.

The paranormal

We naturally tend to fear that which is beyond our understanding, like the paranormal. Edgar Allan Poe offered up ghost stories like 'The Black Cat', Pluto, a pet and playmate that is stabbed and hung, and returns to haunt. In Poe's 'The Flayed Hand', Pierre B., a student, returns home and goes to bed. His valet awakens at midnight to a fierce ringing of the bell and finds Pierre B. on the floor, imprints of five fingers around his neck:

> Dr. Bourdean was called immediately, and his report says that the aggressor must have been possessed of prodigious strength and have had an extraordinarily thin and sinewy hand, because the fingers left in the flesh of the victim five holes like those from a pistol ball, and had penetrated until they almost met. There is no clue to the motive of the crime or to its perpetrator. The police are making a thorough investigation.[4]

In this story, a sorcerer's artefact, a long, black hand stripped of skin, dry and shrivelled, attempts to murder its new possessor. In Eleanor Lewis' paranormal tale 'The Vengeance of a Tree', an innocent man's hanging renders the oak tree from which he swung an instrument of justice.

Director Hong-jin Na's film *The Wailing* (2016) unveils a personification of evil in a dark comedy. *The Wailing* employs archetypal horror tropes of cruel and unusual death, the haunted house, ineffective barricades against evil—even a shaman cannot dispel the demon—a creepy child and cannibalistic zombies. When a Japanese stranger arrives in a South Korean village and evil surrounds him, a laughing stock cop must toughen up when that same evil threatens his family. *The Wailing* is a somewhat appropriation of director Wes Craven's cult film *Scream* (1996) in its mystery, horror and comedy blend, but that's as far as similarity goes. Opening scenes are parodic, with laconic, dry humour. But the mood grows increasingly sombre when the audience must confront darkness in a child. Enter the primitive and the obscure with shamanism, faith and mind play, twist after twist. Hong-jin Na reinvents the supernatural in a genre hybridization that contains a who-dun-it, exorcism and ancient traditions in an unsettling wallow in evil. The narrative goes full circle, and assuages a hitherto undecided audience dissuaded by its jesting start. Cinematic effects and the disquiet they bring add to the success of this crossing of mystery, crime, drama and horror that emerged a pleasant find for the Cannes 2016 critics, and was a box office pick in Korea, also stealing the spotlight in the Hollywood movie scene as a foreign hit at the box office.

King likes psychological horror and the paranormal, where—an example—protagonist Carrie White has telekinetic powers and seeks revenge in *Carrie* (1973); or John Coffey in death row has powers to heal in *The Green Mile* (1996); there is an invisible force sealing a town from the world in *Under the Dome* (2009).

In Mary Shelley's science fiction horror, Dr Frankenstein's toils pay off in the creation of the undead from lifeless things:

> It was on a dreary night of November that I beheld the accomplishment of my toils. With an anxiety that almost amounted to agony, I collected the instruments of life around me, that I might infuse a spark of being into the lifeless thing that lay at my feet. It was already one in the morning; the rain pattered dismally against the panes, and my candle was nearly burnt out, when, by the glimmer of the half-extinguished light, I saw the dull yellow eye of the creature open; it breathed hard, and a convulsive motion agitated its limbs … Oh! No mortal could support the horror of that countenance. A mummy again endued with animation could not be so hideous as that wretch. I had gazed on him while unfinished; he was ugly then, but when those muscles and joints were rendered capable of motion, it became a thing such as even Dante could not have conceived.[5]

The creature is a thing of horror because it was once dead.

Are there rules in horror and the paranormal?

World building: Horror is all pervasive; it is an easy genre to cross with another. Whichever genre you cross it with, setting is vital in planting the seeds of terror. Often location is an abandoned or isolated place: thick forest, lakeside at night, haunted house on the hill, dilapidated mansion, solitary farm, empty field, cabin in the woods … Shirley Jackson's *The Haunting of Hill House* (1959) is set in a gothic house, dark, that stands by itself against the hills. Stephen King's *Pet Sematary* (1989) is set in an old farmhouse in rural Maine. His novel *Salem's Lot* (1975) has a haunted house in a vampire-infested hometown, and creepy events in *It* (1986) occur in sewers, storm-drains and a haunted house. Bram Stoker's *Dracula* (1897) is set in a solitary chilly house with a gloomy courtyard, a great old door studded with iron nails, a projecting doorway of massive stone, great winding stairs that lead to room after room, empty. A combination of gothic, suspense and macabre works particularly well.

Characterization: The macabre should not overshadow the relatable quality of the characters. For example, stuttering Bill in King's *It* appeals to young adult and mature adult readers alike, and strengthens the audience's fascination with Bill's quest to hunt and destroy the balloon-clasping 'Pennywise' that feeds on fear. Serial killers do not come with a stamp on their forehead; they blend with society, live normal lives inside the abnormal. A sinister baby, all plump-legged and kicky in the pram, associated with mysterious deaths (as in the 1975 British horror *I Don't Want to be Born*), may be more ominous than a grown-up brandishing an axe and wearing a death mask. The more 'normal' the perpetrator of horror, the more shocking their crime. No one will forget Heath Ledger's Oscar-winning performance in what the Academy termed his 'menacing, mercurial, droll and diabolic' performance as the Joker in Christopher Nolan's *The Dark Knight*. He was a believable character, how sinister.

Hook/tension: The reader is looking to be surprised. Like King, withhold information; reveal gradually. Maintain the reader's curiosity, hold secrets that even the characters themselves may not know. Psychological horror is most effective (unlike popular zombie stories) where it's not all gore and bloodshed but something is left to the readers' imagination (and their own fear). Death and the afterdeath is generally a shared fear, hence its recurrence as a popular theme in horror fiction.

A good horror trope is the use of ineffectual barriers. The tension is lost if victims get away easily. You need trapping mansions, doors that give to assailants, guards that dark forces can easily dispose of, victims whose weapons malfunction. Monsters that don't die.

Plot/theme: Real life offers a good source of horror stories—you have only to turn on a television, listen to the local news on the radio, see the headline on the front page of a tabloid to grab an idea. In one of Australia's worst cases of serial murder police discovered eight bodies in six plastic drums hidden in a bank vault, and more in the backyard of a house. The eight in barrels were steeped in hydrochloric acid, the killers' macabre way of destroying the victims after having tortured and killed them. Serial murderers provide a trove of stories: Tsutomu Miyazaki with his human Dracula fantasies abducted and murdered little girls in Japan; John Wayne Gacy, the Killer Clown, sexually assaulted and murdered young men and teenage boys—Stephen King leveraged on this trope in *It*, where the shape-shifting child killer also masquerades as a clown; Ted Bundy indulged his necrophiliac tendencies in various states of the United States during the 1970s; Jack the Ripper and his slasher murders terrorized London's Whitechapel in the late 19th century; Russian Alexander Pichushkin's 'chessboard' killings included hammering victims on their heads and inserting vodka bottles into their skulls ...

The latest news articles may have stories of a prison riot where inmates behead a snitch; a baby born with a face like a goat's and hooves for feet; a train stuck two hours in a tunnel (and you imagine: what if?); an alien creature in a city sewer (as in King's sewer-dwelling monster targeting children in his novel *It*); a live spider in a toddler's ear; a rabid dog (King uses this idea in his 1981 novel *Cujo*); a pregnant boy carrying his own twin in his stomach (Bradbury's 'Skeleton' comes close); unexplained sightings, sounds, smells. Paramedics and law enforcement officers see the stuff of horror novels daily. An intense backstory will help support the main theme and add to conflict, conflict, conflict.

Fear, revulsion or spook: Horror appears particularly effective when cast with supernatural elements, and masters of psychological horror really play on this. Magical realism with black magic or voodoo would fall into this category.
    In *Danse Macabre* (1981) King explained how he leverages fear:

> I recognize terror as the finest emotion ... and so I will try to terrorize the reader. But if I find I cannot terrify him/her, I will try to horrify; and if I find I cannot horrify, I'll go for the gross-out. I'm not proud.[6]

First-person narrative can be quite effective in horror, as it puts you in the perspective of the victim. However, this can also be confronting, and easier for the reader to take if written in third-person and supported by taut or conversational dialogue that moves the story along.

A good horror story takes on things *most* people dread: spiders, sharks, height, crowded places, rats, mice, disease, viruses, cruel and unusual death, a calculating serial murderer, being alone, blood, God, Satan, evil gods, demons, bugs, amphibians, rot, cockroaches, darkness, thunder, bogeymen, hairy creatures, legless creatures, empty rooms, graves, coffins, distorting mirrors, unusual sound, dark lakes, ghosts, pain (serial killer torture stories), wasps, computers, drowning, being buried alive, ants, being trapped, man-eating wild animals, man-eating humans, worms. Butler's alien T'Gatoi in 'Bloodchild' has wormlike movement—twisting and hurling in controlled falls. Take the object of fear and make it a hundred times worse: a raping worm that is giant and seeks human hosts for its eggs; a monster snake (as in director Luis Llosa's 1997 movie *Anaconda*); a body-shifting alien masquerading as an attractive human that will infest you with a life form that tears out of your body (as in Ridley Scott's 1979 movie *Alien*); an undead little girl who is vindictive (as in Hideo Nakata's 1998 Japanese psychological horror *Ringu* or *The Ring*); a man-gobbling shark (as in Spielberg's 1975 movie *Jaws*); a poisonous snake in an improbable, inescapable place: a plane (as in David Ellis' 2006 film *Snakes on a Plane*); a clan of giant apes more intelligent than humans; a vicious baby-faced doll (as in director Tom Holland's 1988 film *Child's Play*). *Tick-tock. Tick-tock.* Zombie stories continue to mesmerize horror fans with reusable post-apocalyptic plots of people coming back from the dead with intention to harm. And they are reeking, decaying, malforming, infecting.

Tell a compelling horror story, because you love to write good stories. King, who gets his ideas from everywhere, says on his website, 'I was made to write stories and I love to write stories. That's why I do it.' Like King, research. King sees two things, brings them together in a new light and asks the question: 'What if?' In *Danse Macabre* (1981) he explained horror, terror and the gross-out:

> The finest emotion is terror, that emotion which is called up in the tale of The Hook and also in that hoary old classic, 'The Monkey's Paw'. We actually *see* nothing outright nasty in either story; in one we have the hook and in the other there is the paw, which, dried and mummified ... It's what the mind sees that makes these stories quintessential tales of terror ... Horror invites a physical reaction by showing us something which is physically wrong ... But there is a third level—that of revulsion. This seems to be where the 'chest-burster' from

Alien fits … So: terror on top, horror below it, and lowest of all, the gag reflex of revulsion.[7]

King also commented on the nature of evil, dividing horror into stories in which horror comes out of an act of free will, the decision to do evil; and horror that is fate, external, like thunder or lightning. What's your horror or paranormal story?

This book capitalizes on examples—let us consider a few stories.

Stephen King's *The Body*

One first reads King's novella *The Body* (1982), later adapted into the film *Stand by Me* (1986), potentially anticipating a horror story. King, right? Wrong. This is more of an adventure, a coming of age story that includes the finding of a dead little boy. The story contains elements of body horror and illustrates the tropes of King, a masterful storyteller.

World building: We get a vivid picture of the tree house, the planks on its side pinched from Make Lumber & Building Supply on Carbine Road. We know its corrugated tin roof and the heat it emanates in a summer of no rain. We understand the Back Harlow Road that comes to a dead end by the river, the fields that lead up a cindery embankment to the rail tracks, where the boys make big jumps and leap over brackish water. There is the Castle Rock Dump and its tainted brass bedstead, a little girl's doll with stuffing on its crotch, a flipped over automobile with its bullet nose glittering in the sun, giant water bottles, plump rats, big crows, loads of seagulls, stray dogs … We see the old well at the back of the dump and the dirt road through the gate at the front … The dirty collars of foam along Castle River's edge … The rain, thunder, marshy undergrowth with a bad smell where a pale, white hand is sticking out.

Characterization: King is a master of characterization, interspersing it in the dialogue and actions of primary and secondary characters. There is Teddy, a big, impulsive dumb-head who has ears like lumps of war wax, burned by his father; Teddy, who can't see very well beyond his glasses, who first thinks with the red in his eyes before his friends haul him to reason. Gordie, an insightful creative who writes stories and is happy to share these with his friends, who enjoys surrealist painting, who tries to do the right thing, who sometimes cries and feels second best to a dead brother his parents will never forget; who is ridden with guilt for being the one who stayed alive. Vern, casual and playful, always quibbling over one thing or the other with big Teddy, but full of fear; he always gets nightmares. Chris, whose father was always a mean streak, who hates his dad like poison, who may have stolen the milk-money at school but is kind to his friends; the friend who is always there, the peacemaker who knows the right words to say, wise beyond his 12 years. King takes time to develop secondary characters like the thieving storekeeper when Gordie goes to get provisions; like the soft-spoken Ace, the Spartan shaped, Apollo-faced bully who later grows to become a 32-year-old buried in an avalanche of flesh.

Hook/tension: 'You guys want to go and see a dead body?' Vern's easy question to his mates as they are playing cards. Everybody stops, pays attention. The story unfolds a series of events that forever changes four lives. The boys discover life as much as they discover death.

Plot/theme: This is a story of friendship, and a coming of age account from the eyes of the adolescent narrator Gordie, going on 13. King baits you, puts the concept of a dead little boy in your head, tells you the boys are going on an adventure to see a dead body. He then hangs you out with stories-within-a-story: Gordie's storytelling. The boys clown, brawl, energy after energy, much merriment, conflict, conflict, conflict. Gordie stops blind-as-a-mole Teddy from dashing in front of a train. The four boys race each other, collapse in laughter. Gordie goes to the store for camping provisions where he challenges a thieving shopkeeper. There's a dumpster keeper and his vicious dog. The reader is still waiting, keenly aware that the boys are off to see a dead body.

But King is pitiless. The boys chase each other some more, let slip in their dialogue and actions their individual flaws beyond the tightness of their friendship. They come to a place where the embankment stops and the trestle starts ... From noon to 3 pm, 6.30 pm to night and then dawn, the horror quotient remains a hunger in the reader's mind. King feeds it in dribs with a crawl of fear at night when a piercing shriek awakens the boys. No, not a ghost. Or is it? Then there is a river swim, ghastly slugs in the boys' privates (that's a gross-out), a near-death experience when Vern and Gordie narrowly leap from the tracks to escape an approaching train ...

At this point the reader is just about giving up when King whips out the main gross-out: a missing little boy face down on the ground, hair matted red, swollen torso full of farts, eyes open, ants and bugs all over his face, beetles crawling out of his mouth.

Fear, revulsion or spook: The boys are not afraid of their bullying siblings or parents or dogs or law enforcement. But the idea of a dead boy about their age petrifies them, and Vern will have nightmares. They cling to each other when a faraway scream, perhaps the ghost of the dead boy, awakens them in the night. Yet a morbid curiosity to see body horror is bigger than their fear. There is a scene of slugs that will test, if not repulse, the most hardcore.

Dialogue here is pert, excitable, conversational, as you would expect from boys being boys, the kind of banter that moves the story along and discloses much backstory.

Overall in this story King employs short, sharp sentences, sometimes a single word, never verbose. The writing is easy, readable, tackling with levity sombre topics like bullying, family violence and fear. He pays attention to setting, the glary heat to wary chill and then hailstones fat as pebbles. He weaves in humanness in this story of friendship, offers insight to human nature, excellent at the human touch in all his plotting even as he plunges you straight into skin cringe.

Stephen King's 'The Breathing Method'

World building: King walks the reader through the narrator David's journey. The story opens on a snowy, bitter night in New York. The wind whistles and whines, it means business. The sidewalks are bare. In the club at 249 East 35th Street where the elderly gentlemen meet to tell stories is a dark library with reading lamps and a roaring fire. King sets up this novella for elements of horror.

Characterization: True to form, King takes keen interest in primary and secondary characters, robustly developing them. The protagonist David is a 73-year-old who works in a law firm with modest expectations of more career development. He is comfortably ensconced in his life with wife Ellen, warm, amused, old. George Waterhouse heads the law firm, a baffling, sporty gentleman well in his 70s. Odd as ever. Stevens at the club is reliable as a butler, reserved, brutally proper. His small smile, his ancientness.

Hook/tension: The story is set with scenes as if it is a play: 1: The club … 2. The breathing method … Told in first-person, it heightens the reader's insight on what is going on, stories within stories, dark stories. There is hook all right.

Plot/theme: King is at it again: he plants a seed and keeps the reader waiting. We know there is something very important about a breathing method in this story, but what? He teases us, holds us hostage as we drink one Martini and then a second. Even a third is offered before we get to hear the first story: a man drowned in a telephone booth. Drip by drip, months go by, a second story: a woman trapped in a portable toilet that is taken away, airborne, and the door bursts open. Weeks pass. Brandy. More mild stories. Drip by drip, a revelation. Now it is Thursday before Christmas. Brandies, eggnog punches, groups form and reform. Finally a meaty story of a senator who stumbles into an office and looks the worse for wear. His shirt is matted with blood, his eyes falling from the sockets:

> 'There's something in the trunk of my car ... something I found out at the Virginia place. I've shot it and stabbed it and I can't kill it. It's not human, and I can't kill it.'
> He began to giggle ... and then to laugh ... and finally to scream.[8]

Narrator David is affected and dreams of the story afterwards, crying out: 'His head! His head is still speaking in the earth!'

But this is not *the* story we are waiting for. And when it arrives, it is worth the wait.

Fear, revulsion or spook: Blood, limbs blown off, a dead face embossed with a map, decapitation and things that will not die. Everything about the library where the club runs is surreal. David can find none of the publishers of the books he has been reading on any listings. The library has rooms and more rooms ... These are some of the unsettling concepts in this story.

The first-person narrative allows an easy dialogue that reveals the natures of the primary and secondary characters. Overall, King continues his light, conversational tone, some wry humour. He writes easy, takes liberties on suspense with the coolness of a stunning model on a catwalk, a film star on a red carpet. He knows he will get away with it. After all he is *King*!

Bram Stoker's *Dracula*

World building: We follow Jonathan Harker's journey from Buda-Pesth and its station and the bridge over the Danube, to Klausenburgh and its Hotel Royale, through countryside towns and castles atop hills, past rivers, streams, forests and all the way to a creep of night as we approach Count

Dracula's castle. Inside, the castle has room after room, each empty, and the fortress juts from the edge of a precipice, a prison. There is much darkness, gloom and isolation in the setting.

Characterization: Count Dracula is perhaps the most developed character in the book. He is clad in black, head to foot; he stands tall, thin, ancient; his skin is pale as a corpse's, his hand cold as snow. The bay of wolves is to him music, the wolves like children. He neither eats nor drinks. He lives in the loneliness of a servantless castle and its impregnable walls. He sleeps in a coffin. He has fangs in his mouth and at night crawls face down along the castle wall, cloak spread like wings. His eyes burn red. He snatches children (the reader knows this from Dracula's bag with a living thing within it, a gasp and a wail as of a child coming from it), and commands his wolves to attack women. He has girls with scarlet lips, sharp teeth and ribald laughter living in the castle. He shows strength and is manipulating, and he holds his guest Jonathan Harker prisoner. The rest of the characters, like Jonathan or his fiancée Mina or her friend Lucy or Dr Seward, reveal first-hand accounts of their nature through letters, diaries, journals, interviews and logs. We understand Jonathan's curiosity and his fear. Mina's longing, and compassion. Lucy's fragility …

Hook/tension: The opening of the story with Jonathan Harker's diary piques the reader's curiosity and invites them to inside knowledge of an otherworldly encounter.

Plot/theme: A man's visit to his friend Count Dracula changes his life forever. Stoker maintains an air of expectancy from the onset, with the animals' unease and crowds at an inn door making signs of the cross and performing a charm to guard Jonathan against evil. One woman puts a crucifix on his neck. The style of narration from multiple viewpoints across different media adds to the story's tension. We learn about the weird case of Dr Seward's patient Reinfield, who has much madness, gloom and cruelty. We learn about mysterious deaths all around, victims petrified by what they have seen.

Fear, revulsion or spook: The narrator foreshadows evil as horses neigh, snort and plunge; dogs sound out agonized howl after howl. The count's coachman has blood-red lips and sharp teeth white as ivory. Suddenly mountains wall the narrow roadside, and the place is deserted. Further afield into darkness are trees, tunnels and an air of mystery as a moon sails through black clouds. Before you know it, there is a ring of wolves, teeth bared, tongues lolling, responsive to moonlight. Inside the castle, everything about it and the count is sinister. There are phantom shapes and ghostly women with fangs. There is death, much death, all of it strange, victims found dead with fear and horror on their faces. There is sighting of a strange woman in black, wandering children vanishing to reappear with some tear or wound in the throat. The attacks on children add to the reader's abhorrence. The supernatural is evident in the count's effect on Jonathan, his hallucinations and strange dreams. The count clearly has strange powers that afford him strength, an ability to crawl down walls and command wolves, as well as to morph into a younger version of himself.

There isn't much dialogue, a result of the book's structure that adopts a first-person point of view from the multiple viewpoints of different narrators. Overall, Stoker uses a unique style of letters, diaries, journals, newspaper clippings and ship's logs to unveil unusual happenings. The logs and clippings are matter of fact: for example the account of the strange man aboard a Russian ship (who fits the description of the count); the crew's unease; the crew's vanishings; the death of the captain, lashed at the helm of the abandoned ship sailing through the night.

The horror in *Dracula* is not gross-out blood and guts. It is more psychological fear, the kind associated with Satan-kind evil, against which the reader feel powerless along with the characters; yet remains morbidly curious as they reveal their stories.

Like Stoker's *Dracula*, Mary Shelley's Promethean-themed *Frankenstein* shows elements of gothic horror. It also adopts a descriptive narrative approach that uses both letters and the first-person perspectives of primary characters like Dr Frankenstein and the beast he has created from the dead. Offering personal insight through this first-person point of view, Shelley shares with the reader her curiosity in the characters she has developed: like Dr Frankenstein and his clinical attitude but deeply feeling nature; he is a scientist who feels heart and soul, ardent in his pursuit of an experiment that brings to life a monster. Like the creature Frankenstein has created, that is drawn to him but whom he abhors, calling it a daemon. It is shaped in the figure of a man, runs bouncy. It is yellow-eyed, muscles and arteries visible through yellow skin. It is proportionate-limbed, its hair a lustrous black, its lips straight and black. And it too feels, just as deeply, and becomes fiendish when it is miserable. And the doctor's abhorrence keeps it miserable. The reader understands its solitude, its longing, its repugnance with itself and its deformity. There is world building, aesthetic descriptions of valleys and glaciers and hill summits and vast mountains, precipitous ascents and places of desolation. *Frankenstein* elicits a mild kind of fear, largely arising from its dealings with a creature resurrected from the dead (paranormal effect), one that the reader can both relate to (in its pining) and loathe (in its manipulations). Perhaps for this reason it is more visible as a gothic science fiction than a horror.

Ray Bradbury's 'The Long Rain' is not horror but contains elements of psychological horror and 'gross-out'. A lieutenant and his crew are shipwrecked on Venus, a planet of incessant rain:

> It was a hard rain, a perpetual rain, a sweating and steaming rain; it was a mizzle, a downpour, a fountain, a whipping at the eyes, an undertow at the ankles; it was a rain to drown all rains and the memory of rains. It came by the pound and the ton, it hacked at the jungle and cut the trees like scissors and shaved the grass and tunneled the soil and moulted the bushes. It shrank men's hands into the hands of wrinkled apes; it rained a solid glassy rain, and it never stopped.[9]

And then a beast comes out of the rain. It is an electrical storm, 'a thousand whips would fall out of its belly, white-blue whips, to sting the jungle'. The lieutenant says, 'Lie down, everyone.' Someone cries, 'Run!' The lieutenant says, 'Don't be a fool. Lie down.' The men flop. 'Is it coming?' they ask each other, after a moment. 'Coming.':

> The monster came and stood over them. It dropped down ten blue bolts of lightning which struck the rocket. The rocket flashed like a beaten gong and gave off a metal ringing. The monster let down fifteen more bolts which danced about in a ridiculous pantomime, feeling of the jungle and the watery soil.
> 'No, no!' One of the men jumped up.
> 'Get down, you fool!' said the lieutenant.
> 'No!'
> ... The man who had leaped up was now running, like someone in a great hall of pillars. He ran and dodged between the pillars and then at last a dozen of the pillars slammed down and there was the sound a fly makes when landing upon the grill wires of an exterminator. The lieutenant remembered this from his childhood on a farm. And there was a smell of a man burned to a cinder ... The body was twisted steel, wrapped in burned leather. It looked like a wax dummy that had been thrown into an incinerator and pulled out after the wax had sunk to the charcoal skeleton. Only the teeth were white, and they shone like a strange white bracelet dropped half through a clenched black fist.[10]

First there is the ghastliness of insistent rain that pelts, gropes, hacks, slithers. Then there is the savagery of being burnt alive. Finally there is gruesomeness, body horror, the remains of a human all charcoal, fist clenched, teeth bared.

Tossing up typical tropes is Director Kiyoshi Kurosawa's *Daguerreotype* (2016), a fantasy horror: a dilapidated mansion that houses secrets, a creaking door that opens itself ajar, a mysterious dark room that sees women die, the ghost of a beguiling woman climbing up and down an s-curled stairway: she is wearing an old-fashioned flowing dress. She is the dead wife who noosed herself to escape husband Stéphane's fixated photography. Lone wolves with much to lose, dim-lit rooms and desolate lakes at dusk, billowing leaves on a windless night, swirling lamp shades no one has touched ... Set in the present, this ghost story weighs up madness and obsession, vacillates between the real and the hyperreal to an unsettling climax.

Horror is subjective. One person's fear is another's glee. Learn about the things most people fear, and exaggerate them. You might get it a bit right, attract a broader audience. Build the fear in your characters, make it personal to them. Patience—don't rush the clues. What clues? That's right: your characters are clueless. Get the netting right, toss in your hook, bait with suspense, ensnare with the paranormal. Employ riveting dialogue. Haul into your boat a darn good story that's as fine as it gets. And the reader just might swallow it.

Exercise 8

Write a 500-word speculative fiction based on the following:
- You are paying last respects to the body of your best friend and his eyes suddenly open.
- You are alone in a place called Lollipop Creek and a whisper in the horizon unsettles you.
- A child is walking along a beach and suddenly sees a face in the sand.
- You sit up, unfocused for a moment. Something just happened ...
- A man leaps into a ravine fleeing a ...
- A priest holds out an orange-lit lamp, stunned at the desecrated sacred place ...
- A tsunami of sand howls its way into the dim-lit city, tonnes and tonnes of bad temper ...

9

Cross genre

Crossing genre means deconstructing traditional modes of fiction, as theorist Hans Bertens would have it.[1] Crossing yields a type of writing that breaks 'boundaries between different discourses', in the words of theorist David Carter.[2]

When you tell someone you're writing a cross genre fiction, they might fall back.

'A what?'

'A literary speculative novel.'

'Is it science fiction?' they might ask.

'There are aliens and little girls with non-human powers swirling interspace. But I wouldn't call it sci-fi.'

'Is it fantasy?'

'There are no wizards or dragons. But there's magical realism and dark fantastical things that happen to innocent characters.'

'Not horror or paranormal then?'

'There are no zombies or axe-wielding maniacs, no inane pretties running screaming up the stairs of a trapping mansion. No—not paranormal or horror. But there's a whole bunch of literary writing.'

For a moment, a very brief moment, they nod as if they understand. But do they?

The reader's generic expectation of a writer, a publisher or a publication influences the perception of the individual text. Authors, publishers and other players in the literary act apply what French theorist Gérard Genette termed 'paratexts' of interpretation in his book in *Paratexts* (1997),[3] meaning liminal devices and conventions, within and without the book, that form part of the complex mediation between the book, its author, publisher and reader. The publisher's branding, the work's title, foreword, epigraph or jacket, are all part of the work's private and public history that contributes to the work's sorting, determines its placement on a bookshelf. Genette discerned that a literary work consists of text that has been endowed with significance by its core players.[4]

Like typecast actors, renowned authors sometimes find it tough to cross genre, as J. K. Rowling must have figured when she chose to publish her crime fiction novel *The Cuckoo's Calling* (2013) under a pseudonym: Robert Galbraith, targeting a 'neutral audience, free of expectation or hype'. [5] When you first read King's *Different Seasons* (2012), you may find disillusionment that your skin is not crawling. If you endowed significance to the book based on King's notoriety as a horror writer, you might trivialize the storytelling when it did not meet those expectations. But there are strong stories in this non-horror book, like 'Rita Hayworth and Shawshank Redemption' that was adapted into a 1994 film starring Tim Robbins and Morgan Freeman. A reader may anticipate anything Stephen King writes to be horror or relating to horror and, inclined to this notion, one might argue whether *Under the Dome* (2009) is science fiction, overlooking that it might be cross genre. King writes non-horror stories. He crosses genre. If you started with a blank canvas, no 'genre' label, a non-history on King, would you revise your approach to his work?

Are there rules in cross genre?

There is no prescription for hybrids other than seemly literary and commercial appeal. Who decides? The market you are writing for. No one will snatch you into a chamber of secrets and fervently whisper urgent tips to 'writing different'. Imprint your cross genre fiction with your writerly voice, style, choices and instinct, and tell a darn good story, a self-sufficient artefact that is complex and varied in its interaction with other genres and subgenres, and is viable as speculative fiction. Let us look at Kris Ashton's dark fantasy horror 'Howling Mad' (2017), [6] that also has elements of literary writing:

> *World building*: The story begins in a post-apocalyptic world, desert country silhouetted in the morning sun. An old man sits rocking in an antique rocking chair on the porch of a weatherboard house. This sets the premise of an outback story, aligned with a tint of the literary in its use of metaphor (hunger as a companion/dust storm of shock and grief) and a flowering of prose (pain that is hot and bright, a magnesium flare/perfect silence of the outback prevailed, marred by the caw of crows and the sibilance of a breeze passing through the button-head grass).

Characterization: Protagonist Billy in his one-man exodus from carnage is desolate, insecure. The world is not as he knew it, his past full of skeletons. Parched in the desert heat, Billy is also unquestioning, gullible or careless to drink the old man's lemonade. The old man, Ron, is cunning, too late Billy finds.

Hook/tension: As the story progresses, the reader gets uncomfortable with the old man. As Billy cocks his head, all at once uneasy, so does the reader, way before the text makes visible the zombies (creepers) lying face up and eyeless on the ground. As Billy slumps, paralysed, and the old man steps down from the porch and arranges him face up, the reader is already waiting for the caw that breaks the outback silence, the crow that lands on the barbed wire and turns its hard silver eye on Billy.

Plot/theme: An old man is also a serial killer who lures innocent wanderers to a crazy game of creepers: which paralytic baking in the sun will outlive the others. But Billy has a secret that summons his resurrection. Suddenly, it becomes a werewolf story, and Billy gets his revenge.

The fantastical/Fear, revulsion or spook: As a dark fantasy, 'Howling Mad' offers up a serial killer, zombies (creepers) and a werewolf. There is fear, revulsion and spook to the reader in the fate that befalls victims to the old man: paralysed with spiked lemonade, left face up in the blistering sun, eaten alive by crows that love the eyes. It is almost a relief when Billy turns out not dead but a werewolf.

In this story, the dialogue is the kind of vernacular you might expect in an outback town:

> Billy unslung his rifle. He pointed the muzzle at the ground to show he meant no malice, but intended to take no chances. 'Morning,' the old man said, lifting his hand in a lazy greeting. 'Morning,' Billy said back. He stopped at the bottom of the porch stairs and then glanced over his shoulder to observe the bodies littering the road and the grass verge. 'You won't need that thing,' the old man said, motioning at Billy's rifle. 'Haven't seen a creeper around here in ages. Crows got 'em all.' [7]

Neither Billy nor the old man are verbose, and dialogue moves the plot along. Where Ashton blends the fantastical/fear, revulsion or spook in 'Howling Mad', he takes fear, revulsion and spook and applies science to 'The Larval Stage' (2018), his science fiction horror that is about a human host to flesh-eating alien larvae, a story of terminal illness. [8]

Let us consider K C Grifant's dark fantasy western 'A Dusty Arrival' (2018), inspired by the '80s movie *Gremlins* (and its sequel) and competitive gaming in the weird west card game Doomtown: Reloaded:

World building: The story begins on a foothill at the edge of a town, where the protagonists are uneasy about a sunbathed mountain gorge out west. There are taverns and there is gunslinging, and there is no doubt the story is a western.

Characterization: Protagonists Melinda and Lance have an easiness about each other in their role as gremlin slayers:

'Strange to be the heroes for once, ain't it?' Lance said with a chuckle as he paced around the detonator. He rolled tobacco in a paper with one hand. He wouldn't light it so near their trap, just tuck it into his pocket with half a dozen more.
   'Don't know why you're making so many,' Melinda called over to him.
   'Just preparing for our victory shindig is all, love.' [9]

Effective in their mission, they are a duo couple a reader can identify with.

Hook/tension: Suddenly a kid rides up and warns of creatures coming from the south. Action, action, action, it's a trap, Melinda and Lance are in a fight for their lives. The story's tension endures to the end.

Plot/theme: The western hero plot works well in a story where the protagonists save towns from the gremlins and their attacks that leave infestation.

The fantastical/Fear, revulsion or spook: As a dark fantasy, 'A dusty arrival' offers up a beast fable with the gremlins and their sickness that makes people go berserk or drop dead. One scene examples the revulsion quotient:

But that wasn't the worst of what Melinda had seen at Greybends and what gave her nightmares every night since: the gremlins, their mouths full of more teeth than any creature on this earth needed, liked to tear into human bodies and fornicate in some devilish mating ritual. She'd never forget seeing a small gremlin the size of a prairie dog wiggling out of an old woman's torso as two adult gremlins, basking in the red guts, ogled Melinda with orange eyes. [10]

By human standards, the gremlins are monstrosities, the killings of human beings carnage. Dialogue in the short story is easy, slang, 'ain't' it?' Whaddya know, it gives authenticity to the story in its setting, as the gremlins come straight outta hell.

These examples of cross genre fiction show it's an open book. There are no instructions on writing cross genre. No one will tackle you to the ground for your inventfulness: you can blend any themes or genres. Award-winning speculative fiction writer Nora K Jemisin's genre-bending fiction explores themes spanning cultural identity and 'common' heroes. In her debut novel *The Hundred Thousand Kingdoms* (2010), where gods dwell among mortals, an outcast becomes a heroine. Pouring new wine into old skins, Jemisin borrows from mythologies of gods and mortals, and from character archetypes, like the trickster Sieh in the story, in a world of role reversal where the gods are enslaved. In this first book of an inheritance trilogy, Jemisin borrows from a northern African tribe in designing the traditions of the fictional barbarian Darre—protagonist Yeine Darr's people. Stealing from Christianity's the Holy Trinity and concepts of resurrection, as well as from Hinduism, Egyptian mythology and Greek mythology, Jemisin hurls in the appeal of a demonic lover, forging a romantic plot that is fundamental to the speculative work.[11, 12]

Romantic plots make good deviants—don't matters of passion thrive anywhere? Look about you, online (eBooks and author websites) and in physical stores: see the offerings of paranormal romance, fantasy romance, suspense romance, historical romance, science fiction romance. In each of these categories, the work is a romance novel where the speculative element plays a central role, or a speculative novel where romance plays a central role. Author Anne Marble wrote about the growing fans of fantasy, futuristic and paranormal (FF&P) romances, particularly thriving in electronic publishing. Whichever crossing, whether a blend of romance with fairies or genies or zombies or werewolves or magic or future science, lines haze. In true speculative fiction form these genre crossings are about what Card terms the infinite boundary.

Other crossings may place works as erotic paranormal romances, creations that arrive with jacket or blurb warnings that might say: *This story contains explicit sex with dominant males.* And sizzler texts that might read, '*She moaned into his mouth, how greedy. Her need riled the werewolf beyond measure.*' Or '*His vampire tooth ripped her chemise. "Destroy you, I will," he said.*' Or '*She strained under the creature's cold grip, frenzied by an emotion that was not ... terror. One tentacle brushed her lips, another stroked her breast, another found its way to her wetness as an altogether stray one inched toward her backside ...*' And tantalizing titles that might be named *Paramour Awakened, Desire Unchained, Enticing the Fiend, Cravings Unfettered, Taken by a Werewolf, Forbidden Ecstasy.* Publishers like Carina Press, Harlequin's digital-first adult fiction, are constantly on a call for submissions for erotic romances across subgenres, erotic thrillers, erotic psychological fiction ...[13]

Genre crossing is stepping out, going beyond genre. It crosses between audiences and teases out multiple ideas. It is being resourceful, and it rewards. It is rewarding for Douglas Adams in *The Hitchhiker's Guide to the Galaxy* that is literary science fiction; for George R. R. Martin in *A Game of Thrones* that is literary fantasy; for Tolkien in *Lord of the Rings* that is literary fantasy and also arguably science fiction; for Le Guin in *The Dispossessed* that is both utopian and dystopian and just as literary; for Golding in *Lord of the Flies* that is general fiction, literary fiction and science fiction; for Atwood in the futuristic fantasy or science fiction *The Blind Assassin* that won the Booker Prize in 2000, and in the apocalyptic *Oryx and Crake* that is literary science fiction, shortlisted for the Booker Prize in 2003.

It is rewarding to King. Don't worry about pleasing other people, he advocated in *On Writing: A Memoir of the Craft* (2000). Just write as truthfully as you can, he said. First write for yourself—if your story is good, it will *fit* somewhere. Imagine Andy Weir's, let alone Matt Damon's, bewilderment when in 2016 the film *The Martian*, based on Weir's sombre book about an astronaut stranded on Mars and presumed dead, won 'Best motion picture—music or comedy' in the Golden Globe Awards. The story was so extraordinary it bent the prescription of an award!

American science fiction and horror writer Ray Bradbury's cross genre work has seen translation into more than 40 languages and sold millions of copies around the world, with 89 credits on his filmography on IMDb. Bradbury first wrote for himself. He 'wrote different', bent genre with productive results. He took risks, was playful with text. Blending genre is subverting expectations. It steps you out of your comfort zone as you experiment with unfamiliar hybrids. And it's not novel: way back in the 19th century Robert Louis Stevenson bent genre in *Strange Case of Dr Jekyll and Mr. Hyde* (1886), a work that still today falls under the labels of fiction, horror, psychological fiction, fiction, physician fiction, self-experimentation in medicine fiction and multiple personality fiction.

Works of modern speculative fiction writers like King, Le Guin, Atwood, Borges and Bradbury span multiple genres. Other 'straight' authors surprise you with the speculative. In her literary novel *Song of Solomon*, Morrison yanks the ground from your feet and takes you soaring to the air with protagonist Milkman. Andrew McGahan in *The White Earth* (2004) hurls you into the ethereal when William finds himself face to face with a shape, dark against the sky, a thing with the head of a horse or a lizard, half standing, half crouching and towering above him; it is a bunyip—a mythical creature of the Australian indigenous people. Margaret Atwood in *Stone Mattress: Nine Wicked Tales* (2015) offers up stories within a story where 'Alphinland' evokes the wonder of folktale in protagonist Constance, a fantasy novelist whose invented world climbs out of her book and into the real world.

Japanese author Haruki Murakami 'writes different', an element that stands him out, as he crosses genre in works like *After Dark* (2004), a literary novel that exposes elements of speculative fiction in an all-night Tokyo story with its sleeping beauty Eri and her sister protagonist Mari, and its exploration of pervasive hallucinatory dualism. Anne McCaffrey's Dragon series enjoys classification as science fiction, fantasy, science fiction fantasy, romance. Stephen King's *The Dark Tower* series is horror that is also considered dark fantasy, science fiction fantasy and spaghetti western, where post-apocalyptic Mid-World's last gunslinger Roland Deschain is on a quest for a magical edifice. *Under the Dome* continues to thrive as a novel and television series in the categories of science fiction, mystery, horror suspense, even general fiction. Robert Kirkman's *The Walking Dead* horror series has seen adaptations into apocalyptic fantasy games. Ursula Le Guin's *The Dispossessed* is a cross between the subgenres of utopia and dystopia, and is bestselling on Amazon among both science fiction and fantasy books. Margaret Atwood's literary speculative novel *The Handmaid's Tale* still sits well, despite the author's protestations, as science fiction.

These works silently queer genre to loudly expose crossings in literary speculative fiction along merits of creative play and poeticity. Where traditional definitions of genre focus on textual regularities, on conventions of content and form, genre bending means resisting the potentially fixed parameters and rigidity of a singular genre. It means destabilization, taking a risk and assuming a convincing 'multiplicity' with one or more dominant genres. It means embracing the concept philosopher Gilles Deleuze and his collaborator psychoanalyst Felix Guattari explored in *A Thousand Plateaus* (1987), one that rejects the idea of a stable, fixed self, or a fixed subject position, one that insists the 'multiple must be made'. These intuitive thinkers break from traditional thought and resultant binaries. Deleuze and Guattari emphasize the nature of knowledge as rhizomatic—offering an infinite number of possibilities.

To these philosophers, deviation (from language, textual discourse or genre) is only a natural occurrence in a pattern of multiplicity. After all, literature is what fellow philosopher Roland Barthes termed an 'assemblage', 'made up', 'multiple writings'. Literature is, according to French literary theorist Gérard Genette, recycled, 'endowed with significance'.

Cross your genres, be playful, inventive: anything goes.

Exercise 9

Write 500 words of a cross genre work that combines two distinct genres or sub-genres. Choose ONE of the following as the first line of your story:

- She stepped into the room, felt the tension.
- A beast climbed out of the yawn of her dream.
- You found a diary in the bottom drawer of the kitchen shelf.
- Out in the woods, the sun had come out ...
- 'What are you talking about, crazy?'
- The scream was over in seconds.
- Her eyes sparkled like silver coins. There was something not right about them.

10

Literary speculative fiction

This chapter extends the discussion of cross genre fiction, and considers how literary writing might contribute to the quality of speculative fiction. Earlier chapters reveal Atwood's and Golding's works as snapping literary awards, where the 'literary' here is not about a grouping of books on a shelf.

Are there rules in literary speculative fiction?

To answer this question, one must first determine what is literary speculative fiction. An approach may be to shrink the phrase to 'literary' and 'speculative fiction' to distinct definitions. Earlier chapters loosely broke down speculative fiction into fantasy (and subgenres), science fiction (and subgenres), horror and the paranormal (and subgenres) and cross genre. That leaves the term 'literary' to illuminate. There is seemingly no clear definition of what constitutes literary writing or poetic language, nor consensus in the proper determination of literariness within a given work. The context of 'literary' in this book is as a phrase synonymous with 'poetic language', but without alluding to having the qualities of poetry. Rather, within this work the interchangeable terms focus on linguistic structures such as the breadth of vocabulary, vernacular, voice and an interplay between metaphor and metonym, all narrative tools that introduce to the reader complexities, ambiguities or parallels.

Literary in written material, for example poetry, novels or essays, is characterized by excellence of structure, language and style in the given literature, is aligned with quality of form. *A Dictionary of Literary Terms and Literary Theory* sees 'literariness' as the object of literary studies in the early phase of Russian Formalism, where linguist Roman Jakobson defined 'literariness' as 'the transformation of a verbal act into a poetic work and the system of devices that bring about such a transformation'. Employing the term 'device' (where a device generally refers to a thing made or adapted for a particular purpose) signals that the concept of literature is something made up, created, crafted, rather than literal. Focusing primarily on linguistic structures, Jakobson's reference, in the context of interpreting the work of a poet through the prism of language, referred to textual elements. Literariness, according to Jakobson, is about *form*, that which makes a given text a work of literature. It is not about linguistics, defining ordinary language. Poetic language in the context of this work is about the interplay of language and text, where language is 'style' or expression—tools the author uses to convey meaning to the reader. Language within this context is aligned with communication and expression of ideas, a style of expression, rather than a tongue or vocabulary of a people.

Another Russian formalist, Viktor Shklovsky, in his 1917 essay 'Art as Technique', saw art (including poetry) as thinking in images, where images belong to no one and poets can use the resources of language by 'arranging images'. According to Shklovsky, poetic imagery helps create the strongest possible impression. Let us retain the concept of poetic language/literary writing as inherent linguistic structures (such as vocabulary, voice, synonyms and metaphor) that allow an author to use language creatively. Barthes aligned language with an idea of play, a 'blissful enjoyment of fabrication and function'. When reading, he found himself writing down passages, moments, words that held power to move him. This immersion in a 'readerly' pleasure of reading, equalled his 'writerly' pleasure of writing.

In alignment with Barthes' playfulness in the language of writing, literary writer Toni Morrison in her Nobel lecture saw narrative as radical, 'as creating us at the very moment it is being created'. In this space where language is infinite, where language begins before language, Morrison employs what Barthes must have envisioned when he said, 'Literature is never anything but the deepening and extension of language'.[1] Identify with Barthes' type of fascination with language, with Morrison's attention to narrative as genesis, and link these with the notion of poetic language.

Pay attention to another author, Bill Ashcroft, who used the metaphor of a horizon to refer to literary texts. According to Ashcroft, while a horizon confines our view of the earth or our field of vision, it also gives us a 'permanent sign of spatial possibility'. To Ashcroft language is familiar with near or far, with a boundary of perception, with a phenomenon of meaning that opens possibilities relevant to the limits of language. Literary language blurs the boundaries that normal language imposes; it allows change in what he terms a 'constant horizon of our experience, unreachable but already there at the beginning'. Literary language, and creativity in general, is open to the horizon, is what Ashcroft terms a 'projection of our imaginations' where metaphor, for example, is 'a constant intimation of possibility' and 'opens a space for the future'. Bill Ashcroft's metaphor aligns with Shklovsky's notion of imagistic thought.

Literary writing in the context of this book is about greater poetics of writing, and reading, where it embraces Shklovsky's meaning of 'imagistic thought'; literary critic and semiotician Mikhail Bakhtin's considerations of language as play; Jakobson's transformation of a verbal act into a poetic work, an interplay of language and text where literariness is about form; Barthes' *The Pleasure of the Text* (1975) that aligns literary writing with creative play, counting what he describes in *The Grain of the Voice* (1985) as a 'blissful enjoyment of fabrication and function'. In borrowing from Barthes his pleasure of writing and pleasure of reading, his enchantment with unique articulation, where the author is the text's very first reader, the meaning of literary speculative fiction in this chapter is speculative fiction entwined with poeticity and the pleasure of text.

Now—are there any rules to writing literary speculative fiction?

The answer arrives in the form of examples, as this book promised to provide from the onset.

Bradbury continues to be a relevant example in representing an author who wrote literary speculative fiction, with productive results. What is it about Bradbury? Poetic language, quality of form, playfulness with language. He uses irony, parody, imagery, metaphor ... and could not help himself in a prologue to *The Illustrated Man* (2008), a telling of how on a warm afternoon in early September he first met the Illustrated Man: 'Walking along an asphalt road ... he was tall, once well muscled, but now, for some reason, going to fat. I recall that his arms were long, and the hands thick, but that his face was like a child's, set upon a massive body.' Tongue-in-cheek he introduces 16 visionary tales, startling in their beauty of language and imagination. Years before, English novelist Christopher Isherwood saw Bradbury's potential and gave him an enthusiastic review in *Tomorrow* magazine, describing him as being 'very little of a scientist and very much of a philosopher-poet'.[2] In its deliberate philosophical and poetic style, *The Martian Chronicles* bent genre and stood out for its literary writing. Bradbury chose art as language. He crossed genre by integrating literary with speculative writing, with productive results. In a *Los Angeles Times* eulogy, Lynell George described Bradbury as the author who 'lifted fantasy to literary heights'.[3]

Consider George R. R. Martin's fantasy short 'The Lonely Songs of Laren Dorr' (1976) earlier discussed:

> There is a girl who goes between the worlds.
>
> She is grey-eyed and pale of skin, or so the story goes, and her hair is a coal-black waterfall with half-seen hints of red. She wears about her brow a circlet of burnished metal, a dark crown that holds her hair in place and sometimes puts shadows in her eyes. Her name is Sharra; she knows the gates.
>
> The beginning of her story is lost to us, with the memory of the world from which she sprang. The end? The end is not yet, and when it comes we shall not know it.
>
> We have only the middle, or rather a piece of that middle, the smallest part of the legend, a mere fragment of the quest. A small tale within the greater, of one world where Sharra paused, and of the lonely singer Laren Dorr and how they briefly touched.[4]

There is imagery in the worlds the girl goes between. Martin likens the colour of her hair to coal, its texture to a waterfall. He toys with the reader's thinking and refuses to offer the beginning of the girl's story, or its end—rather, he offers a middle ... Similar beautiful descriptors exist in other Martin fantasy works like *A Game of Thrones* (2011),[5] rolling text that reads easy, rich with metaphors and allusions, even when he is killing off his darlings. Poetic descriptors allow the work to be considered literary writing. In one scene Ser Waymar Royce, an anointed knight of House Royce, serving as a member of the Night's Watch, is with Will as they range the north of the Wall when they come across White Walkers, also known as Others:

> Ser Waymar met him bravely. 'Dance with me then.' He lifted his sword high above his head, defiant. His hands trembled from the weight of it, or perhaps from the cold. Yet in that moment, Will thought, he was a boy no longer, but a man of the Night's Watch.
>
> The Other halted. Will saw its eyes; blue, deeper and bluer than any human eyes, a blue that burned like ice. They fixed on the longsword trembling on high, watched the moonlight running cold along the metal. For a heartbeat he dared to hope.
>
> They emerged silently from the shadows, twins to the first. Three of them ... four ... five ... Ser Waymar may have felt the cold that came with them, but he never saw them, never heard them. Will had to call out. It was his duty. And his death, if he did. He shivered, and hugged the tree, and kept the silence.
>
> The pale sword came shivering through the air.[6]

What identifies 'literariness' in this excerpt includes the metonym of a dance for a swordfight; the imagery of eyes that burn blue like ice; the trembling of the longsword, its paleness as that of a living being; the moonlight running cold along the metal, the attention to rhythm ... Will's hug of the tree in symbolic fear ...

J. R. R. Tolkien's writing is equally rich, literary, in *Lord of the Rings* (1954), where he constructs languages for Middle-earth, invents languages such as Qenya and Sindarin, the language of the elves. Reading Tolkien, a reader comprehends this writer's fascination with language, with culture.

H. G. Wells, whose novels eccentric author Jorge Luis Borges saw as speculations on 'future probability' and a symbolic representation of features inherent in all human destinies,[7] in *The Invisible Man* (1897) writes in flowing, descriptive prose: long sentences, dense paragraphs with the heavy English of his time, using words like 'portmanteau' for a travelling bag. Enter long segments of dialogue. A similar trajectory of long descriptive sentences informs *The Time Machine* (1895) and phrases such as 'expounding a recondite matter' or 'incandescent lights' or 'trammels of precision'.

At first glance Adams' *The Hitchhiker's Guide to the Galaxy* (2002) seems not at all literary, yet the writing is 'mock serious' even when he offers poetry:

> Vogon poetry is of course the third worst in the Universe. The second worst is that of the Azgoths of Kria ... The Vogon began to read—a fetid little passage of his own devising. '*O freddled gruntbuggly* ...' he began ... '*thy micturations are to me/As plurdled gabbleblotch-its on a lurgid bee.*'[8]

Classified as a children's book but rated PG in its movie adaptation, Adams' novel crosses readership to include pre-teens, young adults and adults with an affection for adventure, comedy and science fiction. What attracts these readers to the novel is possibly Adams' creative play, the incredulity in his text. There is irony, even literary parody, where on imitative impulse he appears to reference Shakespeare or Lewis Carroll (*O freddled gruntbuggly* ...) in the Vogon poetry. Adams immerses himself within a creative space and shows no restraint in his inclusion of footnotes in a work of fiction (a 'poke'—sly criticism). He leaps into experimental writing, where his leap is one of tactic and faith.

The author is playful, shows no restraint in his inclusion of footnotes in a work of fiction, demonstrating metafiction. As a form of postmodern writing, metafiction gained popularity in the '80s and '90s, and might comprise 'self-aware' fiction in which the author or narrator self-consciously alludes to the text's artificiality, as in a narrator's mock use of footnotes to expound a point to the reader:

> *President: full title President of the Imperial Galactic Government.
>
> The term Imperial is kept though it is now an anachronism. The hereditary Emperor is nearly dead and has been for many centuries. In the last moments of his dying coma he was locked in a stasis field which keeps him in a state of perpetual unchangingness.[9]

He offers descriptions within descriptions:

> *The Hitchhiker's Guide to the Galaxy* is a wholly remarkable book. It has been compiled and recompiled many times over many years and under many different editorships [*sic*] ... The introduction begins like this: 'Space,' it says, 'is big. Really big.'[10]

Adams' science fiction work—with its irony, parody, imagery, elision, metaphor, opposition, metafiction, rhythmic writing and overall creative play—showcases a literary speculative form. Like a poet, Adams refuses to be constrained by (mis)conceptions about language or genre. In his eccentric protagonists, he challenges traditional hierarchies between word and logic, and his controversial novel is able to offer a textual montage that challenges traditional hierarchies of genre.

The *Guardian* review appreciated Adams' 'refreshingly light approach to embarking on some of the worlds' biggest philosophical problems', his 'amazingly amusing and bizarre novel that will leave you speaking gibberish'.[11] Adams celebrates and exemplifies art as a tool (the literary as critique, when in comes satire) to address social tensions, such as those protagonist Arthur Dent experiences when the council wants to knock down his house and build a bypass instead. The tensions in the narrative, hilarious, some in unearthly worlds, exemplify ordinary issues and the complexities of existence in playful language.

In a nutshell, literary speculative fiction is about writing with joy, with a great sense of fun, as Bradbury urged. To him writing was not a serious business. 'All of my books have been surprises,' he said in *An Evening with Ray Bradbury*. 'I've never known where the hell I'm going. That's the great fun. When I write my mysteries, I start out with some characters ... But they are fascinating. That's the reason we read mysteries, isn't it?'

Literary writing outside speculative fiction

As guiding examples of literary writing, let us consider some works outside speculative fiction.

Literary writing is rewarding to Australian author Peter Temple whose crime novel *Truth* (2009) won in 2010 the Miles Franklin Literary Award, Australia's most prestigious literature prize. Temple disoriented the reader with 'multiple plots and elliptical exchanges', according to the Miles Franklin panel. But the panel also savoured Temple's narrative, embedded in voice and rich dialogue, a work 'written with all the ambiguity and moral sophistication of the most memorable literature'.[12]

The work received much commendation:

> In the case of Peter Temple's *Truth*, the divide was so comprehensively crossed that we did not think much about the conventions of crime fiction except to note that Temple was able to observe them rather as a poet observes the 14-line convention of the sonnet or a musician the sonata form: as a useful disciplinary structure from which to expand, bend or depart. (Morag Fraser, Judge of the 2010 Miles Franklin Literary Award, *The Guardian*)[13]
>
> ... consistently arresting ... tautly constructed and compulsively paced ... His dialogue is entirely distinctive, full of the mangled poetry and beautiful solecisms of ordinary speech. His images can catch in the mind like things glimpsed under lightning. (Edmund Gordon, *Observer*)[14]

Temple had written literary crime fiction. He teased the reader's expectation and cared about how the text communicated itself to the reader. He created *Truth* artistically. In first writing for himself, experimenting with imagery, elision, metaphor, oppositions and playfulness contrary to genre expectations, Temple offered quality of form the judges could not discount.

Literariness is evident in Michael Ondaatje's *The English Patient* (1993), and in *Divisadero* where, at Lucien Segura's wedding, Marie-Neige—the woman who is not his wife—pulls a note from her cotton sleeve and pushes it into his breast pocket:

> It would burn there unread for another hour as he danced and talked with in-laws who did not matter to him, who got in the way, whose bloodline connection to him or his wife he could not care less about. Everything that was important to him existed suddenly in the potency of Marie-Neige ... She had stepped into more than his arms for a dance, had waited for the precise seconds so that it was possible and socially forgivable—the sunlit wedding procession, the eternal meal—and she had passed him a billet-doux as if they were within

a Dumas. The note she had written said Good-bye. Then it said Hello ... She had, like one of those partially villainous and always evolving heroines, turned his heart over on the wrong day.[15]

There is beautiful style structure, playfulness and metaphor (sunlit wedding procession; billet-doux within a Dumas; 'goodbye' and then 'hello') in the excerpt, much for a reader to accept the work as literary writing.

In the novel *A Million Windows* (2014), the reader finds literariness in Gerald Murnane's shrewd countering of wordiness and repetition with delicious phrasings such as 'dazzling points of light on a distant hillside' and 'the common-room was suddenly in gloom after the last shafts of sunlight had passed from the nearby panes'.

Literariness is in the work of Morrison; in Haruki Murakami; in Andrew McGahan; in Peter Temple; in Alice McDermott; in Edgar Allan Poe; in Kate Grenville; in Margaret Atwood; in Isabel Allende; in Gerald Murnane; in C. S. Lewis; in Lewis Carroll. Literariness is in Gay Talese's 'Frank Sinatra Has a Cold', narrative that climbs outside the norm of journalistic feature stories of the time to pioneer new journalism. Talese transforms the article on Frank Sinatra into a piece of creative non-fiction that reads like a long short story.

Literariness is in the works of F. Scott Fitzgerald, Ernest Hemingway, William Golding, Mark Twain, Jane Austen, D. H. Lawrence, Charles Dickens, Harper Lee, Alice Walker, Alexandre Dumas, Gustave Flaubert, Marcel Proust, William Shakespeare ... All these are writers who play with language, who extend the borders of language and accepted literary genres.

It is this play with style, with structure, with imagery, elision, parody, metaphor and opposition that you can emulate within your speculative fiction.

Exercise 10

Consider the following excerpts:

Excerpt 1:

It might have been easier if they'd fought. If she were tight-faced and blaring, shrew-like and abusing, spitting out words that not only goaded but stuck. Abuse that returned to haunt in little bursts: in the stillness of the bath, between pages of a novel, in the heart of a dream.

Excerpt 2:

It sifted in, fine as baby dust. He noticed it unexpectedly. At first it was the way the girl held herself: her soft waist and new face too. Then it was the angle of her neck when he stepped into the room.

Excerpt 3:

You listened fiercely to your instinct to run, but took the wheel.

Choose one excerpt as the opening of your cross genre story.

Give the story a catchy heading.

Give the characters fitting names.

Create something unique about their character.

What is your setting? Where are your characters? Weave this setting subtly into your story, taking care on vivid descriptions.

Pay attention to sound, metaphor and rhythm. Let the writing sound poetic. Hear how it sounds: read it out loud.

Tip:

Listen to a real-life conversation and take the words out of context. Add them as witty dialogue in your story.

11

Short story

This chapter considers the unique features of the short story, and its potential in speculative fiction because of the market and opportunities that continue to welcome this form.

One of the shortest famed shorts in history is by Ernest Hemingway:

For sale: baby shoes, never worn.

This original short short story was apparently written on a dare. In the 1920s, Hemingway's colleagues placed a bet that he couldn't write a whole story in six words. Guess who won. Hemingway is believed to have prided himself on this creative piece as his best work.

Renowned novelists of speculative fiction have some amazing collections of their own short stories, and these authors include Orson Scott Card, Stephen King, Margaret Atwood, Ray Bradbury, George R. R. Martin, Harlan Ellison, Ursula Le Guin, Mary Shelley, Marion Zimmer Bradley, Edgar Rice Burroughs, Lewis Carroll, William Golding, Hugo Gernsback, after whom the award for the best science fiction and fantasy is named, Isaac Asimov... Among his novels, Murakami's surrealist short stories are still hot merchandise in online and physical stores, with his first collection *Onna no inai otokotachi* (*Men Without Women*) comprising five tales. J. G. Ballard's science fiction legacy is mottled with his other genre works and many, many short stories, including Locus Award nominees *The Best Short Stories of J.G. Ballard* (1978) and *The Complete Short Stories of J. G. Ballard* (2002). Noticed earlier was Jorge Luis Borges' existential and surreal collection *Labyrinths*. Octavia E. Butler sold short stories as well as novels, and won the 1984 Hugo Award for Best Short Story for 'Speech Sounds'. Her story 'Bloodchild' is part of her only published science fiction collection, *Bloodchild and Other Stories* (1995).

Short stories work particularly well in speculative fiction in their welcome of adaptability, flexibility, experimentation, where your first focus is on beginning, middle and end, and the rest is on your art as a storyteller. In *An Evening with Ray Bradbury*, the author couldn't reiterate enough the power of short stories: 'Write a hell of a lot of short stories,' he said, and warned of the dangers of starting straight up as a novelist without ample writing practice. Short stories explore compact ideas; if you write a story a week, 'every week you'll be happy,' said Bradbury. 'At the end of the week you'll have done something. With a novel you don't know where the heck you're going. You can spend a whole year writing one and nothing comes out of it.'

At the end of 30 weeks, he smiled, a decent story will come. At the end of a year ... he laughed: You can't write 52 bad stories in a row. What he meant was that practice is about finding the discipline to persevere at your craft until a gem happens. Bradbury honed, waited until he was 30 to write his first novel *Fahrenheit 451* (1953), a classic dystopian novel whose film adaptation was nominated for a 1967 Hugo Award in the Best Dramatic Presentation category. 'Worth waiting for, huh?' he said.

Bradbury was not implying that younger people are unable to write great stories. What he was illustrating is that writing short stories is a great way to hone the writing craft. The nature of the short story allows a writer to form a robust narrative in a constrained space (length of the writing) and time (timeline across which events occur), so you end up refining your craft. Bradbury encouraged aspiring writers to examine 'quality' short stories, and suggested Roald Dahl, Guy de Maupassant, Edgar Allan Poe, among others.

Master storyteller Stephen King has about ten collections of short stories (at the time of this book's publication), including his first and award-winning *Night Shift* (1978), also nominated as best collection for the Locus Award and as anthology/collection for the World Fantasy Award in 1979. *The Bazaar of Bad Dreams* (2015) features the 2016 Edgar Award-winning best short story 'Obit'. Of the collection, King is quoted as saying, 'while I love each and every item, I'm happy to sell them, because I made them especially for you. Feel free to examine them, but please be careful. The best of them have teeth.'[1]

Answering questions on his fan site, George R. R. Martin offers the following tip:

> Given the realities of today's market in science fiction and fantasy, I would also suggest that any aspiring writer begin with short stories. These days, I meet far too many young writers who try to start off with a novel right off, or a trilogy, or even a nine-book series. That's like starting in at rock climbing by tackling Mt. Everest. Short stories help you learn your craft. They are a good place for

you to make the mistakes that every beginning writer is going to make. And they are still the best way for a young writer to break in, since the magazines are always hungry for short SF and fantasy stories. Once you've been selling short stories for five years or so, you'll have built up a name for yourself, and editors will start asking you about that first novel.[2]

Martin in his statement aligns with the mindset of Bradbury and all those other writers who see the power of the short story, and of honing your writing. As you refine your art in this form, you get better equipped to apply precision, create convincing characters and craft hooking narrative into a larger piece of work. Le Guin, Shelley, Burroughs, Golding, Murakami, Butler, Borges or Ballard were not practising when they wrote short stories, evident in the body of works they produced.

Let us consider misconceptions about short stories and the novel. In this subjective field, author Mary Louise Pratt, in 'The Short Story: The Long and the Short of It' (1981), considered asymmetries in the relationship between the short story and the novel. There is, for example, a misreading of the short story as incomplete or fragmentary, and of the novel as whole.[3] Pratt took liberty to determine there is no single consistent use of the term 'genre' and that genre is not solely a literary matter; it applies to verbal behaviour and all realms of discourse.[4] With this determination, Pratt allowed for the flexibility of the short story, a thing that short story writers appreciate.

Pratt argued against four propositions that critics of the short story may apply with respect to the novel: the novel tells a life, the short story tells a fragment of a life; the novel deals with many things, the short story deals with a single thing; the novel is the whole hog, the short story is a sample; the novel is a whole text, the short story is not.[5] One's respect for the short story may align with Pratt's view of it as an artistic construction with its own form of totality.[6] Are you drawn to the knowing that a short story is complete in its incompleteness? Some readers find this aspect of the form exasperating. According to Pratt, a short story is autonomous in its own genre without needing anything about the novel to explain itself.[7]

The following section seeks to examine definitions of a short story.

Are there rules in a short story?

In other genres, a short story is largely a brief story that comes along with immediacy and focus on a single theme. In speculative fiction, readers may doubt your storytelling if you offer them an imagined narrative without world building, and all those things earlier discussed (characterization, hook/tension, plot/theme, dialogue), *plus* the fantastical or science fiction or philosophy or fear. This adds complexity to what makes a good speculative fiction short story, one befitting the lengths of a short, short story rather than a long, short story or a novella. On defining the genre, *A Dictionary of Literary Terms and Literary Theory* says, 'when it comes to classification this is one of the most elusive forms ... One is confronted with the question: How long (or short) is short?'[8]

There are no cast iron rules about short story writing, particularly with the explosion of other short form 'cousins' such as flash fiction or the 'short short' story or sudden fiction. Author A. L. Kennedy in her article 'Small in a Way that a Bullet Is Small' asked where one formally draws the line between 'a novella and a long short story and a short-short story and a literary letter?'[9] Kennedy exposed in her question the continually blurring boundaries of the short form. In an example, Helmut Bonheim at the University of Cologne—while conceding that some of his labels are debatable—determined the following genres in his book *The 200 Genres of the Short Story* (2001): academic, anecdotal, character, comic, cowboy, fable, plotless, postmodernist, pre-modernist, rethorical [*sic*], romantic, crime story, e-mail story, spy story, non-resolution story, telephone story, he-didn't-look-back story, I-saw-the-world-wrong story, twist-in-the-tail, utopian, vampire, vignette, writer-as-ventriloquist (to name a few). Despite such complexity in labelling and classification, conventions exist that a publisher or competition judge might look for, including length, characterization, point of view, timeframe or voice.

On the *New York Times* website, Raymond Carver spoke of his trouble in concentrating attention on long narratives—hence his focus on poems and short stories. Carver told of his love of the short form's ability to find intensity in the everyday:

> It's possible, in a poem or a short story, to write about commonplace things and objects using commonplace but precise language, and to endow those things—a chair, a window curtain, a fork, a stone, a woman's earrings—with immense, even startling power.[10]

A fascination with the everyday, or relatability with the ideas an author explores in their narrative, is a significant part of the reader's enjoyment of a novel. Carver argued that for both readers and writers the short form demands intense concentration, even in writing about the everyday, and for that reason it is a potent form in contemporary literature. Carver was also affirming that the precision and mutable nature of the short form allows its writer to experiment.

CUT, an e-publishing platform by writers for writers, was developed in collaboration with the National Association of Writers in Education (NAWE). CUT, as an e-publishing forum, specializes in short stories and has over 300 registered writers, and has published hundreds of ebooks (of which a few are collections) and hundreds of stories 'in progress'. In online profiles, writers share what they love about the short story/stories and mention the 'combination of the compact form and the possibilities for innovation' (Michael Thomas); 'pocket sized epics ... sympathetic to a sustained, intensive vibe' (Don Rintoul); 'a glimpse ... of a wider story' (Sandra Horn). Paul Ariss writes that short stories 'come to visit for a while, take you somewhere you didn't expect and then put you back where you started before you'd even realised you were gone'. Alistair Canlin appreciates that 'you can throw the reader straight into a world, and pull them out again just as quickly, leaving them asking questions, and constantly thinking'.

The diversity in these responses offers more than a hint of the complexity of the short form and its reception, in particular for critics absorbed with definitions. Author Paul March-Russell in *The Short Story: an Introduction* (2009) fondly posited the short story as a 'literary fragment', one whose size emboldens people to dismiss the complexity of writing it. To March-Russell, the short story is a form that captures immediacy, 'the passing moment'. As such, the genre is close to poetry and allows for more 'poetic language'—the integration of tropes ranging from metaphor to elision.

March-Russell proposed a mutual relationship between the short story and postmodernism:

> *The postmodern is ... undecidable*: The short story leaves meaning to be uncovered. In its form, the short story can suspend an act of deciding, can 'defer the moment of decision into an indefinite future', thus offering 'multiple options within the act of judging'.[11]

> *The postmodern is ... decentred*: The short story's 'undecidability' dissolves centralization; it throws text off-balance and proposes new centres of meaning.[12]

> *The postmodern is ... simulation*: The short story's decentralization allows distinction from reality and enables artistic representations of reality.[13]

> *The postmodern is ... surface*: The brevity, economy and technique required in its writing renders the short story capable of hinting at underlying truths while staying 'curiously inexpressive'. For example, a short story can reveal something completely disturbing with emotional detachment.[14]

The short story allows one to explore the arteries of human existence through the metaphoric potential of poetry. It holds such immediacy that personal experience can catalyse the short story's writing, in order to transform that initial experience into art and allow the artist distance from the chaos of history. March-Russell offers Franz Kafka and Isaac Babel as examples of authors who embrace the marginality of the short story as an aid, not a hindrance, to artistic expression, to writing in code in a unique literary style, to embodying alienation and aligning with otherness. For instance in 'A Report to an Academy', Kafka's character of an ape, and his estrangement in a human world, is an allegory to 'satirise the politics of cultural assimilation'.[15]

March-Russell explained that, in alignment with Poe's or O. Henry's 'well-made story', the short story allows incompleteness that is self-sufficient, lightness that is not banal, technique that is not difficult to read, and accessibility that is eloquent. Despite its small cast and narrow parameters, a good short story is not narrow, but is highly crafted and accessibly told. It is designed, March-Russell explained, to be read as a single and stand-alone unit, but may receive a degree of permanence in the form of an anthology, or a collection of short stories.

In coaching about the short story, tutors encourage writing students to have that crucial beginning, middle, end. Jessica Cunha in a workshop opened her story thus:

Warnings
Everything was black on black on black. Midnight hair fell in sheets across her shoulders. A cascading waterfall, deadly straight. It blended with the shadows of her dress, the one that clung so well it was difficult to tell where her body ended and the night began.

In this short story, Cunha applies repetition (Everything was black on black on black) as a literary device. Her title foreshadows events in the story. She immerses the reader in the story with a sharp beginning, offers mystery in the middle, and unveils all in a twist ending. She applies clipped sentences to convey urgency:

His body. Her hand. His blood. Her dress.
Her warnings. Her anger.
My gun.

Dialogue is equally terse.

Understanding that beginnings can be the hardest, Cunha takes time to choose the right one, and then stretches out the suspense to an unsuspecting reader. As the story's first reader, Cunha confessed she loved the surprises, hence was an experimental writer who found footing as she went, discovering rhythm and following it through. Discussing the story, she confirmed that 'Warnings' began with a sketchy concept and a loose character design, but was a stereotypical detective story, this one with a damsel in distress and a corrupt law enforcement officer. In experimenting, she borrowed from typical storytelling tropes while keeping the direction of the narrative a mystery even to herself until the end.

On the *New York Times* website, author Susan Sontag offers tips on good writing in her article 'Directions: Write, Read, Rewrite. Repeat Steps 2 and 3 as Needed'.[16] To write is to practise, she says, 'with particular intensity and attentiveness', the art of reading. Because you are your work's first reader, and ought to be its severest. Through writing, rereading, editing and rereading, you see your work with different eyes and fix it before you make it public. Practice sets the moorings of something solid.

Stories within a story

One technique of writing your speculative fiction is starting it as a stand-alone short story, and then embedding it into a novel. Award-winning writer Derek Neale in an interview with CUT, said:

> I write scripts and I'm also a novelist. However, short stories are central to the way I think about writing. I think they're very much connected to novel writing, as well. I'm very interested in the crossover between what is a chapter and what is a story and whether or not they can be the same thing.[17]

Neale converted a chapter from a novel into a short story and wrote it in a different character voice. He offered the example of another writer:

> Louis De Bernières said, maybe rather playfully, that for one of his novels, he laid out all the chapters on the floor and arbitrarily picked the order in which they would go. To his mind, they were all short stories and independent of each other. I'm not sure that's entirely true, but I can certainly connect with the point he's making, that relationship between stories and chapters.

Embedded stories as chapters or parts of a chapter are a viable accomplishment for the short story writer who wants to create a novel within their strengths. Linkages and layering make the composite resemble a novel, not an anthology. Borrowing from linked stories in the story cycle, embedded stories can work as a novel where you distinguish individual stories and continue to integrate them into the composite. The art is in a careful choice of where you place a short story within the novel, and then how you form correlations with all or integral parts of the composite.

While not offering the work as linked stories in a short story cycle, embedded stories exhibit features of the 'rhizome' that Deleuze and Guattari produced in *A Thousand Plateaus* (1987). According to these philosophers, the rhizome 'has no beginning or end; it is always in the middle, between things, interbeing, intermezzo.' The main principles of the rhizome are connection, heterogeneity and interconnections between everything. In Deleuze and Guattari's principle of multiplicity, the rhizome continuously adapts to other multiplicities. Perceiving text or genre as a rhizome makes deviation a natural occurrence in the pattern of multiplicity. What this means in a model of stories-within-a-story as a rhizome is that each embedded story is like a 'plateau', where multiple plateaus make up the rhizome. Perfectly, if wholly distinct, the stories in a heterogeneous collection are connected.

This model of hiding or embedding short stories in a novel welcomes the writer whose form is experimental. In applying it, the writer is able to take advantage of their familiarity with the merits of the short story—such as economy, concentration and succinctness. Writing story by story, the writer is creating in a discipline already familiar, while layering the novel with characters, timelines, motifs and interplay—a sum of the parts.

Exercise 11

Step 1. Visit the website **50wordstoriesuk.wordpress.com**

This is one of many online sites that offer free bite-size stories for your enjoyment. The first creative piece of exactly 50 words is by an anonymous London writer:

His Last Words
'I won't be a minute', he said, slamming the front door.

By 11pm she'd called the police, having exhausted all possibilities. They searched. Nothing.

His credit card untouched for the next four years before expiring.

They'd been so happy, she thought, but she'd never escape those (now) ambiguous last words.

Read a few more stories on 50wordstoriesuk.wordpress.com.

Notice how they have a beginning, middle and end.

See how the short story stays away from adverbs and adjectives. Less is more … if you can say it in fewer words …

Step 2. Use an online search engine to get writing exercises online. The website **writingexercises.co.uk** is one of many online sites that offer free writing prompts and exercises to help you get started on your creativity and nudge you out of a writing block. It offers random first line prompts, random subjects, quick plot generators, making connections between random nouns, and more.

Begin with a random first line prompt, follow instructions and generate a first line. Here are examples of what the generator fashioned:
• She had no intention of choosing sides until she was sure who was going to win …
• The little boy's idea of heaven was …
• He could hear everything, but dare not open his eyes …
• They had to work together, so they would need to …
• She'd only given in because she was lonely …
• There was a strange wailing sound coming from the next room …

Step 3. Choose a first line. Use it to write a 50-word science fiction, fantasy, horror or paranormal story. It is okay if you wind up with a longer story—just edit it to down to fifty words!

Repeat with another first liner, and write a 100-word story.

Repeat, and write a 200-word story.

In cropping word count, here is a general rule: First get rid of adverbs and adjectives. Next get rid of words, phrases or sentences that do not add to the story.

12

Targeting young adults and new adults

Speculative fiction tends to be popular in readerships classified as young adults (YA) or mature young adults, perhaps because of the novelty of its extraordinary stories or the ease of its accessibility in bite-size fictions across cyber and technological channels and devices that certain age groups are particularly adept with. It could be that the developing mind is inherently more curious and less rigid on reading preferences, or that young adults—unencumbered by all those things (like careers) that occupy adults—are better able to make time for escapist stories in fantastical worlds!

Boundaries of YA novels are continually being redefined, now including classifications of the 'new adult' reader, generally 17+ and capped at 25, and the contemporary young adult reader to whom Random House targets novels such as John Green's *The Fault in Our Stars* (2012), Lesley Livingston's *The Valiant* (2017) and James Dashner's dystopian novel *The Fever Code* (2016). Goodreads.com lists speculative new adult fiction as stories with paranormal or fantastical elements and featuring 18–25-year-old characters. Adult themes (such as drugs, alcohol and sex) surrounding the interests of a maturing adolescent or 'new adult' invite crossover text that transverses audiences.

YA literature will typically have a young adult protagonist playing out themes that tackle ideas and transitions that young adults might experience. In our dynamic worlds of technology, autonomy and opportunity, young adults experience conflicting feelings and face 'grown-up' challenges such as drug use or sex crime where they are victims or perpetrators. You would think a writer could write in any genre and target them. Uncensored, this author could travel on themes for young adults, particularly on the premise that if it happens to a young adult, some young adult out there will identify with it, so it is writable as a YA novel. But no. Thrusting a YA protagonist into the narrative is not enough for a guarded publishing industry.

Crossing audiences means finding ways in which to productively adapt 'adult themes' into YA fiction or new adult fiction, potentially along the premise of the writer as a champion of change.

YA literature—an important conversation

It is intrinsic that individuals within society are inclined to package and classify; it is inevitable they will question something that falls outside 'normal' classifications. Cataloguing of fiction depends on publishing sortings or marketing ploys, and a YA readership is generally aged between 12 and 18. But YA literature has had its share of authors who have stretched boundaries. Take the example of the Harry Potter novels that started off as children's stories. They gathered fans in adolescents and adults—not simply in the UK but in the global market. Novels like *Harry Potter and the Goblet of Fire* (2002), with its 752 pages rather than the typical 200 pages of a successful YA novel, stepped young adult literature into a new horizon.

YA literature now includes classifications of the new adult reader, the mature young adult reader and the contemporary young adult reader. These new classifications have not succeeded as they should in opening YA boundaries, in helping to dissolve borders so that readership is targeted based on effective storytelling and remarkable narrative rather than a prescription of what subject matter, narrative style or theme is suitable for teens, for example. A novel, any novel, that can promote awareness and conversation around contemporary adolescent issues is a worthy read for young adults and new adults.

Adapting adult themes to young adult fiction

Youth empowerment arrives through learning, doing and socialising. The diversified YA fiction market offers writers an innovative way to tap into and interact with the curious youth, the budding adult who is still negotiating values and applying learnings. The quest for empowerment allows for both receptiveness and vulnerability.

A good YA novel will speak to a higher order, a desire for more, for different—this yearning is what our youth are potentially consciously or subconsciously experiencing today in an impersonal world ridden with accessible 'harms': isolation through social media and technology, easily obtainable drugs, malicious strangers a click away on cyber, permissible societies that do not set imitable foundations of moral living … In their bleakest moments, the youth are overwhelmed and will drown unless they find empowerment, something to clutch. And they know how to find choice—there is much information online, but is it resourceful? Young adults are hungry to know. Censored or not, they will find what they seek. While it is presumptuous for a writer to assume a mentoring role, the very element that may stimulate the rebellious nature of a young adult, if such mentoring is skilfully woven into engaging narrative written to evoke hope, resilience, self-awareness, optimism, expression ... rather than tragic thought—if it does not penetrate vulnerability and derail self-esteem but proffers insight, it is workable for young readers.

As a writer, whatever plight you mean to thrust on the young adult in your story, do not devastate them to no end. No Macbeths. Give them a rake, a hose, a pruner, a pair of secateurs. Give them a portal they can open to enter, a fist they can lock to hurl fireballs, magic they can summon to go undetectable, physical strength to combat monsters, mental ability to dispel fear and tackle the undead ... give them something, anything, someone. A mentor (wise old man or woman) as in the frequently used character archetypes that Vogler explores. The mentor is your sage (like Hagrid or Dumbledore in *Harry Potter*) who guides your protagonist.

How you portray their characters and their value systems, and what you aim the reader to gain from them can be a productive way to integrate adult themes. If you build into your protagonist a quest for more, or integrate plotlines that address the challenges adolescents encounter in the real world, you can become a motivating author who encourages transformation in the developing reader.

A motivating author offers ideas about survival, combats ignorance with knowledge, opens up conversation about confusing 'adult' situations that could happen to young adults. The writer as a champion of change can first break the circle of silence and then equip the young adult—and society—with awareness that destructive situations are resolvable with self-awareness and as simple an action as a call for help in the right direction.

A productive YA novel will help combat helplessness. In today's era, the young are exposed early to matters once considered pertaining to grown-ups. Today you will find young people walking around with all-manner-of-hopelessness. *Come, let us compound the hopelessness of a young person*, says no one aloud ever. Society, of whichever cultural, sociological, political slant, does not condone it—not without ideological malfunction.

While the debate on human nature versus nurture is far from settled,[1] is a separate sociological and physiological discussion outside the scope of this chapter, one might argue for survival and moral certainty. This argument is not suggesting a Darwinian approach to survival of species (and the fittest shall live), but an innate instinct to protect the young. Is nurture common sense? Do individual human beings, as 17th-century French philosopher René Descartes set out, possess certain in-born 'ideologies' (like caring for their young, as do most animals) that underpin our approach to the world? Descartes was likely an optimist.

What is most probable is the notion that we are intrinsically geared by our nature to nurture forming beings, groom them to adulthood. When we do the reverse, we do it silently, maliciously, dislodged from witnessing.

The written word is on a path or in the direction of a public statement. Think of writers as heralds, as inclined to speak for social change. As answerable members of a society, any society, it is not our duty, anybody's duty, to inspire a troubled young mind, any troubled mind, to jump off a cliff. As authors we offer, in our stories, possibility. We offer insight. This is how we can adapt adult themes to be productive elements of YA fiction.

Look back to renowned speculative fiction authors George R. R. Martin and J. K. Rowling, and contemplate their portrayal of characters and events of young adult protagonists and secondary characters in the novels they create. While in Martin's *Game of Thrones* there is encounter with the pitiless boy king, Joffrey Baratheon, there is also the vulnerable young like Sansa, who matures and learns to play her cards; there is Arya, who attains survival skills that would shame a commando; there is Rickon, whose direwolf hauls him out of peril; there is Bran, whose visions give insight to the future and help inform choice. Rowling has Harry Potter and his friends, who must face off a potent wizard. These stories offer hope and resilience in the heart of tragedy, evil or abomination. They are templates to learn from.

Good literature—irrespective of subject, style or theme—will offer a forum for open minds. According to Freud, the artist is a unique individual in a 'process of sublimation': refining basic drives, such as those of sex and aggression, and converting them into creative and intellectual activity.[2]

Exercise 12

This exercise is about dialogue.

Step 1. Listen to one of the following:
- lyrics of a song
- conversation among people in a room or a space (for example, in a bus or a train carriage)
- a catch-phrase in an advertisement on television, billboard or radio
- words of a nursery rhyme

Take the words out of context. For example, if the intent was:
- merry, make them spooky
- angry, make them romantic
- romantic, make them loony

Step 2. Use the words in the new context as dialogue in a 250-word science fiction, fantasy, horror or paranormal story.

Step 3. Give your story three possible endings.

Tips:
- Notice how people do not speak in perfect grammatical sentences or long-winded monologues. We often speak to advance our agenda, irrespective of the other person's response.
- Focus on a:
  - catchy heading
  - sharp opening
  - active speech
  - edit, edit, edit—read and rewrite your story.

13

Critical and cultural theories

This is not a book about literary theory. There are many books on critical and cultural theories, including Nigel Krauth and Tess Brady's edited collection of essays *Creative Writing: Theory Beyond Practice* (2006), a divergent collection that speaks to frameworks that shape creative writing in the 21st century; Dani Cavallaro's *Critical and Cultural Theory: Thematic Variations* (2001), a radical book on key concepts, issues and debates; David Carter's *Literary Theory* (2006), that offers insight to ideas behind postmodernism, queer theory, feminism, intertextuality, deconstruction and literary theorists like Baudrillard, Althusser, Foucault, Freud and Jung; and Hans Bertens' *Literary Theory: The Basics* (2013), a comprehensive analysis and historical capture of methods and issues in poststructuralism, Marxism and new criticism. This is not such a book.

The aim of this chapter is to connect critical and cultural theories and how they might apply to the writing of speculative fiction. But why is it important?

Aspiring writers might find interest in critical approaches to human language and thought, factors that potentially influence how a reader approaches your work. Students in literature or postgraduate study in creative writing disciplines often find themselves catapulted into an in-depth study of theory where they must scrutinize text and understand their own writerly and readerly roles. For students of writing, the discernment of literary theory may involve a stumbling and a questioning at the necessity of this enterprise. Take the analogy of a child undoing a knot, as illustrated in Malcolm Sparrow's *The Character of Harms* (2008), habits of mind:

> Give a knotted mass of string to an adult, who has developed all of the relevant cognitive skills (and maybe had some experience too), and watch how they behave. Notice how they hold the whole object up to the light, and look at it this way, then that way, turning it around and around, examining it diligently from all sides—careful all the time not to pull or tug or to make matters worse—until they begin to understand the structure of the thing itself. As the

structure of the knot becomes clearer, so the components or stages of a plan begin to form in their minds … If they understood the structure correctly, and fashioned a plan accordingly, the knot eventually falls apart, and is no more.

By contrast, give the same knot to a child, who has yet to develop this particular set of cognitive skills, and observe their behavior. Witness their frustration as they tug and pull and generally make matters worse. Note the relative lack of attention to observation and discernment of the nature of the thing, or the particularities of its structure. Note the alacrity with which the child jumps into action, applying crude methods that usually fail.[1]

Aligning this analogy with the learning of literary theory, a skilled scholar will hold a text up to the light, look at it this way, then that, turn it around and around, examine it diligently until they shape clearly where they want to go, how they want to go. A person new to theory approaches it with the cognitive skill of a child, frustrated as they tug and pull, make matters worse. Enthusiastic to get going, they might forget to hold the text up to the light, instead jumping in with alacrity and a lack of attention, and finding mis-starts and non-conclusions.

Deciphering critical and cultural theories is no mean accomplishment, and the diversity of debate on the range of this or that theory's meanings and implications rages among critics. To a student, literary theory may pose as a white elephant: burdensome, deemed necessary by some, more trouble than their worth. Where skilled pundits understand them, pull them apart, quibble, a novice's effort to grasp them, let alone pull them apart, is rife with mishaps and non-conclusions. To the determined, one day, gradually, something falls into place. Amidst the diversity of thought, the often dry exposition surrounding literary theory, you finally find positioning with which to align your creative work and the theories that influence it. And then one day you astonish yourself by thinking literary theory in the everyday.

Let me share an immersive experience.

Something ruffles up at the aquatic centre today:

I am in the spa, legs stretched out, arms folded behind my head. My mind is sharp as a blade. Heated beads of water volcano up the chemical-rich tub. A cold stream beneath my thigh gurgles from a spout, blends with hot to create an even 36 degrees of temperature.

The philosophers Roland Barthes, Paul Ricoeur, Jacques Derrida, Gilles Deleuze and Félix Guattari emerge before me. They are immersed as I am: legs spread out, hands behind their heads. Barthes' eyes have a shimmer in them. Ricoeur, Derrida … prolific writers, scholarly debaters of deconstruction and hermeneutics—the art of interpreting—are these thinkers here for me now?

Ahead on a far side, a guard's eye abandons its watching. A little girl steals the moment with a water bomb, splashes where only moments ago a young woman wearing a swim cap the colour of red liquorish speared into the lap pool. The girl clambers out of the pool as the guard's eye returns to its monitoring. Oblivious, the swimmer continues her five-stroke-breathe lapathon. I ignore the pulse in Barthes' eyes, look upwards towards the staves. I blink at the bright light of the facility, gaze into an all-windowed upstairs gym. An elderly man in grass green pants and a firm t-shirt pedals in the aerobics class next to Robert Redford—correction, next to a Redford look-alike. *Grass green pants Barthes Barthes Derrida.* My eyes are back to the beating heart. *Construction deconstruction intertextuality.* The elderly man pedals, pedals and pedals in the gym, his pants gleaming sweat. *Bright pigment that makes grass green.* The little girl arranges herself to do another water bomb. Man pedal, pedalling in the gym. *Chlorophyll absorbs blue light ... and red light ... but mostly reflects green light ...*[2]

In the lap pool: My arms start first against the water tide. I push off the wall to a breaststroke cycle, my mind still on the philosophers. *The text is demonstrated, is spoken according to certain rules (or against certain rules) ... Barthes.* My head and shoulders come out of the water. I lunge forward through the kick. My head and shoulders come out again, and Barthes—eyes still pounding—leans towards me from the edge. He is speaking: *the work is a fragment of substance ... the text is held in language: it exists only when caught up in a discourse.* Arms first, I lunge forward through the kick, unfazed by the seeming unreality of Barthes in his togs by my poolside. *I am the story which happens to me: freewheeling in language, I have nothing to compare myself to ... Barthes.*

Under the quick rinse shower: I press the button, water gushes out of the faucet in a one-minute blast. I rub my body. *The text is structured but decentred, without closure ... The text is plural ... Barthes.*

Inside the changing cubicle: I move to fasten the lock but Deleuze clasps the door from without, pushes himself in. He and Guattari would like a word: *when one writes, the only question is which other machine the literary machine can be plugged into, must be plugged into in order to work ... Literature is an assemblage. It has nothing to do with ideology. There is no ideology and never has been ...* Guattari rests an elbow on Deleuze's shoulder. He has a principle of multiplicity. *The two of us wrote Anti-Oedipus together. Since each of us was several, there was already quite a crowd.* And principles of connection and heterogeneity: *any point of a rhizome can be connected to anything other, and must be. Write, form a rhizome, increase your territory by deterritorialization.* I think of my artefact: stories-within-a-story—connection, heterogeneity and interconnections ...

It is Ricoeur who seizes the last word outside the aquatic facility as automatic doors glide shut behind me: *I will speak about the difficulties linked to translation ... easier said than done and occasionally impossible to take up. These difficulties are accurately summarised in the term 'test' [épreuve], in the double sense of the 'ordeal' [peine endurée] and 'probation': testing period, as we say, of a plan, of a desire or perhaps even of an urge, the urge to translate.* What is knowledge, Ricoeur? I silently ask.[3]

Now, dear reader, please reflect on immersion. In this example, creative writing plays out from within to without, joins the everyday, moves into the lived experience to enter this space in the pool.

Theory 101

Sometimes referred to as 'literary theory', 'critical theory' or simply 'theory', there are many schools of thought, often linked to philosophy or philosophers. Theory potentially dates back to Plato and beyond, before finding popularity with the Russian formalists in the 19th century, rising in emerging trends towards comparing culture and forms of artistic expression among open-minded scholars in the 1920s and seeing legitimization as a scholarly discipline around the 1970s.

Around this time literary theory gained ground in continental Europe, a result of social and political upheaval that led to examinations of contemporary culture and critical approaches to literary meaning, cultural identity and history. Russian formalists like Viktor Shklovsky (1893–1984) or Boris Tomashevsky (1890–1957), explored formal methods in the approach to literary art, seeing art as science with its devices of rhyme, repetition, metaphor and symbol. Theory debate comprised concepts and intellectual assumptions with which to explain or interpret literary texts, and theories delved into matters encircling language, semiotics, signification, political, feminist, ethical, even psychoanalytical fields. The early focus of debate was on hard theory, but its span swiftly enfolded cultural understandings—where culture manifests itself in our knowledge and characteristics, as defined by our language, society, religion, diet, external influences and so forth.

Culture—how or who we are—informs how we perceive. Culture as a template forges our behaviours and perceptions, and language supports this template by shaping a system of meaning. From birth, potentially even before—as early as your nurture in the womb—your formations may already have been imprinted by external influences. Self-experience, kinfolk, education, peers, influential storytellers all play a role in the way you think, in your way of being, so that everything social, political, religious and economic becomes a construction, makes you a sum of many things.

Even the language you learn or speak influences your preconditioning; and this an important aspect of one theory, the 20th-century Saussurean model named after Swiss linguist Ferdinand de Saussure and his theories on semiotics, where language is a social contract. This underpins your deconstruction of text: the meaning that you assign to the text, the assumptions you make, the perspectives you bring to it, the importance you assign to it. And this meaning might change according to context or a process of intellectual maturity, and encounter or intermingle with other cultures because we are dynamic, not static, and our learnt culture is equally dynamic, constantly evolving.

Critical and cultural studies take into account these influences that shape what we do, how we do and where we attach value, and connect them with our approach to literature, our deconstruction of it, where deconstruction is breaking it down, challenging it, in order to better understand it.

Theories arrive hand in glove with critical practice. They offer an intellectual approach, extend our ability to think critically and offer a richer perspective to the literature we encounter—local and global. Text is static. Theory helps the reader to interact with text, to interrogate the role of the writer, the reader. But why? French philosopher Michel Foucault answered this question shortly before his death:

> There are times in life when the question of knowing if one can think differently than one thinks, and perceive differently than one sees, is absolutely necessary if one is to go on looking and reflecting at all.[4]

If a looking and reflecting author understands text as more than it is, will they write differently? Will the perceiving reader approach the text differently? The choice, urged author and theorist Thomas Schmitz, is not whether we want to do theory or not: the choice is whether we want to do good or bad theory.[5]

Hans Bertens in *Literary Theory: The Basics* looked at literary theory, closely linked to literary practice—the practice of interpretation, where interpretation goes beyond 'What does it mean?' to 'What does it mean and to whom?' and 'Who wants it to have this meaning and for what reasons?', and considers reading for meaning, the self as the source of value and meaning.

A few dominant literary theories in a nutshell:

Feminist theory: This is used to counter the marginalization of women, against dominant ideologies of male supremacy. The dominance of one leads to the repression of the other. You can use it to fashion stories such as Atwood's *The Handmaid's Tale*, set in a totalitarian and theocratic state; or *The Edible Woman*, about women and their relationships to men, diet and society. Octavia Butler was a feminist whose writing targeted three groups: 'the science-fiction audience, the black audience and the feminist audience'.[6] She cast strong female protagonists in her work, for example Shori, the young black vampire girl in *Fledgling* (2005) or Lauren Olamina in *Parable of the Sower* (1993).

Inspired by Robert Tapert's fictional character Xena, the warrior princess,[7] speculative fiction writer Maddison Stoff applies a feminine perspective to influence how she develops characters and storylines, purposefully weaving strong female protagonists and representing minority groups. She says, 'I try to make space where there wasn't space before for different kinds of characters traditionally under-represented in the genre. I also try to question sexist tropes and the political assumptions that go into making fictional worlds.'[8]

Discussing feminism, another writer Faith Mudge says:

> What I remember most clearly about watching *Return of the Jedi* is my mother's quiet but fierce sense of betrayal at what that storyline did to Leia. I still can't watch the movie without a bad taste in my mouth. Much of the science fiction I loved as a child used the humiliation or disparagement of women as a plot device, or worse, as a joke, and it was clear you were supposed to think less of the women for it, rather than the writers. It was infuriating then and it's grown more infuriating since, but my understanding of sexism is more nuanced. There are all kinds of ways to disrespect agency. I never want to be lazy with any character I write, of any gender.[9]

Feminist theory is about critically assessing the patriarchal social order and its use of terms that connote weakness, passiveness or gentleness, for example, with the feminine, and privileged terms denoting strength, dominance, or success, for example, with the masculine. A writer of speculative fiction can use this theory to address themes of gender, as master storyteller Ursula Le Guin did in her Nebula and Hugo award-winning feminist classic *The Left Hand of Darkness* (1968)[10] that takes place on an alien world without sexual prejudice, where inhabitants of the planet can shift between genders on choice.

Autobiographical theory: Artistic formations are sometimes imprinted by personal history or external influences of family, self-experience, education, culture, society ... The language we speak (and write) influences and exposes our preconditioning, as per French philosopher and theorist Michel Foucault's idea of discourse as a loose structure of interconnected assumptions that makes knowledge possible. The writing and interpretation of a text may be influenced by a number of contexts which underpin the deconstruction of a text.

Autobiographical theory is used in understanding personal discourse, for example in a memoir, where the self or subject is the principle referent. It interrogates the theory of mind and narrative skill, the ability to tell a coherent and structured life story factually, or stories at a point in time. Often it involves a study of event memory and the narration of that past, revelations of self and form through personal stories, in the act of recounting and reminiscing. Narrative fiction with supernatural or fantastical elements can be particularly potent when written in first-person, offering insight to the protagonist's mind, preconditioning influences in the assumptions they make, the perspectives they bring, the importance they assign, their reasonings. An example is Stephen King's psychological horror *Duma Key* (2008), about a man whose life is disintegrating; he rents a deserted house where weird things happen, including in his paintings.

The autobiographical can be used to fabricate realist fiction that measures up to a real person or event. In an example of self-experience (the autobiographical), novelist and short story writer Kris Ashton had an illness and a dream: two unrelated things that combined to inspire his story. In his science fiction horror 'The Larval Stage' (2018) Ashton translates true experience into fiction: in real life he woke up one day to find his hands and feet were so tender he could barely use them. A blood test revealed nothing, and the mysterious condition cleared in a day or two. In fiction he invents haemoglobic fever:

> His back ached like an infected tooth and the flesh on his legs and buttocks throbbed in time with his heartbeat. Rhys was very pleased when the line of blue light dropped off his naked toes and disappeared.
> 'You can sit up now,' Dr Blackman said. 'We'll have the results in a few seconds.'
> 'Thanks,' Rhys said.
> He slid off the cushioned platform and stood up. Adjacent to Dr Blackman's desk was a chair, but for now Rhys had no desire to sit…
> Dr Blackman looked up. His eyes almost disappeared in the black foliage. 'I'm afraid I don't have any good news, Rhys.'[11]

How long till I'm dead? Rhys asks and, in his terminal illness, offers himself up as a human host to alien larvae, with dire consequences. In another example of the autobiographical fictionalized, short story writer Dan Malakin's daughter was barely one when he left her for less than a minute in the bath. He heard a crash as she tried to stand up and slipped. He wondered what if ... and came up with 'Deleted Lives' (2018), a science fiction story about artificial intelligence, a Julia that isn't real, that is a refinement of photos, videos and memories. An expensive replica that claps her hand and babbles in baby language. A version that looks like her, acts like her, but is not Julia, the one that was left in the bath for a minute, just a single minute.[12]

Postmodernism: In Roland Barthes' context of text as a marriage of writings, postmodernism comes along with associations, a non-originality of the text, its interdependence with other literary texts, where text is a multidimensional space and writers only assemble, pre-mix, borrow from, draw upon what is already written. According to Barthes—who was a strong proponent of postmodernism, with his revelations of text as a marriage of writings drawn from many cultures—a text is approached, is experienced, is plural, is metonymic.[13] Science fiction as hyperreality is a good example of postmodernism. Douglas Adams in *The Hitchhiker's Guide to the Galaxy* (2002) exploits postmodernism through metafiction (e.g. footnotes in a work of fiction), creative play, irony, even literary parody in text that bears subversive themes.

Without intending to be reductive in this example, but attempting to simplify a complexity, one can also think of postmodernism as 're-mixing', adopting new forms for old: a questioning of what is originality. Seth Grahame-Smith's novel *Pride and Prejudice and Zombies* (2009), that started out as online fan fiction, combines modern zombie narrative with Jane Austen's classic *Pride and Prejudice* (1813) in a romantic satire that is also a comedy of manners. In her short story 'A Small Problem' (2018), Carine Heidmann borrows from a simple fairy tale to put new wine into old skins in a remake of the Brothers Grimm's story of a frog prince:

Her pretty shoes squelched in the mud. She sat in the wet grass by the pond.

Filth everywhere. It covered her feet and smeared her dress. Her entire outfit would be ruined. She wrinkled her nose. And the smell...

There was no help for it. She'd already agreed to do it.

She breathed through her mouth, smoothed down her dress. Lifted her chin and faced the creature. 'This had better be worth it.'

It stared at her, said nothing now, after being so garrulous moments before, imploring, hard-selling its proposal.

'Okay,' she sighed. 'No point delaying this.'

She leaned forward, inching closer, inwardly writhing. She imagined what it would feel like. She trembled, every fibre of her being resisting what she was about to do.

At the last moment, she scrunched her eyes. She didn't have to look while she was doing it.

She puckered her lips and kissed the frog.

A worm of revulsion forced its way through her being as her lips touched a cold wet mouth. She recoiled, squirming. 'Ew. Yuck. Yuck!' What was she thinking? Gagging, she spat into the grass, wiped her mouth with the back of her hand, wished she could rinse it out, brush her teeth and gargle with a strong antiseptic mouthwash.

A force knocked her backwards. Golden white light blinded her. She shielded her eyes, craned to see but couldn't make out a thing. Magical radiance bathed the world. Sprinkles of fairy dust appeared from nowhere and snowed everywhere. Magic soared and zoomed through the air, creating trails of glittering fairy light, lifting her hair, the fabric of her clothes, and erupting goosebumps all over her body. Excitement fizzled through her and she could've sworn she heard the swell of an orchestra somewhere. She loved the thrilling buzz of ecstatic power that came with a manifestation of magic. Her heart leaped in anticipation of its outcome.

But her mind spewed worries. Would she be able to live with the memory of what he'd been? A creature living in a muddy morass? Would he be able to?

She so dearly wanted everything to be pure and noble and perfect but... Could she ever banish the memory of their awful first kiss? Would it haunt her every time he came near?

As suddenly as it started the lightshow ended. The noise died down.

She blinked. Half-blinded, she looked around. Where was he? Her prince.

A flash of colour drew her gaze downward to the grass.

Her mouth gaped. 'Wha—'

She leaned closer, stared at the magnificently dressed, square-shouldered, blonde-haired, picture-perfect, but ridiculously undersized, prince. Hardly taller than the frog had been, even his frog-sized crown was too big for his head, lying aside in the mud.

She waited for the magic to complete its work, make him grow bigger, bring him to a full manly size, preferably a good few inches taller than her.

It didn't happen.

Instead, he did a gallant doll-sized curtsy. 'My lady,' he said in a deeply melodic male, but small, voice.

Her horror even greater than when she'd kissed the frog, her dreams splintered. 'What am I going to do with you!'[14]

True to postmodernist thinking, Heidmann determined that no story is fully told—you can always recraft it. She looked at the scene when Tiana kissed the frog in the Disney version of this fairy tale, and an alternate outcome to the classic popped into her head. Postmodern theory comes along with a freedom of thinking and embraces experimentation with new insights and perspectives. It is about remaking, connections, contradiction. Imitation, reproduction, reiteration. Enters a new version of the fantasy in 'The Young Prince':

'Falada, falada, where art thou hangest?' cried the young prince, face up to the tower.

'Fa—! Falada? Where art thou hangest?' chided a voice from a window. 'That fluff is from The Goose-Girl and the person who wrote that story is most ungrammatical.'

'Open the door, my princess dear, open the door to thy true love here!' cried the prince.

'Careful, my prince dear, I'm stuck up in a tower, there's no door here!'

'Let down your hair, dear Rapunzel.'

'My name's not Rapunzel. But…'

A magnificent long strand, fine as spun gold, fell to the ground.

'One hair is of no use to me, I must have the whole head,' cried the prince.

'That line's from The Golden Bird, and the exact wording is: One feather is of no use to me, I must have the whole bird.'

'Do not jest, dear princess. I've come from a great way off and rode all this way.'

'Okay. Wait a minute.'

After more than a minute, fifteen to be precise, a mane of braided tresses, fine as spun gold, fell to the ground.

The prince looked at the curls aground, and then at the window aloft. 'My dear,' he cried, 'the idea was to wind your hair round one of the hooks of the window, and lower it so I could climb up.'

'Not to shear it?'

'No.'

'My hope falls away. You can't communicate. Thankfully, that was just a wig. Hold out your hands if you will.'

The prince followed her bidding.

Plash! Something wet fell onto the prince's palms.

'There's a nasty frog!' cried the prince.

'Just shush it and kiss me,' said the frog.

The prince hesitated.

'I know it doesn't feel right,' said the frog, 'but go with the flow.' The frog closed its eyelids and pushed out its lips. When nothing happened, an eyelid opened. 'I guess this is the point you say, "Don't call me, I'll call you" before you ride into the sunset? Alone? But listen, at the core of our unique differences, we each have a deep desire to… to…' The frog fell silent.

'I admire your hopefulness,' said the prince.

He closed his eyes and puckered his lips and nearly threw up at the moist spread on his mouth.

Nothing like a sprinkle of golden dust fell upon him. No princess murmured against his lips, 'You have broken a cruel charm. I was enchanted by a spiteful fairy who changed me into a frog.'

All he saw was an avocado-green frog.

'I don't know what you expected,' said the frog, 'but I've always wanted to try a prince's kiss. If you ask me, I'd say it's a bit overrated.'

'A kissed frog... is still... a frog,' said the prince slowly. 'Even a well-read one.'

The frog regarded him. 'You might be too young for me. We're talking like light-years.'

'Well then,' said the prince. 'How about friends?'

The frog considered for a moment. 'With benefits?'[15]

In a new approach to writing that is part of postmodernist thought, this parodic flash fiction borrows from the Brothers Grimm's 'The Goose-Girl', whose horse's name was Falada; from 'Rapunzel', whose hair she could let down from atop a tower window; from 'The Golden Bird', whose tail feather was not enough for the king; and from the modern phrase of 'friend with benefits'—a friend with whom one has an occasional and casual sexual relationship. Postmodernism welcomes adaptations and creative works in contemporary appropriation, including pastiche and parody, and creative art that stimulates a scrutiny of 'originality'.

Queer theory: Simone de Beauvoir (1908–1986) was a woman before her time and in *The Second Sex* ([1949] 2010) explored concepts of otherness, ambiguity, embodiment, disclosure, temporality and situation. Queer theory borrows Beauvoir's concepts, such as ambiguity, embodiment, self and other, in stories and discussions from the perspective of engaging with difference. Philosophy scholar Mary Sirridge discussed Beauvoir and her place in philosophical thought, pointing out that, according to Beauvoir, the differences between information and literature are linked with the basic features of the human condition and the distinctive way in which literature functions.[16] We are each individually situated in a singular relationship with the world, where the world is an 'interplay of all the individual situations as they overlap and envelop each other'.[17] Our individual situations are not closed with respect to each other, because we are not islands, and language gives us a way of communicating, of engaging despite our differences. The power of literature, argued Sirridge, is that it 'allows us to pass beyond our separation from one another ... although we coinhabit a point of view'.[18] Readers 'adopt the novelist's situation'; they become inside out. By engaging with difference within a novel, an author invites the reader to engage with difference, to welcome 'otherness'.

Queer theory accommodates the notion of queer as not something confined to identity or sexuality, but rather a way of seeing things. Queer theory is about what literary critic and social theorist Michael Warner termed 'resistance to regimes of the normal', focusing on the politics of identity and inclusion. Stoff, who is also transgender and autistic, found inspiration in speculative fiction because it didn't 'other' her. She said, 'In a galaxy where robots and aliens were commonplace, no one was going to worry about a minor neurological divergence and, if they did, I could hop on a ship and take myself away to somewhere else. I found that feeling quite empowering. That sense of endless possibility.'[19] Stoff was talking about using the power of literature to overcome her sense of alterity (being different from and in opposition to), to welcome otherness and a reinvention that channels ways to 'belong' while still being different: an outside that is also an alongside, and is okay.

Any work of speculative fiction that engages with difference or encourages a different way of seeing things, a denormalized way, breaks the shroud of silence and embraces queer theory irrespective of whether it is LGBTQIA (lesbian, gay, bisexual, transgender queer, intersex and asexual)-themed, or simply about an outcast protagonist like Yeine Darr in N. K. Jemisin's *The Hundred Thousand Kingdoms* (2010).[20] Marginalized Yeine is denaturalized because her mother, once the heiress in a dynastic family, married a man from the barbarian north and faced disownment. By casting Yeine as the heroine of a story in which she shifts the dynamics between the gods and the people, Jemisin addresses the 'being different' and denormalizes the reader's expectations.

Narratology: Narratology relates to a school of thought, a humanistic discipline generally associated with the term. It can also relate to the study of narrative structure, closely linked to the study of rhetoric, structuralism and semiotics. Still a contentious terminology, it took prominence when Tzvetan Todorov in *Grammaire du Décaméron* (1969) (*Grammar of the Decameron*) referred to it as the 'science of narrative', an instrument of codifying texts.[21] Narratology comes into play when you start interrogating King's, Bradbury's, Atwood's or Shelley's writerly signatures or styles. As a method of inquiry, narratology comes with devices, such as voice, point of view, imagery, comparison, symbols, style and structure, that the author applies to their storytelling craft in their own unique articulation.

You apply narratology to any work of speculative fiction when you query how the writer is telling the story or manipulating its content by using devices such as chronology of events and characterization.

In August Fell's paranormal horror 'The Devil Girl' (2018), the narrator's manner is conversational, colloquial:

> I saw her just after the sun cut below the hills. The sky was still light, but the place where I stood was dark as a cellar. I was looking for crawfish, but I wasn't finding any. The flood had just dropped after the big storm, and the grass beside the creek was laid over flat and brown like the fur on a dog. The trees were all dead halfway up, green above that. They had drowned in the flood, same as all the cows and pigs, and some trees were going to live, and some weren't…
>
> I was beside the creek with my old net, turning over rocks underwater and watching for craws to shoot out. The sun went behind the hills and I looked up, saw nothing but the rocks and the half-dead trees. When I looked up next she was there, right there by the dead sycamore tree on the other side of the creek, close…
>
> She was white, like I'd heard, white as a new sheet or a January moon, and didn't look any taller than me. She was naked, and had little breasts, and I got all hot in the face because she had nipples pink as roses. I'd never seen a girl naked before, not even once. Her hair was white too, almost silver it was so shiny. She turned her head to look at me, and I seen her horns. Oh yes, just like the story, little horns all twisty like a goat's, no bigger than the ones on a yearling. I was thinking she was pretty, and that I already kind of liked her. I said she looked at me, and when she did I forgot everything else, and so would you, friend, so would you.
>
> She had eyes like mouths, big and dark with no white anywhere, they were the only thing I recall about her face, even now, close as I've been to her. And they're the one thing I wish I could forget, the absolute worst thing. They were eyes with no soul in them, nothing but empty. The way a doll's eye looks, only she was looking at me sure enough.[22]

Fell's voice conveys the wonderment and simplicity of a poorly educated 10-year-old encountering for the first time Lucifer's spawn. The first-person narrative gives it relatability, immersion. It draws the reader from the role of witness to participant, poignant in this unsettling account. And later when the horror amplifies, as the night comes down and the cicadas are buzzing and the devil girl is standing behind Billy who is talking to George, and only the narrator and you can see her, she hooks you with those eyes and puts her little white hand and touches Billy's face. And then she opens her mouth and a sound like you are in a cave, and a hundred thousand people and dogs and cats and everything are in there with you, all howling, all crying, all screaming, it comes over you like a wave or a wind and blacks out everything. This is what Fell and that boyish, conversational, inviting voice does to you.

Hamilton Perez applies a similar boyish appeal that is compelling in first person to create the kind of friendly ghost you want to laugh and cry with, in 'Me & the Dead Boy' (2018):

> Three days after my best friend killed himself I found him standing outside my house, throwing rocks at my bedroom window. He was bone-pale and partially transparent. The streetlights cast beams through him like swords through a magician's assistant.
>
> There was no mistaking. It was Ronnie...
>
> I opened the window and leaned out, unsure at first what to say. 'Can I help you?'
>
> 'David. It's me. Ronnie. I'm a ghost!'
>
> 'I know that, stupid. What do you want?'
>
> He shrugged. 'Thought we could hang out?'
>
> That's when I decided what this was. After days of too little sleep and too many people asking how I was doing, my subconscious had joined the ever-growing comfort-choir to make me talk about my feelings.
>
> 'No thanks.' I shut the window.
>
> I flopped onto my bed, ready to forget Ronnie's suicide and his ghost altogether, when a rock crashed through my window.
>
> I started at the sharp crack and all in an instant, I knew: This was real. Everything just piled on after that. Ghosts are real. There's life after death. Ronnie was back. And the glass breaking had probably woken Mum.
>
> I rushed to the door, cracked it open, and listened for the creak, the groan of her climb from bed. How would I explain this? *Sorry, Mum, Ronnie just broke a window. No, he's still dead. Just a ghost is all.*[23]

Perez, intrigued by the 'unfinished business' of the average ghost story, figured he hadn't read many stories where the ghost still felt like a person, used well his authorly voice to create a coming of age fantasy more focused on relationships than the supernatural.

The narrator helps the reader understand the nature of a character, to form an impression and a judgement. This is the power of narratology.

The psychoanalytic: There is no such thing as psychoanalytical theory. But there are many schools of psychoanalysis whose concepts emerge from clinical practice. Discussions on psychoanalytical criticism, for example by

Elizabeth Wright,[24] focus on the relationship between a literary text and the psychology of its creator. Psychoanalytic and philosophical appraisal of characters, their personas and Jungian archetypes, inform their roles in relation to a template of the hero, the shadow, the herald, the shapeshifter ... as explored in Christopher Vogler's *The Writer's Journey* (1998).[25]

This type of literary criticism offers a means of understanding the application of psychoanalytical methodology to literary texts. It welcomes Jungian and Freudian frames, for example in fictional character formations and interrogating the drivers that influence archetypal behaviour. Linkages between narrative and the mind can allow a writer to shed insight on a character's intentions, influencing the unsuspicious reader through judgements programmed into the text. An intelligent author can generate 'norms' that guide the reader to approach the text with encoded expectations. Louis Stevenson's novel *Dr Jekyll and Mr. Hyde* (1886)—a good/ evil multi-person—that stages Jekyll and Hyde as a double-life man whose persona swings from distinguished to repulsive—is a fine example of the psychoanalytic in fiction. Ruth Rendell's murder mysteries broke new ground with her psychological approach to thriller writing, revealing the author's enthralment with crime. In a 2005 NPR (formerly National Public Radio) interview, Rendell said:

> I'm fascinated with people and their characters and their obsessions and what they do. And these things lead to crime, but I'm much more fascinated in their minds.[26]

There is the psychoanalytic in Lucy Mackey's depiction of the new queen in 'The Ferrymen' (2018); the reader doesn't need a spelling out to figure out the queen's sadism:

> The first time the new queen held court, she put the marmosets in a great cage hung from the ceiling on chains, and with them a grey timberthrall. The marmosets flew against the bars but the timberthrall clawed its way up, driven by their screams. Some had learnt a few words—the king's name. They called for him. Nobody was allowed to leave the court for the entire hour it took all the marmosets to die. When the last marmoset succumbed to exhaustion and fell to the cage's floor, no courtiers dared to look away. It lay panting among the bloodied and scuffed plumage of its fellows. The timberthrall—its frenzy cooled—took its time. After the deed was done, the queen let the timberthrall out. It coiled sinuously around the foot of her throne, carrying its bloody prize. The queen reached down to stroke its fur, her expression gentle.[27]

The narrative portrays what Jung calls 'individuation', a process in which the individual harmonizes (or disharmonizes) his/her 'persona'—the self as presented to the world—and 'the shadow'—the darker, potentially dangerous side of the personality that exists in the personal unconscious.[28] The queen's gentle expression as she strokes the timberthrall is in disharmony with her darker self that thrived in a public display of the marmosets' massacre. Using the psychoanalytic to inform characterization, a good writer can leverage from light and shade in a character to weave complexities into a plot. Psychoanalytic theory is also comfortably ensconced in Stephen King's subliminal horrors and thrillers.

Postcolonial theory: This theory illuminates the human consequences of colonisation and imperialism. Ashcroft and colleagues' *The Empire Writes Back: Theory and Practice in Post-Colonial Literature* (1989) is a diverse body of literature that takes into account colonial writing in India, Australia, the West Indies, Africa and Canada, scrutinizing language as complicit in the act of colonisation. Apocalyptic, post-apocalyptic, utopian or dystopian novels, for example Le Guin's *The Dispossessed*, can exemplify the effects of established colonies that subjugate other beings. Take Sheldon Siporin's speculative poem 'Sanctuary' (2018):

You were abandoned
drifting, alone in starlight
fatherless
once
before the adopted family
before the alien strangers
a blue woman with one
breast, a man with square
diamonds for eyes
stared and
took pity, held you
gave you a home
Grown up
you did the same
once
a spiny scarecrow from Mars
tangerine-faced bawling
moved you
But so many lost
ones
like dusty-faced comets

pale as pinpoints of paste
Consulting with Father who
took you aside
his sibilant advising
Not one child
a generation
not one group of siblings
a village
Your bloodstream
your organs
now home to a
nation of
nano-tots[29]

A synthesis of the modern American trend of adopting Third World infants along with the phrase 'it takes a village', drawn from an African proverb and popularized by Hillary Clinton to emphasize the impact of society on a child's well-being, the poem is a showcase of applying postcolonial theory in fiction.

Marxist theory: This theory is about a shift from capitalism to socialism and originates from German philosophers Karl Marx and Friedrich Engels. Characters and events in George Orwell's speculative fiction *Animal Farm* are comparative to Marxism and the 1917 Russian Revolution, so the novel can be perceived as a criticism of Marxism and the anarchy that can govern a socialist society. The reverse is true in that fiction can contravene a literary theory; for example, Harlan Ellison's 'I Have No Mouth, and I Must Scream' applies the opposite of Marxism with its Promethean theme of a demigod machine that exploits its human captives, and depicts a state of disorder resulting in mutiny aimed towards social revolution, with dire effects for the perpetrators.

Existentialism: One can take this theory in its simple form (this is, after all, theory 101) to be about meaning and purpose, exploring the philosophies of choice and the human being's freedom to determine how they exist. Existentialism is about the self and the meaning of life, with focus on free will.[30] Earlier this book mentions the unconventional author Jorge Luis Borges and the surrealist and existential concepts in his speculative works like *Labyrinths*. Existentialism is in Ray Bradbury's 'The Man' with its philosophical theme of science versus religion, where a man in a search for meaning fails to see the answer to his questions when he arrives at a remote planet and discounts the profoundness of a prophet's visit. Existentialism is in Matthew R. Ward's adaptation of an old sci-fi trope, where the crew of a generation ship forget they are on a ship; Ward wondered what would encourage the crew to stay on mission generations after it started… and came up with 'To the Stars' (2018), a story about a pilgrim's visit to the 'Ark', an intergalactic vessel led by an old priest. In this story, the pilgrim has a revelation for Father Wheeler:

'Your people need you, you know that. They've never needed anyone more.' The pilgrim held up a hand to silence Father Wheeler's reply. 'The way they speak about you with such love. And concern. They need you, but you can't be the man they need while you're in such a state. That's why I'm going to share with you a secret. A secret you must never tell anyone.'

This time the pilgrim allowed a pause. Father Wheeler did nothing but stare at the floor.

The pilgrim continued. 'This mission of yours, the great voyage. You know why the mission began? Why we sent your ancestors into space, to never return?'

'The Lord asked for brave men and women to make the journey, so His people could spread to another planet. Go forth and multiply.' Father Wheeler did not look up as he spoke.

The pilgrim sank into a chair. 'That's an old story. Older than you know. But that's all it is. A story. Men thought up your mission. Only men. I should know, I'm one of them.'[31]

'To the Stars' is a story of precession and purpose, true to motivational speaker Marshall Thurber's concept of everything in motion: Where is the self in perspective?[32] The pilgrim's confession unveils to Father Wheeler that what he thought was an immutable theory of the Ark and its mission, the origins story that took his ancestors into space, is nothing but a man-made lie. Father Wheeler must now shape his own story of predicting the unexpected; there is something bigger in front of him, he just needs to see it. The old priest faces a philosophy of choice surrounding man's belief in the mission of the Ark, and the priest's role in perspective.

Literary theory and after

Consider reading as a quest for meaning, with the self as the source of value and interpretation. According to scholar David Carter, what a work communicates to its reader 'depends on what questions we put to it'; it also depends on our understanding of historical context and how we assimilate it into our worlds.[33]

The works of reflexive authors like Edgar Allan Poe, Jorge Luis Borges, Isabel Allende, Toni Morrison and Salman Rushdie carry underlying political statements, as do the works of realistic writers such as Ernest Hemingway and George Orwell. It may take reflexive competence in a reader to assimilate those underlying concepts. This type of reader will encounter texts with awareness and openness. The intellectual grounding of academics, such as their exposure to critical and cultural theories, may predispose them to this type of reading. With persistence, your eyes open to feminist, postmodernist, autobiographical, queer and other theories and, unlike earlier reading for sheer enjoyment, suddenly you can reflexively scrutinize texts and draw conclusions. Writer and scholar Wenche Ommundsen supersets the idea:

> The theoretically literate reader is the reader most likely to seek out moments when the literary text theorises itself, reflexive moments when the difference between fiction and theory, between fiction and criticism, becomes blurred, and the text echoes the reader's own preoccupations.[34]

Despite Ommundsen's theoretically literate reader, whether or not texts are intended to be reflexive, sometimes authors simply write. Critics may take issue with the next supposition—it's a child of a thought; go ahead, smash that child—but there are many schools of theory: envision a reporter on live TV interviewing the late B. B. King on his music, barging double-barrelled questions on the artist's own style, his borrowed styles, his genre influences, lyrical structures, string bends, chord progressions, left hand vibratos, quarter notes, measures, phrasing and shimmering ... King might take a breath and say, 'I just play blues, man.' Artists may not want to dismember or interrogate their art; they might simply want to enjoy it.

How many academics are open to indulge this possibility: that perhaps an author just 'wrote', that there is no intrinsic critical or cultural theory that enthused their work? Imagine waking up one day to discover you're not the only one who determines, as in Hans Christian Andersen's fairy tale,[35] that the emperor with his new suit is, in fact, naked. Le Guin did, as FAQ on her website suggest:

Q. What themes and ideas recur in your writing?

A. This is a question for critics not for the author. Two obvious things often pointed out by critics: Taoist thought runs quite deep in the structure of many of my fictions. And many of them put the viewpoint characters into a different society and culture, where they have to figure out what's going on, how things work.[36]

Le Guin's response implies that she did not go out, headlights on, hunting the themes inherent in her work. Perhaps she integrates them subconsciously, influenced by one or other preconditioned 'template', a sum of many things, a construction that plays a role in the way she thinks.

The ordinary reader may not care about how this 'template' influences Le Guin's work, may simply desire a narrative with appeal, without caring to dismember its form, structure or intent. The reader, you, me, may merely yearn to derive from the work Barthes' pleasure of writing, pleasure of reading, an enchantment with unique articulation.

In an interview with Stephen W. Potts, Octavia Butler said:

> As far as criticism goes, what a reader brings to the work is as important as what I put into it, so I don't get upset when I am misinterpreted. Except when I say what I really [*sic*] was so-and-so, and I am told, 'Oh, but subconsciously you must have meant this.' I mean—leave me alone! I don't mind attempts to interpret my fiction, but I am not willing to have critics interpret my subconscious. I doubt they're qualified.[37]

In the interview Butler conceded that she avoided all critical theory because she worried about it feeding into her work. She didn't want its influence in creating 'a vicious circle or something worse'. She didn't want people reading more into her story than existed, for example critics took her short story 'Bloodchild' to be about slavery; but it was really about love, an idea of possibilities in a narrative of reverse sexism where a human boy—in a world colonised by aliens—offered his body in an act of choice, rather than enforcement, to become pregnant with the bug-eyed monster's children.

In his essay 'The Still-Breathing Author', Gerald Murnane—who has received many reviews for his books—stated he did not care about the reviews. Why? For the simple reason that he found them 'mostly incomprehensible'. He said: 'The fact is that I see my books from a standpoint wholly different from the reader's standpoint.'[38]

So who determines the interpretation of a text, and why? How do we know the text means anything, if at all? Perhaps like the imagined B. B. King, who just plays blues, man, an author, whichever author, just writes. Whatever they write, it need not be postmodern fiction like Rushdie's *The Satanic Verses* (1988) to be read reflexively. But according to Ommundsen, in order for reflexive potential to be realised, 'the reader has to bring to the text a certain kind of interest, a set of expectations and a specific competence'.[39]

Text can be more than it is. But if authors are not present to explain their intention—their constructive or deconstructive positioning in formulating their text—readers must form their own interpretations. Different readers may form different interpretations of the same text, leading to multiple readings, or misreadings, of text of whichever genre where meaning is lost in translation. Readers approach the text with pre-constructed frames that contain their perceptions and reality, and use these contextual frames to decipher familiar or unfamiliar referents within the text.

Even if authors were present to offer an explanation, their interpretation may have shifted from the time of writing to a new reading of that same work. But criticality can enhance creativity, argued author Amanda Boulter, because literary theory addresses 'what writing does and why and how it works'.[40] Reflexive reading means approaching text with openness, a manner of approach that independently offers both the author and the reader a richer perspective and a basis for global intellectual understanding.

Exercise 13

- Take a familiar fairy tale and rewrite it in a different genre for a different audience. Write in a genre you wouldn't normally pick.
- Take a familiar story and change the gender and characteristics of the protagonist. Give the story a completely new ending.
- Take a familiar historical narrative (e.g. The six wives of Henry VIII or the story of Moses of Egypt or the assassination of Franz Ferdinand Carl Ludwig Joseph Maria, Archduke of Austria-Este, Austro-Hungarian and Royal Prince of Hungary and of Bohemia) and write it in a modern setting.
- Take a familiar story that is not speculative fiction and write it as a fantasy, science fiction, horror or paranormal story.
- Take a familiar story and write it in a gender neutral way (e.g. gender neutral characters, character names and pronouns).

14

E-publishing

Electronic publishing, also termed e-publishing or epublishing, is about producing, storing and distributing books, journals and magazine electronically rather than in print. This type of publishing is a promising and intuitive way of exploiting technology and offers immeasurable platforms for speculative fiction. Electronic publishing empowers authors and publishers, with cheaper and faster ways to package and market digital books, also termed e-books, ebooks or electronic books.

E-books may be full-length publications comprising multimedia (text, image, video and interactive content) that are downloadable onto a reading device such as a computer or tablet or smartphone. An e-book does not need to have a hard print counterpart, although 'print-on-demand' options offer a cost-effective way to print individual copies or limited quantities of text to order, using digital technology. Ingram, with its subsidiary business unit Lightning Source, is a viable printer and distributor of print-on-demand books, offering high turnaround print solutions that fulfil global distribution requirements and capture all sales.

Digital publishing may also include online text on a social media platform or a website.

History

E-publishing has flourished since it gained ground in the 2000s in a changing landscape of digital technology and a pervasive cyber world. Suddenly the developed world saw the rise of mobile platforms, electronic magazines (then called ezines), multimedia and interactive text and different models of content authoring.

As more and more individuals and organizations moved to the internet, e-publishing opened up as an alternative or complementary mode to traditional publishing. A self-publishing bubble surfaced, where questionable boutique companies robbed you blind and helped themselves to a kidney—never mind your spleen—to publish your work. Others like Publish America (now America Star Books) did not ask for money but became factory-like conveyer belts that flooded the online market with poor quality print-on-demand books, secure in the knowledge that proud authors, family and friends would bulk buy the publications. An inundation of unedited drafts in paperback, hardcover or digital jacket covers continued to sully the perception of e-publishing and self-publishing—also termed vanity publishing—and few reputable authors could consider e-publishing or self-publishing without wrecking their credibility.

Things have changed, the result of a competitive market, shifting publishing practices and the rise of independent publishers who continue to reinvent the book and publishing business with an offering of electronic books and print-on-demand options. In an unlimited world of e-commerce and an increasing saturation of traditional publishing, picky on who to publish based on consumer appetite and marketing trends, some exceptional writers are now employing alternate authoring options and taking advantage of the electronic creation, packaging and distribution of content to a borderless world. The proliferation of author websites, social media platforms and online resources for writers, including offerings of editing services and tools for file formatting, now allows quality digital publications even from self-published authors.

We are in the heart of an ongoing digital revolution that continues to stagger traditional publishing. Events have led to major trade publishers like Penguin and Random House merging to stay alive. Large publishing house are seeking from authors world rights in all forms to accommodate paperless offerings of bestsellers as e-books to ravenous consumers.

The paradigm shift in publishing has allowed a steady growth of e-publishers and e-book retailers like Fictionwise, Hard Shell Word Factory and Diesel eBooks, most of which have since seen a takeover: for instance, in 2009 Barnes and Noble absorbed Fictionwise, one of the largest electronic booksellers in North America with an estimated 1.5 million e-book content units sold in 2008 alone. As an e-book retailer, Fictionwise offered a comprehensive collection of popular fiction, including Hugo Award and Nebula Award nominees, and early short stories by authors like Marion Zimmer Bradley, Harlan Ellison and George R. R. Martin. It quickly evolved to manage other e-book websites and offer custom reading devices to secure e-books against piracy.

E-publishing options for speculative fiction today

Today e-publishers continue offering opportunities to aspiring writers. Electronic platforms for publishing speculative fiction include CUT (www.cutalongstory. com), an e-publishing forum that specializes in short stories; Smashwords (www. smashwords.com) that offers e-books from independent authors and publishers and attracts you with the slogan 'Your ebook, your way'; Flipsnack (www. flipsnack.com) that offers free bookmaking software; and Amazon's Createspace (www.createspace.com), a self-publishing and free distribution company that also offers paid professional services in editing, layout and design.

Other speculative fiction markets online and print, in particular for short fiction and novellas, include award-winning magazines or magazines whose stories have won awards, such as *The Magazine of Fantasy & Science Fiction* (www.sfsite.com/fsf), *Analog* (www.analogsf.com), *Asimov's Science Fiction* (www.asimovs.com), *Uncanny* (uncannymagazine.com), *Strange Horizons* (www. strangehorizons.com), *Apex Magazine* (www.apex-magazine.com), *Aurealis* (aurealis.com.au), *Space and Time Magazine* (spaceandtimemagazine.com), LightSpeed Magazine (www.lightspeedmagazine.com), Beneath Ceaseless Skies (www.beneath-ceaseless-skies.com), the British SF magazine *Interzone* (ttapress. com/interzone) and science fiction and fantasy magazine *Clarkesworld* (clarkesworldmagazine.com). These magazines, and many more like *Daily Science Fiction* (dailysciencefiction.com), *Bards and Sages* (www bardsandsages.com), *AntipodeanSF* (www.antisf.com), *Albeido One* (www.albedo1.com), *Shimmer* (www.shimmerzine.com) and *PerihelionSF* (www.perihelionsf.com) continue to accept work in electronic form for digital publication. Reading the types of work a journal publishes will help determine if your own work is a good fit.

There are also reputable online literary journals that encourage submissions by students and scholars of creative writing, have periodic calls for submission of papers on specific themes that may include or allow speculative fiction, and carry out peer reviews of submitted work.

Why e-publish?

E-publishing is an effectual way for speculative fiction authors and publishers to tap the cyber market that promises:

> *Speed*: e-publishing allows faster publication, supporting a quick turn-around to a published version. With access to free online style guides, dashboards and content converters, you can publish easily and immediately.

Multimedia: Multiple content forms that may include text, images, graphics, videos or animations. You can also offer readers accessibility options using existing software and devices compatible with a range of digital content formats.

Immediacy and broad reach: Once published, work may be available to a diverse audience and an international readership at the click of a button. Content is instantly searchable. Electronic publishing and social media platforms encourage loyal online communities of writers and readers.

Low cost of production and storage: Free online tools and resources enable cheaper publishing and distribution options compared with traditional publishing which also demands physical storage.

Easy edit: You can correct a digital publication and make a brand new version live online in minutes. It is equally easy to manipulate font size to suit reading on a range of devices.

Marketing: You can use social media platforms, your author website, email alerts, distribution or subscription lists to tell readers of your new publication.

There is a growth of work in the public domain. An example is Project Gutenberg (www.gutenberg.org), a digital library of free e-books, including literary classics, in a range of formats. YouTube is another public domain medium, this one supporting audio books.

Writers like Mieko Kawakami in Japan have shot to fame after a lowly start in e-publishing. Kawakami started off with prose poetry in the form of internet diaries and blogged her way to a literary prize. In 2008 she won the 2008 Akutagawa Award, Japan's most prestigious honour for a new writer.[1] This same prize was previously awarded to the legendary Japanese author Kobe Abe in 1951 for his short novel *Kabe* (*The Wall*). A growing fan base put Kawakami in the spotlight and publishers noticed. Her debut novella *My Ego Ratio, My Teeth, and the World* (2007) won the Tsubouchi Shoyo Prize for Young Emerging Writers for its lyrical poetic prose. Kawakami is now one of Japan's renowned literary authors, like Haruki Murakami.

Discouraged by rejections from traditional publishers, Amanda Hocking self-published her e-books on Amazon's Kindle and wound up selling over a million copies. Unable to resist a self-made success story, St. Martin's Press bought publishing rights to her books, awarding her $2.1 million in her first contract.[2]

Erika L. James, author of *Fifty Shades of Grey* (2011), is believed to have matured her writing as a *Twilight* fan, growing her book from an online fanfic (fan fiction, a trend of the digital era) series named *Master of the Universe* on FanFiction.net under the pseudonym Snowqueens Icedragon.

Fan fiction is popular and is understood as the phenomenon behind Meg Cabot's *The Princess Diaries* (2000) and Lev Grossman's *The Magicians* (2009), both adapted into television series, and Seth Grahame-Smith's *Pride and Prejudice and Zombies (2009)*, adapted into director Burr Steers' 2016 post-modernist movie.

Yet, like access to Hollywood for actors, the path to novel success is a tough one. E-publishing opens avenues for digital creation, distribution and marketing, but it does not guarantee you will fanfic your way to literary stardom. What is important is that you understand the formats in which you can make your work available to readers.

Popular e-book formats

An online publishing platform like Smashwords can easily convert your e-book to your required format. Digital content types include:

PDF: Portable Document Format, or PDF, is a file format readable by most devices. Most word processors will easily convert your document into a PDF. This format is, however, unsecured, which means that you have limited control on how your work is shared.

ACSM: Relatively new and fiddly to access, Adobe Content Server Message (ACSM) files are formatted for use with Adobe Digital Editions, an e-book reader from Adobe Systems. Major publishers are beginning to adopt this format for e-books, as it allows greater security of digital content where the reader must be authorized to download and read the copy.

Epub: This is an open industry format that works with a range of tablet devices.

Kindle (.mobi): Kindle is an Amazon.com product that reads e-books in Mobipocket format, also accessible on a Microsoft Windows device.

Plain text: This is an unsecured format that is accessible on most electronic devices and to most readers due to its lack of formatting.

HTML: This is text written in hypertext markup language (HTML), a kind of coding that tells a web browser how to display text on a page.

Be mindful

A few things to beware:

- Avoid e-publishers who ask you for money to publish your work.
- Choose the right publisher who will referee or edit your work to ensure you receive a quality product that is available at a reasonable price in formats accessible to a broad audience.
- Consider a secure digital format that protects your work from digital piracy, but remember that secure e-books may limit readership to those with access to a specific reading device.
- Research e-publishers, see who are in their author lists. How recent are 'new' publications? Take a step back and question if there have been no publications in the past year or more. Read an excerpt of published work and ask yourself if you would like to see your own work alongside it. Check out the publisher's news section and assess how published work is promoted and if any publication has won or been shortlisted for an award. Use a search engine to find out what people are saying about the e-publisher. Online forums (named 'writer beware' or something similar) are one way to background check a publisher.
- Weigh the royalty percentage an e-publisher is offering, taking into account that they have low publishing overheads.
- Bear in mind that, while the internet is a global medium, developing countries may still be disadvantaged in technological and financial areas, and their readers may not have easy access to your digital publication.
- Remember that publishers, and competitions, seeking first or exclusive rights may disallow previously published work, including that presented on an author's website or through self-publishing.

E-publishing generally pays less in sales than traditional publishing. An e-book may sell in cents for instant download, so your sales largely depend on successful marketing. Stephen King offered a timely reminder in *On Writing: A Memoir of the Craft* (2000) that writing is not about making money or finding fame. It is a passion that *might* pay. Le Guin on her website affirmed this: 'most writers don't earn enough from writing to buy catfood.'

Be practical

Write for love. As Ray Bradbury would say, don't plan on making money. He once joked that his wife 'took a vow of poverty' to marry him. He was 37 before he and his wife could afford a car, and was living hand to mouth when he got an advance of $750 for *The Martian Chronicles*.

Surround yourself with the right people who will support (or tolerate) your passion. Join a local writers' group. Use an online search engine to find resources for writers. Subscribe to relevant magazines and journals that give you lists of publishers of the genre(s) in which you write. Hunt contests and calls for submissions to which you can submit your work.

And you will not run short of other writers, as mentors, with their tips. Hilma Wolitzer shared her thoughts:

> Writing fiction is a solitary occupation but not really a lonely one. The writer's head is mobbed with characters, images and language, making the creative process something like eavesdropping at a party for which you've had the fun of drawing up the guest list. Loneliness usually doesn't set in until the work is finished, and all the partygoers and their imagined universe have disappeared.[3]

Writing is cathartic in a creative process that drives itself. Author and scholar Dominique Hecq looked at the potential usefulness of psychoanalysis for the creative writer, and at writing in particular.

> I write to answer incipient questions that trouble my mind ... I write to relieve some form of anxiety, the question of anxiety being the unanswerable question par excellence, since the object cause of anxiety, the shadow of *Das Ding*, cannot be symbolized ... In this sense, I write because I must do so, exhilarating, detestable or painful though this might be. That writing is my jouissance, the paradoxical satisfaction that I derive from my symptom and the excesses of an enjoyment that is closer to pain than pleasure, would hardly be surprising. But the question that arises concerns the status of this symptom and the place of the real—hence the vexed question of pathology. Might my writing be a mere symptom, or does it fulfil some more fundamental need, as Joyce's sinthome[4] does by way of a littering of the letter?[5]

Like Hecq, write to cure your curiosity. Look at your work with honest eyes and bring it to its best light. Fall in love with what you write, because how do you expect others to love it if you don't?

In an afterword to *Different Seasons* (2012), King said of his love for his stories, 'part of me will always be in love with them'. He wrote:

> I hope that you liked them, Reader; that they did for you what any good story should do—make you forget the real stuff weighing on your mind for a little while and take you away to a place you've never been. It's the most amiable sort of magic I know.[6]

Perhaps you too can know this genus of magic. Reading this book is only a beginning to heart and passion, vibrant storytelling in speculative fiction that crosses genre. You don't know what's in you until you test it. Go forth and tell your story.

Exercise 14

i.

This is an exercise on dialogue. Write a 500-word speculative fiction. Reveal character in what is said (or not said)—show, don't tell.

Does your character have a distinct speech pattern?

Use silence as words. Use a full-stop rather than an exclamation mark (in an argument or a shout). Use a full-stop rather than a question mark (in a question).

Do something unique to denormalize your writing.

Tip: Create your own words as metonyms (substitute for something else)

- Form a verb out of a noun. Examples:
  - Tissue—She *tissued* the spillage
  - Helmet—He *helmeted* the child and put her on a bike
  - Bowl—He *bowled* the peas and placed them on the dinner table
  - Bottle—She *bottled* the idea
  - Tray—He *trayed* the cakes
  - Paper—She *papered* the wall (applied wall paper, stuck posters)
  - Moon—He *mooned* the dough (made it round—don't let your mind wander!)
  - Myth—She has *mythed* (told fiction/lied)
  - Toe—She *toed* the water surface, considered for a moment and then dived
  - Tomorrow—He studied his task list and *tomorrowed* a few to-dos
  - Ladder—She *laddered* up the attic
  - Horn—She *horned* a few pedestrians

  Can you think of other examples? Use them in your story.
- Form a noun out of a verb. Examples:
  - Write—That was one hell of a *write*

Can you think of other examples? Use them in your story.

- Form a noun out of an adverb or adjective. Examples:
  - Ginger (colour)—He was a *ginger* with a stutter
  - Purple (colour)—He wore a *purple* with a flower
  - Ugly/beauty—The world is full of pretties, uglies and in-betweens; he was totally an ugly

Substitute curse words—'*sprew* you', 'son of a *biscuit*', 'mother *fowler*, that hurt' ...

Can you think of other examples to create your own words?

ii.

This is an exercise on point of view. Write a 100-word speculative fiction in third-person past tense. Example:

MAVERICK
Killing was an art.

She found him at the beach, a black man with laughing eyes.

'Maverick,' he said. 'You have a name?'

'Maybe.'

'Takes money to know it?'

She laughed. 'Ivy.'

She suggested the forest, he held no objection.

Fingers together tip on tip, they sank beneath a silver birch. As she pondered ripping his spleen or pulling his heart, he rose.

'Gotta wee,' he said, a chuckle as he moved into the dark.

The quiet broke with a murmur of wings as Maverick leapt. He glided above her head.

A bloodshot gleam in his eye settled her conviction.

—Eugen Bacon[7]

Rewrite the story in second person past tense.
Killing was an art.

You found him at the beach, a black man with laughing eyes.

'Maverick,' he said. 'You have a name?'

'Maybe.'

'Takes money to know it?'

You laughed. 'Ivy.'

You suggested the forest, he held no objection.

Fingers together tip on tip, you sank beneath a silver birch. As you pondered ripping his spleen or pulling his heart, he rose.

'Gotta wee,' he said, a chuckle as he moved into the dark.

Quiet broke with a murmur of wings as Maverick leapt. He glided above your head.

A bloodshot gleam in his eye settled your conviction.

Rewrite the story in first person present tense.
Killing is an art.

I find him at the beach, a black man with laughing eyes.

'Maverick,' he says. 'You have a name?'

'Maybe.'

'Takes money to know it?'

I laugh. 'Ivy.'

I suggest the forest, he holds no objection.

Fingers together tip on tip, we sink beneath a silver birch. As I ponder ripping his spleen or pulling his heart, he rises.

'Gotta wee,' he says, a chuckle as he moves into the dark.

Quiet breaks with a murmur of wings as Maverick leaps. He glides above my head.

A bloodshot gleam in his eye settles my conviction.

Review the different versions of your story. Is your writing consistent in each tense for a story?

Notes

Perface

1. Krauth, N. & Bowman C. (2017) 'Ekphrasis and the Writing Process' in *New Writing*. http://dx.doi.org/10.1080/14790726.2017.1317277
2. Krauth & Bowman, p. 2.
3. Hume, K. (2014 [1984]) *Fantasy and Mimesis: Responses to Reality in Western Literature* (New York: Routledge), p. 21
4. Hume, p. 21
5. Derrida, J. (1971) *Positions*, trans. Alan Bass (Chicago: University of Chicago Press), p. 5.

1 The non-introduction

1. Bacon, E. (2018) 'Review: Luminescent Threads: Connections to Octavia E. Butler', viewed 4 June 2018,https://www.breachzine.com/single-post/2018/04/24/Review-Luminescent-Threads-Connections-to-Octavia-Butler
2. Barthes, R. (1977) 'The Death of the Author' in *Image, Music, Text* trans. Stephen Heath (London: Fontana), p. 151.
3. Boulter, A. (2007) *Writing Fiction: Creative and Critical Approaches* (New York: Palgrave Macmillan), pp. 11, 24
4. Pryor, M. (2017) 'Introduction' in Michael Pryor (ed.) *Aurealis: Australian Fantasy & Science Fiction* (Victoria, NSW: Chimaera Publications), 97, p. 2.
5. Association of Science Fiction and Fantasy Artists (ASFA), viewed 7 March 2017. http://asfa-art.org/
6. The World Science Fiction Society, viewed 7 March 2017. http://www.wsfs.org/
7. *Aurealis*, 'Submissions', viewed 28 January 2018.https://aurealis.com.au/submissions
8. Norton, S. (2013) 'Betwixt and Between: Creative Writing and Scholarly Expectations' in *New Writing*, p. 72. http://dx.doi.org/10.1080/14790726.201 2.694451
9. Le Guin, U. K. (1979) *Language of the Night: Essays on Fantasy and Science Fiction* (New York: Putnam).
10. Krauth, N. (2016) *Creative Writing and the Radical: Teaching and Learning the Fiction of the Future* (Bristol: Multilingual Matters).

11. Card, O. S. (1990) *How to Write Science Fiction and Fantasy* (Ohio: Writer's Digest Books), p. 12.
12. University of California Television 2001, *An Evening with Ray Bradbury*, viewed 7 March 2017. https://www.youtube.com/watch?v=_W-r7ABrMYU%26feature=youtube

2 There's a story in you

1. Mathews, R. (2002) *Fantasy: The Liberation of the Imagination* (London: Routledge), p. 1.
2. Carver, R. (1981) 'A Storyteller's Shoptalk', viewed 7 March 2017. https://www.nytimes.com/books/01/01/21/specials/carver-shoptalk.html
3. Ward, M. R. (2018) 'To the Stars' in E. Bacon (ed.) *Andromeda Spaceways Magazine*, 70, 63–74 (eBook).
4. Rodgers, C. (2018) 'Two Inches of Tape' in E. Bacon (ed.) *Andromeda Spaceways Magazine*, 70, 19–20 (eBook).
5. Bradbury, R. (2008) 'The Man', *The Illustrated Man* (London: Harper Collins), p. 33.
6. Gray, P. A. (2018) 'The Last Monster You Shall Slay' in E. Bacon (ed.) *Andromeda Spaceways Magazine*, 70, 97–104 (eBook).
7. Gray.
8. Fassler, J. (2013) 'Why Stephen King Spends "Months and Even Years" Writing Opening Sentences', viewed 26 February 2017. http://www.theatlantic.com/entertainment/archive/2013/07/why-stephen-king-spends-months-and-even-years-writing-opening-sentences/278043
9. Gray, p. 97.
10. Gray.
11. Mathews, p. 1.
12. Bradbury, pp. 77–96.
13. Fell, A. (2018) 'The Devil Girl' in E. Bacon (ed.) *Andromeda Spaceways Magazine*, 70, 105–111 (eBook).
14. Mathews, p. 5.
15. University of California Television (2001) *An Evening with Ray Bradbury*, viewed 7 March 2017. https://www.youtube.com/watch?v=_W-r7ABrMYU&feature=youtube
16. *An Evening with Ray Bradbury*.
17. *Writer's Digest* (2010) *Author Q&A: Orson Scott Card*, viewed 7 March 2017. http://www.writersdigest.com/qp7-migration-books/card-interview
18. Collins, L. T. (2018) 'The Sonata Machine' in E. Bacon (ed.) *Andromeda Spaceways Magazine*, 70, 89–90, (eBook).
19. Ebert, C. (2018) 'A World Where Sandy Never Died' in E. Bacon (ed.) *Andromeda Spaceways Magazine*, 70, 21–34 (eBook).
20. Ashton, K. (2018) 'The larval stage' in E. Bacon (ed.) *Andromeda Spaceways Magazine*, 70, 37–47 (eBook).

21. Le Guin, U. K. (2007) 'FAQ', viewed 26 January 2018. http://www.ursulakle-guin.com/FAQ.html

22. Jonas, G. (2018) 'Ursula K. Le Guin, Acclaimed for her Fantasy Fiction, Is Dead at 88', viewed 26 January 2018. https://www.nytimes.com/2018/01/23/obitua-ries/ursula-k-le-guin-acclaimed-for-her-fantasy-fiction-is-dead-at-88.html

23 King, S. (2018) @StephenKing, viewed 26 January 2018. https://twitter.com/StephenKing/status/955939239857967105

24. Jonas.

25. Murnane, G. (2018), 'The Still-Breathing Author', viewed 18 February 2018, https://sydneyreviewofbooks.com/the-still-breathing-author-gerald-murnane

26. Norton, S. (2013) 'Betwixt and Between: Creative Writing and Scholarly Expectations' in *New Writing*, p. 72. http://dx.doi.org/10.1080/14790726.2012.694451.

27. Card, O. S. (1990) *How to Write Science Fiction and Fantasy* (Ohio: Writer's Digest Books), p. 134.

28. Lahey, J. (2014) *How Stephen King Teaches Writing*, viewed 7 March 2017. http://www.theatlantic.com/education/archive/2014/09/how-stephen-king-teaches-writing/379870

29. Card, p. 121.

30. Morrison, T. (1993) 'Toni Morrison—Nobel Lecture', viewed 23 June 2018. https://www.nobelprize.org/nobel_prizes/literature/laureates/1993/morri-son-lecture.html

31. Callil, C. (2014) '*All the Light We Cannot See* by Anthony Doerr. Review—A Story of Morality, Science and Nazi Occupation'. https://www.theguardian.com/books/2014/may/17/all-the-light-we-cannot-see-anthony-doerr-review

32. Boulter, A. (2007) *Writing Fiction: Creative and Critical Approaches* (New York: Palgrave Macmillan), p. 59.

33. Shopova, A. (2018) 'They Come' in E. Bacon (ed.) *Andromeda Spaceways Maga-zine,* 70, 35 (eBook).

34. King, S. (2013) *Under the Dome* (London and New York: Hodder and Stoughton), p. 1.

35. Bradley, M. Z. (1961) *The Door Through Space*, viewed 26 February 2017. https://www.gutenberg.org/files/19726/19726-h/19726-h.htm

36. Bradbury, R. (2008) 'The Other Foot', *The Illustrated Man*, pp. 47–67.

37. Morrison, T. (1998) *Song of Solomon* (London: Vintage), p. 91.

38. Ghansah, R. K. (2015) 'The Radical Vision of Toni Morrison', viewed 7 March 2017. http://www.nytimes.com/2015/04/12/magazine/the-radical-vision-of-toni-morrison.html?_r=0

39. Collins, S. (2008) *The Hunger Games* (London: Scholastic), p. 3.

40. Hecq, D. (2015) *Towards a Poetics of Creative Writing* (Bristol: Channel View Publications), pp. 2–3.

41. Boulter, p. 74.

42. Boulter, p. 74.

43. Boulter, p. 78

3 Vogler's hero/ine's journey

1. Poe, E. A. (1846) 'The Philosophy of Composition'. www.eapoe.org/works/essays/philcomp.htm
2. Poe.
3. Poe.
4. Vogler, C. (1998) *The Writer's Journey*, 3rd edn (Studio City: Michael Wiese), p. x.
5. Vogler, pp. xxvii–xxviii.
6. Mathews, R. (2002) *Fantasy: the Liberation of the Imagination* (London: Routledge), p. xi.
7. Ommundsen, W. (1993) *Metafictions? Reflexivity in Contemporary Texts* (Melbourne: Melbourne University Press), p. 68.
8. Ommundsen, p. 71.
9. Image courtesy of National Galleries Scotland.

4 The speculative: A problem with definitions

1. Atwood, M. (2014) MaddAddam (The MaddAddam Trilogy), viewed 25 March 2017. https://www.amazon.com/MaddAddam-Maddaddam-Trilogy-Margaret-Atwood/dp/0307455483
2. Potts, R. (2003) 'Light in the wilderness', viewed 7 March 2017. https://www.theguardian.com/books/2003/apr/26/fiction.margaretatwood
3. Blaschke, J. (2000) *A Conversation with Harlan Ellison*, viewed 14 April 2017. https://www.sfsite.com/07a/he107.htm
4. Mabe, C. (1988) *Harlan Ellison: Don't Call Me a 'Sci-fi Writer'*, viewed 14 April 2017. http://articles.sun-sentinel.com/1988-03-13/features/8801160511_1_fiction-harlan-ellison-american-science
5. Walter, D. (2013) *Q&A: Harlan Ellison*, viewed 14 April 2017. https://www.theguardian.com/books/2013/jun/14/harlan-ellison-q-and-a-interview
6. Walter.
7. Borges, J. L. (1964) *Labyrinths: Selected Stories & Other Writing*, in D. A. Yates & J. E. Irby (eds) (Harmondsworth: Penguin), p. 6.
8. Cuddon, A. J. (ed.) (1998) *A Dictionary of Literary Terms and Literary Theory*, 4th edn (Oxford: Blackwell).
9. Ommundsen, W. (1993) *Metafictions? Reflexivity in Contemporary Texts* (Melbourne: Melbourne University Press), p. 68.
10. *Writer's Digest* (2010) *Author Q&A: Orson Scott Card*, viewed 7 March 2017. http://www.writersdigest.com/qp7-migration-books/card-interview
11. *Writer's Relief* (2009) *Genre Fiction Rules: Find Out if Your Novel Meets Publishers' and Literary Agents' Criteria for Publication*, viewed 7 March 2017. http://writersrelief.com/blog/2009/06/genre-fiction-rules-find-out-if-your-novel-meets-publishers-and-literary-agents-criteria-for-publication

12. Card, O. S. (1990) *How to Write Science Fiction and Fantasy* (Ohio: Writer's Digest Books), p. 16.
13. Card, p. 20.
14. *The New South Wales Writers Festival 2015*, viewed 7 March 2017. http://www.nswwc.org.au/whats-on/festivals-2/past-festivals/speculative-fiction-festival-2015

5 Genres and subgenres of speculative fiction

1. Mathews, R. (2002) *Fantasy: The Liberation of Imagination* (London: Routledge).
2. Borges, J. L. (1964) *Labyrinths: Selected Stories & Other Writing*, in D. A. Yates & J. E. Irby (eds.) (Harmondsworth: Penguin), pp. 211–212.
3. Card, O. S. (1990) *How to Write Science Fiction and Fantasy* (Ohio: Writer's Digest Books), p. 22.
4. Card, p. 23.
5. *The Encyclopedia of Science Fiction*, viewed 26 March 2017. http://www.sf-encyclopedia.com
6. Borges, p. 5.
7. Turcotte, G. (1998), 'Australian Gothic', in M. Mulvey Roberts (ed.), *The Handbook to Gothic Literature* (Basingstoke: Macmillan), pp. 10–19.

6 Fantasy

1. Martin, P. (2001) 'The Art of the Storyteller and the Writing of Tamsin', viewed 25 February 2017.http://www.fantasylit.com/peter-beagle-interview
2. Martin.
3. Martin, P. (2001) '10 Secrets to Writing Fantasy', *The Writer*, 114: 11, 34.
4. Martin, G. R. R. (1980) 'Ice Dragon', *Dragons of Light* (New York: Ace).
5. Martin, G. R. R. (1976) 'The Lonely Songs of Laren Dorr', *Fantastic Stories*, p. 7 (eBook).

7 Science fiction

1. *Analog: Science Fiction and Fact* (2017) 'Writer's guidelines', viewed 26 February 2017. http://www.analogsf.com/contact-us/writers-guidelines
2. *Clarkesworld Magazine* (2017) *Submission guidelines*, viewed 26 February 2017. http://clarkesworldmagazine.com/submissions
3. Bradley, M. Z. (1963) *The Colors of Space*, viewed 26 February 2017. https://www.gutenberg.org/files/20796/20796-h/20796-h.htm
4. Bradley, M. Z. (1961) *The Door through Space*, viewed 26 February 2017. https://www.gutenberg.org/files/19726/19726-h/19726-h.htm

5. Parsons, M. (2010) 'Sci-fi Writer Iain Banks Talks Surface Detail's Hell, Creationist Heresy', viewed 26 February 2017. https://www.wired.com/2010/10/iain-banks

6. Jordison, S. (2011) 'Back to the Hugos: The Dispossessed by Ursula K Le Guin', viewed 26 February 2017. https://www.theguardian.com/books/booksblog/2011/mar/29/hugo-award-ursula-le-guin

7. Strauss, V. (2000) 'The Dispossessed: Ursula K. Le Guin', viewed 26 February 2017. https://www.sfsite.com/01b/dis73.htm

8. *The Encyclopedia of Science Fiction*, viewed 26 March 2017. http://www.sf-encyclopedia.com

9. Cuddon, A. J. (ed.) (1998) *A Dictionary of Literary Terms and Literary Theory*, 4th edn (Oxford: Blackwell), p. 791.

10. Oltion, J. (2005) 'Science Fiction Primer: 6 Basic Rules You Need to Know if You Want to Write Science Fiction', *The Writer*, 118: 11, 28–31.

11. Niven, L. (1966) 'Neutron Star', *If: Worlds of Science Fiction,* 16: 10, 3 (eBook).

12. IMDb (1968) *Planet of the Apes*, viewed 17 February 2018, http://www.imdb.com/title/tt0063442

13. Bradbury, R. (2008) 'The Man', *The Illustrated Man* (London: Harper Collins), p. 93.

14. Bradbury, p. 79.

15. Bradbury, p. 83.

16. Ellison, H. (1967) 'I Have No Mouth and I Must Scream', *If: Worlds of Science Fiction*, 17: 3, 467–483 (eBook).

8 Horror and the paranormal

1. *Horror Writers Association* (2017) 'What is Horror Fiction', viewed 2 March 2017. http://horror.org/horror-is

2. University of California Television (2001) *An Evening with Ray Bradbury*, viewed 7 March 2017. https://www.youtube.com/watch?v=_W-r7ABrMYU&feature=youtube

3. Card, O. S. (1990) *How to Write Science Fiction and Fantasy* (Ohio: Writer's Digest Books), p. 19.

4. De Maupassant, G. (2016) 'The Flayed Hand', viewed 3 March 2017. https://www.gutenberg.org/files/53419/53419-h/53419-h.htm#THE_FLAYED_HAND

5. Shelley, M. (2008) *Frankenstein, or the Modern Prometheus*, viewed 3 March 2017. https://www.gutenberg.org/files/84/84-h/84-h.htm#chap05

6. King, S. (1981) *Danse Macabre* (New York: Berkley), p. 35.

7. King, pp. 31–35.

8. King, S. (2012) *Different Seasons* (London: Hodder and Stoughton), pp. 611–612.

9. Bradbury, R. (2008) 'The Long Rain', *The Illustrated Man* (London: Harper Collins), p. 97.
10. Bradbury, pp. 104–105.

9 Cross genre

1. Bertens, H. (2013) *Literary Theory: The Basics* (London: Routledge), p. 145 (eBook).
2. Carter, D. (2006) *Literary Theory* (Harpenden: Oldcastle Books), p. 119.
3. Gennette, G. (1997) *Paratexts: Thresholds of Interpretation* (New York: Cambridge University Press).
4. Gennette, p. 1.
5. Galbraith, R. (2018) *Robert Gailbraith*, viewed 25 January 2018. http://robert-galbraith.com/about/
6. Aston, K. (2017) 'Howling Mad' in M. Pryor (ed.) *Aurealis* 106, 25–34 (eBook).
7. Aston, p. 27.
8. Ashton, K. (2018) 'The Larval Stage' in E. Bacon (ed.) *Andromeda Spaceways Magazine* 70, 37–47 (eBook).
9. Grifant, K. C. (2018) 'A Dusty Arrival' in E. Bacon (ed.) *Andromeda Spaceways Magazine* 70, 75–80 (eBook).
10. Grifant.
11. Jemisin, N. K. (2010) *The Hundred Thousand Kingdoms* (London: Orbit).
12. Jemisin (2010) *The Hundred Thousand Kingdoms*, viewed 21 January 2018. http://nkjemisin.com/books/the-hundred-thousand-kingdoms
13. Carina Press (2018) 'Submission guidelines', viewed 27 January 2018. https://carinapress.com/blog/submission-guidelines/

10 Literary speculative fiction

1. Barthes, R. (1985) *The Grain of the Voice* (California: University of California Press), p. 122.
2. George, L. (2012) 'Ray Bradbury Dies at 91; Author Lifted Fantasy to Literary Heights', viewed 7 March 2017. http://articles.latimes.com/2012/jun/06/local/la-me-ray-bradbury-20120607
3. George.
4. Martin, G.R.R. (1976) 'The Lonely Songs of Laren Dorr', *Fantastic Stories*, p. 7 (eBook).
5. Martin, G.R.R. (2011) *Game of Thrones* (London: Harper Voyager).
6. Martin, *Game of Thrones*, p. 9.

7. Borges, J. L. (1964) *Labyrinths: Selected Stories & Other Writing*, in D. A. Yates & J. E. Irby (eds) (Harmondsworth: Penguin), p. 5.

8. Adams, D. (2002) *The Hitchhiker's Guide to the Galaxy* (London: Picador), pp. 55–56.

9. Adams, p. 32.

10. Adams, p. 66.

11. *The Guardian* (2014) 'The Hitchhiker's Guide to the Galaxy by Douglas Adams—Review', viewed 8 August 2015. http://www.theguardian.com/childrens-books-site/2014/sep/07/review-hitchhikers-guide-galaxy-douglas-adams

12. Text Publishing (2010) *Miles Franklin Shortlist Announced—Congratulations Peter Temple*, viewed 23 March 2017. https://www.textpublishing.com.au/blog/miles-franklin-shortlist-announced-congratulations-peter-temple.

13. Flood, A. (2010) 'Could Miles Franklin Turn the Booker Prize to Crime?', viewed 7 March 2017. http://www.theguardian.com/books/2010/jun/25/miles-franklin-booker-prize-crime

14. Gordon, E. (2101) 'Truth by Peter Temple', viewed 7 March 2017. http://www.theguardian.com/books/2010/jan/10/truth-peter-temple-edmund-gordon

15. Ondaatje, M. (2007) *Divisadero* (New York: Vintage), p. 219.

11 Short story

1. *Goodreads*, 'Bazaar of Bad Dreams quotes', viewed 17 February 2017. https://www.goodreads.com/work/quotes/43116154-the-bazaar-of-bad-dreams

2. *George R. R. Martin fan site*, viewed 17 February 2017. http://www.georgerrmartin.com/for-fans/faq.

3. Pratt, M. L. (1981) 'The Short Story: The Long and the Short of It', *Poetics* 10: 2, 175.

4. Pratt, p. 176.

5. Pratt, pp. 180–186.

6. Pratt, p. 179.

7. Pratt, p. 180.

8. Cuddon, A. J. (ed.) (1998) *A Dictionary of Literary Terms and Literary Theory*, 4th edn (Oxford: Blackwell), p. 815.

9. Kennedy, A. L. (2008) 'Small in a Way that a Bullet Is Small: Reflections on Writing Short Stories' in A. Cox (ed.), *The Short Story* (Newcastle upon Tyne: Cambridge Scholars Publishing), p. 1.

10. Carver, R. (1981) 'A Storyteller's Shoptalk', viewed 7 March 2017. https://www.nytimes.com/books/01/01/21/specials/carver-shoptalk.html

11. March-Russell, P. (2009) *The Short Story: An Introduction* (Edinburgh: Edinburgh University Press), pp. 222–223.
12. March-Russell, p. 224.
13. March-Russell, p. 226.
14. March-Russell, p. 229.
15. March-Russell, p. 71.
16. Sontag, S. (2000) 'Writers on Writing; Directions: Write, Read, Rewrite. Repeat Steps 2 and 3 as Needed', viewed 23 December 2018, https://www.nytimes.com/2000/12/18/books/writers-on-writing-directions-write-read-rewrite-repeat-steps-2-and-3-as-needed.html
17. Neale, D. (2017) viewed 17 February 2017. http://www.cutalongstory.com/authors/derek-neale/1113.html

12 Targeting young adults and new adults

1. McLeod, S. (2015) *Nature vs. Nurture in Psychology*, viewed 18 February 2018, https://www.simplypsychology.org/naturevsnurture.html
2. Carter, D. (2006) *Literary Theory* (Harpenden: Oldcastle Books), p. 72.

13 Critical and cultural theories

1. Sparrow, M. K. (2008) *The Character of Harms: Operational Challenges in Control* (Cambridge: Cambridge University Press), p. 8.
2. Mauk, B. (2013) 'Why Is Grass Green?', viewed 18 February 2017. http://www.livescience.com/32496-why-is-grass-green.html
3. Bacon, E. (2015) 'Practice-led Research, the Ethnographer and Unearthing Knowledge: Crossing the Thresholds', in G. Pittaway, A. Lodge & L. Smithies (eds.) *Proceedings of 'Minding the Gap: Writing Across Thresholds and Fault Lines', the 19th Conference of the Australasian Association of Writing Programs* (Wellington: Australasisan Associaton of Writing Programs), pp. 15–16.
4. Foucault, M. (1985) *The History of Sexuality, Vol. 2: The Use of Pleasure* (New York: Pantheon), p. 8.
5. Schmitz, T.A. (2008) *Modern Literary Theory and Ancient Texts: An Introduction* (Oxford: Blackwell), p. 208.
6. Potts, S. W. (1996) 'We Keep Playing the Same Record': A Conversation with Octavia E. Butler, viewed 15 April 2018, https://www.depauw.edu/sfs/interviews/potts70interview.htm

7. IMDb (2018) *Xena: Warrior Princess*, viewed 25 January 2018. http://www.imdb.com/title/tt0112230

8. Stoff, M. (2017) 'An Interview with Maddison Stoff' in E. Bacon (ed.) *Andromeda Spaceways Magazine* 69, 70 (eBook).

9. Mudge, F. (2017) 'An Interview with Faith Mudge' in E. Bacon (ed.) *Andromeda Spaceways Magazine* 69, 113 (eBook).

10. Le Guin, U. K. (1969) *The Left Hand of Darkness* (New York: Ace).

11. Ashton, K. (2018) 'The Larval Stage' in E. Bacon (ed.) *Andromeda Spaceways Magazine* 70, 37–47 (eBook).

12. Malakin, D. (2018) 'Deleted Lives' in E. Bacon (ed.) *Andromeda Spaceways Magazine* 70, 91–95 (eBook).

13. Barthes, R. (1977) 'The Death of the Author', trans. Stephen Heath in *Image, Music, Text,* (London: Fontana Press), pp. 142–148.

14. Heidmann, C. (2018) 'A small problem' in E. Bacon (ed.) *Andromeda* Spaceways Magazine 70, 57–58 (eBook).

15. Bacon, E. (2018) 'The Young Prince', unpublished.

16. Sirridge, M. (2003) 'Philosophy in Beauvoir's Fiction' in C. Card (ed.) *The Cambridge Companion to Simone de Beauvoir* (New York: Cambridge University Press), p. 129.

17. Sirridge, p. 130.

18. Sirridge, p. 131.

19. Stoff, p. 72.

20. Jemisin, N. K. (2010) *The Hundred Thousand Kingdoms* (London: Orbit).

21. *The Decameron* is a collection of a hundred allegorical short stories written around 1353;ce by Italian writer and scholar Giovanni Boccaccio.

22. Fell, A. (2018) 'The Devil Girl' in E. Bacon (ed.) *Andromeda Spaceways Magazine* 70, 105–111 (eBook).

23. Perez, A. (2018) 'Me & the dead Boy' in E. Bacon (ed.) *Andromeda Spaceways Magazine* 70, 7–18 (eBook).

24. Wright, E. (1984), *Psychoanalytic Criticism. Theory in Practice* (London: Methuen).

25. Vogler, C. (1998) *The Writer's Journey*, 3rd edn (Studio City, CA: Michael Wiese).

26. Mayer, P. (2015) 'Ruth Rendell Dies, Pioneered the Psychological Thriller', viewed 19 February 2017. http://www.npr.org/2015/05/04/377740302/ruth-rendell-dies-pioneered-the-psychological-thriller

27. Mackey, L. (2018) 'The Ferrymen' in E. Bacon (ed.) *Andromeda Spaceways Magazine* 70, 49–53 (eBook).

28. Carter, D. (2006) *Literary Theory* (Harpenden: Oldcastle Books), p. 88.

29. Siporin, S. (2018) 'Sanctuary' in E. Bacon (ed.) *Andromeda Spaceways Magazine* 70, 55 (eBook).

30. All About Philosophy.org (2018), *Existentialism*, viewed 18 February 2018, https://www.allaboutphilosophy.org/existentialism.htm

31. Ward, M. R. (2018) 'To the Stars' in E. Bacon (ed.) *Andromeda Spaceways Magazine* 70, 63–74 (eBook).

32. Thurber, M. (2014) 'Predicting the Unexpected', viewed 25 January 2018. https://www.youtube.com/watch?v=m1Lka28V-vo

33. Carter, p. 85.

34. Ommundsen, W. (1993) *Metafictions? Reflexivity in Contemporary Texts* (Melbourne: Melbourne University Press), p. 28.

36. Le Guin, U. K. (2017) 'FAQ', viewed 26 January 2018. http://www.ursulakleguin.com/MenuContentsList.html#FAQ

35. Andersen, H. C. (1837) 'The Emperor's New Suit', viewed 26 January 2018. http://hca.gilead.org.il/emperor.html

37. Potts.

38. Murnane, G. (2018) 'The Still-Breathing Author', viewed 18 February 2018, https://sydneyreviewofbooks.com/the-still-breathing-author-gerald-murnane

39. Ommundsen, p. 29.

40. Boulter, A. (2007) *Writing Fiction: Creative and Critical Approaches* (New York: Palgrave Macmillan), p. 5.

14 E-publishing

1. The 31-year-old won this year's Akutagawa Award—named for 'Rashomon' author Ryunosuke Akutagawa—Japan's most prestigious honour for a new writer.

2. Pilkington, E. (2012) 'Amanda Hocking, the Writer Who Made Millions by Self-Publishing Online', viewed 19 February 2017. https://www.theguardian.com/books/2012/jan/12/amanda-hocking-self-publishing

3. Wolitzer, H. (2000) 'Embarking Together on Solitary Journeys', viewed 19 February 2017. http://www.nytimes.Com/library/books/013100wolitzer-writing.html

4. A misspelling of 'symptom'.

5. Hecq, D. (2008) 'Writing the Unconscious: Psychoanalysis for the Creative Writer', *Text* 12: 2, 4, viewed 19 February 2017. http://www.textjournal.com.au/oct08/hecq.htm

6. King, S. (2012) *Different Seasons* (London: Hodder and Stoughton), p. 679.

7. Bacon, E. (2018) 'Maverick' in *Dying & Other Stories: Literary Speculative Fiction*, p. 18 (eBook).

Index

Please note: page numbers in **bold type** indicate figures or illustrations

writing short stories, Ray Bradbury on, 125
writing speculative fiction, the basics, 15–40; *see also* basics of writing speculative fiction
Wuthering Heights (Brontë), 65
wuxia, 57

Y
young adult fiction, 133–137
    adapting adult themes to, 134–136
    in Adams' writing, 119

classification, 134
in J. K. Rowling's writing, 57
in Marion Zimmer Bradley's writing, 178
redefining of boundaries, 133
on theme, 73, 96
on tone, 72
writing exercise, 136–137
young adults, 133
'The Young Prince' (Bacon), 147–148
youtube, 162

9781352006056